LIFE IN BLACK AMERICA

LIFE IN BLACK AMERICA

EDITED BY
JAMES S. JACKSON

SAGE PUBLICATIONS
The International Professional Publishers
Newbury Park   London   New Delhi

For information address:

SAGE Publications, Inc.
2455 Teller Road
Newbury Park, California 91320

SAGE Publications Ltd.
6 Bonhill Street
London EC2A 4PU
United Kingdom

SAGE Publications India Pvt. Ltd.
M-32 Market
Greater Kailash I
New Delhi 110 048 India

Printed in the United States of America

Library of Congress Cataloging-in-Publication Data

Main entry under title:
Life in Black America / edited by James S. Jackson.
    p.   cm.
  Includes bibliographical references and index.
  ISBN 0-8039-3537-4. — ISBN 0-8039-3538-2 (pbk.)
  1. Afro-Americans—Population. 2. Afro-Americans—Statistics.
 I. Jackson, James S. (James Sidney). 1944–   .
E185.86.L497   1991
305.896'073—dc20   91-6934
                                     CIP

FIRST PRINTING, 1991

Sage Production Editor: Judith L. Hunter

CONTENTS

FOREWORD

It gives me a great deal of pleasure to write the foreword for *Life in Black America*. As a member of the original National Advisory Panel formed in 1977 and later as a senior postdoctoral fellow in the Program for Research on Black Americans (PRBA), I have experienced firsthand the evolution of the research and growth of the program. This book marks the first large, integrative report of the research findings generated over the decade. It culminates the work envisioned by the researchers, staff, and National Advisory Panel in the late 1970s and presages an important series of such reports still to come.

This volume and those to follow denote a watershed in social science research. This is the first attempt to report on the feelings, attitudes, and behaviors of a national sample of the black adult population, a sample drawn to reflect the distribution of Americans of African descent across the full breadth of the United States. It was a prodigious effort involving technical innovations in sampling, questionnaire construction, and interviewing. But perhaps most importantly, it marks the first time a large-scale social science survey has assessed the depths of African Americans' reflections on their lives from a black perspective. It is the combination of the employment of traditional, well-established social science procedures, technical innovation, and an African American "emic" perspective that makes this research unique and the book a timely contribution to the heritage of the social sciences. There are numerous ideas and issues worthy of further study within the content of this book. The many conclusions drawn by the contributors, and supported by empirical evidence, have clear implications for policy decisions in both the public and private sector. This book is truly an interdisciplinary resource for scientists, practitioners, and policy makers who want an appropriate knowledge base about African Americans. I believe that it will be an indispensable research tool for the social and behavioral sciences for years to come. It can also provide an empirical context that undergirds the work of persons delivering health and human services to African Americans.

Beyond its appeal and contribution to current and future social science endeavors, I think that the book will make an important contribution to the classroom and libraries of all Americans, regardless of ethnic and racial background. These data and interpretations need to find their way into secondary schools, junior colleges, and undergraduate and graduate courses.

I applaud the efforts of the research group and have enjoyed my own role as advisor and collaborator in the program. Equally important to my own participation was witnessing the major mentoring model and supportive climate established by the Program for Research on Black Americans (PRBA). Over the decade the focus of this program brought together many African American scholars for undergraduate, graduate, and post-doctoral research opportunities. Out of this effort has come a significant nationwide interdisciplinary network of African American scholars working collaboratively. As represented by the authors in this book, PRBA is an unique collective effort of predominantly African American researchers. Given the critical shortage of African Americans with these particular professional skills, it is a noteworthy model for developing empirical scholars of African descent. Therefore this book is a hallmark of what can be done given proper support. I believe that you will find the book valuable, and an important theoretical and empirical counterweight to the endless discussions and debates on race. The range of thought and opinion among African Americans is a testament to our diversity, and an affirmation in a world that persists in simplistic generalities about us. I strongly recommend the book to all who desire to gain a better understanding of how Americans of African descent really perceive their world and their lives.

Anderson James Franklin
The City College and Graduate
School of the City University
of New York

PREFACE

This book represents the culmination of over 14 years of research and writing on the economic, political, and social statuses and the physical, psychological, and social responses of Americans of African descent to their life circumstances. From the beginning it has been our intent to conduct the highest quality research possible based on a set of "real world" considerations, in the hope of influencing future research directions, encouraging the entry of new students of color into research careers, and contributing reliable data to the social policy debates and public policies that directly affect the quality of black American life. Thus far we have done this through the contribution of research articles, scholarly chapters, reports to sponsors, conference presentations, and congressional testimony.

This book also represents the beginning of a series of large integrative reports that will provide detailed data, analyses, and policy implications in many of the significant domains of life. In this volume we detail the history of the Program for Research on Black Americans (PRBA), the methodological basis of the data, and provide a substantive glimpse at a broad array of findings on the statuses and responses of a national sample of the black population. Later volumes will build on this work, providing more detailed treatment of these life domains by examining groups of individuals, like the black elderly and black youth, or specific areas of substantive concern, like the family, mental health, stress, physical health, poverty, religion, and political behavior. We believe that the common threads of the assumptions, methodological excellence, and theoretical framework will provide a strong continuity over these several volumes.

The work reported in this book has been supported by research grants from the Center for Minority Group Studies of the National Institute of Mental Health, National Institute on Aging, Ford and

Rockefeller Foundations, and the Carnegie Corporation. Additional support in the form of institutional and individual postdoctoral grants was provided by the National Institute of Mental Health, National Institute on Aging, and Rockefeller Foundation. We are particularly indebted to Lynn Walker of the Ford Foundation, Bernard Charles of the Carnegie Corporation, and Bruce Williams of the Rockefeller Foundation. They had faith in our objectives and efforts and contributed financial and moral support to our work.

I would like to single out Bernard McDonald and William Diaz at the Ford Foundation for special notice. It was their help in providing a grant to conduct analyses on poverty during the height of the federal freeze on social science research in the early 1980s that permitted the Program for Research on Black Americans to survive. Without this grant this book would have never been written and dozens of students would not have received the type and level of training made possible by the research program. We offer our grateful appreciation to Bernie and Bill and to the Ford Foundation for their vision and critical intervention. During this same bleak period of the early 1980s, key administrators at the Institute of Social Research also contributed much to our survival. Invaluable assistance was provided by Steven Withey, then Director of the Survey Research Center; Robert Zajonc, then Director of the Research Center for Group Dynamics; and Thomas Juster, then Director of the Institute for Social Research.

I would like to acknowledge the contribution of Sally Oswald in preparing this manuscript and coordinating the production of this volume. Without her administrative oversight it just wouldn't have been possible. She was ably assisted by Keith Hersh, Linda Shepard, and Monica Wolford. All three took active and instrumental roles in the analyses and tables reported in the volume. In addition they were assisted by a number of graduate and undergraduate students. These include Ursula Barzey, Donna Cochran, Rukmalie Jayakody, and Cheryl Burns. I would also like to note that the current group builds on the work of many other scholars. M. Belinda Tucker, now at the University of California at Los Angeles, and Phillip J. Bowman and Shirley S. Hatchett, now at the University of Illinois, played critical professional roles in establishing the program and in conducting the first national survey.

I would also like to note the prior work of many of our research assistants. Letha Chadiha, our first PRBA employee, is now an Assistant Professor at Washington University. Steven Cardoze, Andrea

Leibson, Jacquelyn Perlman, James Walker, and Carol Sorrel all assisted ably in data collection, establishment of the datasets and analyses. I won't mention by name the hundreds of other pre- and post-doctoral students, undergraduates, and colleagues who contributed so much to our efforts. Many of these individuals are authors of the individual chapters in this volume, are listed in Chapter 2, or are mentioned in our continuing report, "Research and Training Activities of the Program for Research on Black Americans."

Finally, I would like to acknowledge the special role that Gerald and Patricia Gurin played in the formation of an intellectual foundation, and their work and moral support in helping to establish, and assisting in the evolution of, the Program for Research on Black Americans. They have earned and certainly deserve their position as intellectual progenitors of the program and our work at the University of Michigan.

James S. Jackson
The University of Michigan

```
┌─────────┐
│         │
│    1    │
│         │
└─────────┘
```

INTRODUCTION

James S. Jackson

The National Survey of Black Americans (NSBA) is a major research project undertaken by social scientists and students at the University of Michigan to collect and analyze national high-quality survey data on populations of African American descent. The purpose of this undertaking has been to provide a scholarly, interdisciplinary, basic social science research group that is sensitive to cultural and systemic factors in the social, psychological, economic, and political behaviors of Americans of African descent.

The sample survey was selected as the basic empirical research vehicle. This was not necessarily because of its scientific pre-eminence over any other empirical research method but instead because of its potential power in generating large quantities of representative data (Schuman & Kalton, 1985), links to public policy formulation, and the experience and background of the program founders at the Institute for Social Research (Jackson, Tucker, & Bowman, 1982; Jackson, Tucker, & Gurin, 1987).

For example, analyses of these data provide invaluable input to the ongoing debate on the black family and the functions that family and social networks perform in black life in America (Hatchett & Jackson, 1983; Taylor, Jackson, & Quick, 1982). In addition to their general interest, these findings should be particularly significant for their policy relevance.

Background

A decade ago adequate, national social science data with a social and cultural focus sensitive to the nature of black life in this country did not exist. A major assumption of this research is that data of these nature are necessary for basic advances in science and for public policy planning. A related and equally important purpose is to provide research and training opportunities for social scientists and students of African American descent.

In addition to several major data collections, secondary analysis projects have also included work on health, aging, poverty, race and political attitudes, mental health, social support, and unemployment. The work on the first of these studies, the National Survey of Black Americans, provides a model of survey research on national samples of African Americans consistent with basic tenets of an empirical black social science perspective. This chapter includes a discussion of the conceptual and methodological rationale for the NSBA and provides an introduction to the remaining chapters in the volume.

Previous studies of American adults of African descent typically have been restricted to limited and special populations. National data usually have been gathered in the course of surveys of the general population (Jackson, 1988, 1989; Smith, 1987). This procedure potentially introduces serious biases in the representation of blacks, because they are distributed geographically differently than the total United States population. This approach to data collection in national samples of blacks also has meant that concepts, measures, and methods developed in the study of the white majority have been used somewhat mindlessly in the study of African Americans. There has been little theoretical or empirical concern with the appropriateness of this simple comparative approach (Jackson, 1986; Neighbors, 1985). For the most part, prior national studies have not been informed by an awareness of and appreciation for the unique cultural experiences of black Americans; and concepts, measures, and research procedures that reflect this uniqueness have not been developed or employed (Jackson, Tucker, & Bowman, 1982).

Partly because of the small and nonrepresentative samples of blacks, national surveys have not gone beyond superficial analyses of gross black-white comparisons. This cursory treatment and lack of attention in survey instruments and procedures to the cultural context of black life in America has served to perpetuate a simplistic scientific and policy view of the black experience. Thus, in our opinion, poor science (Jones, 1980) and poor application dictated the need for data from large, well designed national probability sample surveys that addressed, in a culturally sensitive manner, major areas of the life experiences of Americans of African descent (Jackson, Tucker, & Bowman, 1982).

Over the past several years members of the Program for Research on Black Americans (PRBA) at the Institute for Social Research have been engaged in the development, execution, and analysis of data from several major studies. This research has attempted to address the major limitations in the existing literature (Jackson, Tucker, & Bowman, 1982). The first of these two national studies comprise the National Survey of Black Americans. The NSBA Cross-Section Study (Jackson, Tucker, & Gurin, 1987), was initiated in 1977. Funding for the study was provided by the Center for the Study of Minority Group Mental Health, the National Institute of Mental Health, and the Ford Foundation. The NSBA was a national probability household survey of 2,107 black Americans, 18 years of age and older, conducted over a seven-month period in 1979 and 1980. The size and representativeness of the sample permitted systematic investigation of the heterogeneity of the adult black population. Substantively, the omnibus survey was concerned with major social, economic, and psychological aspects of black American life.

The questionnaire instrument included items on relationships with family and friends, community life, religion, racial identity, political attitudes and participation, informal and formal help resources, and job and employment history. The 2,107 face-to-face household interviews were conducted by an all black, male and female professional interviewing staff that was trained and supervised by the Survey Research Center of the Institute for Social Research (Jackson, 1989; Jackson & Hatchett, 1986; Jackson, Tucker, & Bowman, 1982; Jackson, Tucker, & Gurin, 1987).

The national Cross-Section Study served as the "parent" study for the second investigation, the national Three-Generation Family Study (TGFS) of 2,443 three-generation lineage family members. This study was conducted in 1980 and 1981 and funded by the National Institute on Aging and the Ford Foundation. When the respondents in the NSBA had living family members from two adjacent generations, one randomly selected representative from each lineage position was also interviewed (Jackson & Hatchett, 1986). The TGFS was a national probability sample of black American three-generation lineage family members, including 510 complete generation triads. Finally, as a part of the three-generation study a reinterview questionnaire was developed and administered to 866 of the original cross-section respondents who were members of three-generation families. The reinterview questionnaire, in conjunction with the three-generation instrument, permitted the intensive examination of topics relevant to two major groups of the black population: youth and the elderly. For the elderly, additional items in the reinterview survey included a focus on such issues as age identification, life review, attitudes toward age-based housing discrimination, institutionalization and the role of the federal government, collective action strategies of older Americans, functional disability, health problems, medical regimen adherence, family interaction patterns, and work-related and retirement concerns. For youth, issues relevant to educational aspirations and expections; job experiences; cigarette, alcohol, and drug use; family relationships; and leisure time were the objects of study.

Having parallel data on individuals in different lineage positions provides an opportunity to test the similarities and differences in attitudes, values, and life experiences across three generations of black American families. The literature records few three-generation lineage family studies of any population, and certainly none of the scope and national representativeness encompassed in this study (Jackson & Hatchett, 1986).

The data provide unique opportunities to explore assumptions and hypotheses in the literature on socialization, intergenerational mobility, and a number of similar issues in different areas of social science. There are also a number of social policy and practical implications of this study. Many public policies and programs devoted to economically disadvantaged groups are based on the assumption that the objective problems of poverty and discrimination are exacerbated by family socialization patterns that transmit attitudes, values, and behaviors that are dysfunctional for achievement in this society. Thus, many of the regulations in these programs are based on resocializing individuals, often involving intervention in, or circumvention of, the family. The three-generation lineage study provides an opportunity to examine the reasonableness, at least in a correlational manner, of these basic underlying assumptions.

A third major data collection related to both the NSBA and the TGFS was completed in 1984 under a contract from the Department of Health and Human Services (Bowman, Gurin, & Howard, 1984).

The purpose of this contract was to investigate the motivation and mobility of black youth. All of the youth and young adults (ages 14 to 24) interviewed in the Three-Generation Family Study were reinterviewed; approximately 229 males and females were questioned by telephone regarding their educational and occupational attainments.

The fourth major data collection of the PRBA was completed in 1984. Funded by the Ford, Rockefeller, and Carnegie Foundations, the 1984 National Black Election Study (NBES) was designed to assess the attitudes and behaviors of a national sample of the black electorate during the 1984 national campaign and elections (Gurin, Hatchett, & Jackson, 1989; Jackson, Gurin, & Hatchett, 1984; Tate, Brown, Hatchett, & Jackson, 1988). A random-digit-dial telephone sample of 1,150 black adults was completed prior to the election, and 866 respondents in this sample were reinterviewed immediately following the election. The design was comparable to the pre-post election component of the National Election Study of 1984 and permits comparisons between the black and general population on many items of common interest. Notable concerns in this study related to support for Jesse Jackson's bid for the presidency, attitudes toward major political issues, feelings of personal and political efficacy, the role of racial consciousness in political ideology and behavior, and the resource base for black political activity.

The fifth major data collection project was a National Institute of Mental Health supported panel telephone study involving the tracking and reinterviewing of all surviving and willing to be interviewed respondents from the NSBA. A total of 953 respondents were interviewed in 1987, representing 70% of the original NSBA sample that could be located and had an available telephone. Over 80% of these same respondents were reinterviewed in 1988 as part of the third wave of the original NSBA. Questionnaire material in both additional waves of the NSBA included content similar to the original 1979–80 NSBA.

The sixth data collection was a 1988 Carnegie Corporation supported 1988 NBES telephone reinterview of 525 respondents from the 1984 NBES who were available and willing to be interviewed. These 525 interviews represented over 70% of the respondents from the original 1984 random-digit-dial study who could be located. The design of this study was similar to the original NBES involving both pre- and post-election interviews. The content of the interviews was also similar, involving concerns with changes in support for Jesse Jackson, attitudes toward major political issues, feelings of political efficacy, ideological positions, and the role of black political leadership (Gurin, Hatchett, & Jackson, 1989).

The attention to such areas as physical health, mental health, employment, family life, individual and group identification, and political behavior provide the first in-depth investigation of these issues in large representative samples of the entire black population. Scientifically, the results of our surveys should have a significant effect on current theorizing about Americans of African descent, as well as on the content and directions of future research on these populations. The inclusion of many policy relevant questions yields, for the first time, individual and group opinions and feelings among the breadth and diversity of black people located in all walks of life across the entire United States.

African American Perspective on Social Science Research

In the growth of social science rooted in an African American perspective (especially black psychology), three major themes have been consistently emphasized: (a) the development of research strategies that proceed from real-life needs rather than from theoretical imperatives; (b) the development of collaborative relationships with black communities; and (c) the development of new research competencies and roles that will facilitate the advancement of collective black interests (Akbar, 1985; Boykin, Franklin, & Yates, 1980; Boykin & Toms, 1985; Gordon, 1973; Jones, 1980; Myers, 1985). Similar principles have also guided the development of community psychology (Jackson, 1985), an area that has strong ties to black psychology (Heller, Price, Reinlare, Riger, & Wandersman, 1984).

Some recent writings (e.g., Wilson, 1987) have pointed to the period of the mid-1960s to the early 1980s as one in which liberal social scientists refused to acknowledge the existence of pathology in the black community. Wilson (1987) suggests that this "oversight" led to nearly two decades in which social science research neither acknowledged nor addressed the serious social disorganization problems that are now noted daily in current periodicals and serious social science literature. Many social scientists doubted then, as we do now, that the continued focus on the deficits and problems in ethnic racial populations actually contributed to theoretical advances in social science knowledge or to appropriate solutions.

We believe that much of the serious social science work during this period has resulted in a more useful approach, one that emphasizes resources and strengths in black communities and in fact seeks to forge a new paradigmatic social science perspective. This perspective simultaneously recognizes the existence of individual pathology and group deficits as well as the omnipresence of systemic constraints and in this context attempts to understand how the resources of the individual and the group are marshalled to address problems due to macro-economic conditions, deleterious public policies (e.g., urban renewal, freeway construction acts, etc.), illegal corporate activities (e.g., red-lining and steering in the housing industry), and both benign and malignant neglect.

It has long been clear to a number of social scientists that social science paradigms of deficit and problems, which were common in the early 1960s and are even more popular today, are not sufficient in the development of frameworks and theory to adequately account for observed race-related maltreatment and pathological reactions of individual blacks and black communities; nor could this approach be helpful in the development of public policies to address the underlying issues and remedies (e.g., the ill-fated "War on Poverty"). A new paradigm was needed, a paradigm that builds on the strengths in black communities to forge theories of race-related behaviors within an oppressive social and economic milieu and points to adequate public policies that result in ameliorative programs that contribute to long-term and lasting change.

In our work we discount the liberal polemicists of the 1960s and 1970s, just as we discount the conservative polemicists of the 1980s. We must attend to the nature of quality social science research today, just as we should have listened to the rational voices of the last two decades. There is a thread here—a theme that is consistent with the value system of this society, one that starts from self-reliance, individual freedom, and equal opportunity. This theme cannot be related in a useful, productive manner to deficits within oppressed peoples, but instead must be linked to their strengths, resources, and human potential. Thus, the social science voices that have called for redefinitions and new paradigmatic approaches have been attempting to build social science paradigms that are consistent with basic American values and more responsive to the nature of ethnic and racial experiences.

The NSBA builds on this consistent thread of quality social science research and has taken as its basic assumptions: (a) the exis-

tence of individual and group pathology among blacks, (b) the existence of deleterious living and working conditions for blacks, (c)
problems in family formation and subsistence, and (d) macro-economic problems and systemic constraints independent of individual and group pathology. Beginning from this set of assumptions,
the NSBA then asked questions regarding the nature of social, psychological, and physical resources that blacks individually and collectively use to address these problems. Theoretically, we are
concerned with how these resources are created and sustained and
what the structural interrelationships are—traditional social science
questions. In addition, we have asked how these strengths and resources are marshalled or not marshalled by the group to address
the individual and group pathologies that exist in the community. In
this latter set of questions, we are concerned with the issues of theory
and social policy that emanate from the oppressed social, political,
and economic history of blacks in this society and explore the structural and psychological interrelationships among these individual
and group resources. We then examine the interaction of these resources with real and perceived individual, group, and systemic barriers to individual and group accomplishments.

Few other studies in the literature have had a comprehensiveness
of coverage comparable to the NSBA, and they have been done on
very limited and narrow segments of the black population, usually
poor blacks in the northern cities. In these previous studies, it is impossible to estimate the extent to which the findings are generaliz-
able beyond the particular setting and group studied.

The chapters in this book are unabashedly empirical, but with a
critical eye to the development of a social psychological resource
theory that may contribute to further predictions of individual and
group behavior and lead to the formulation of more effective approaches to policy formation. We believe that the lack of good quality data on nationally representative samples of African Americans
has seriously impeded the development of adequate theory as well as
meaningful and useful public policy.

Overview of the Book and Subsequent Volumes

The remainder of this chapter and book focuses on the National
Survey of Black Americans. We believe that the use of one major
dataset and a set of sequential analyses provides an overarching

framework for examining the nature of black American life. Chapter 2 details the nature of the methodological approaches used in the process of conducting the NSBA. These include problem conceptualization, the development of the research instruments, the recruitment and training of a national interviewing staff, sampling issues, field methods, and quality control of the interviewing and coding procedures.

Chapters 3 through 13 detail the substantive findings from our survey. These chapters are organized to represent the important role of the social and physical environment as they impact the perceptions, attitudes, and reported behaviors related to the quality of life among this national sample of Americans of African descent. The breadth and depth of the interviews provide the opportunity to trace the interrelationships of events and reactions in different significant areas of life among black Americans (Jackson, in press).

A major theme that serves to integrate the different parts of the NSBA interviews is that of resources and social support (Taylor, 1986b; Taylor, Jackson, & Quick, 1982). This is a concept that is particularly relevant in a study of black Americans. Some writers have pointed to the breakdown of the black family and social networks; others have commented on the strength of the black extended family and pointed to family and friendship networks as providing major supports to black Americans facing the difficult conditions in their lives. There was an extensive focus on social support in the NSBA. It is not only the subject of the section of the interview specifically devoted to family and friendships (Chapters 4 and 5), but appears as an aspect of other sections as well: the support provided by people in one's neighborhood (Chapter 3); one's church (Chapter 6); the availability of informal support for help when one is ill (Chapter 10); the people one depends on in dealing with the stresses of work, joblessness, and retirement (Chapters 7, 8, and 9); the use of informal resources when faced with major personal problems in one's life (Chapter 11); and the importance of collective identity and political organization (Chapters 12 and 13).

In Chapter 3 Milburn and Bowman present the findings related to neighborhood involvement. They note that, although much has been speculated about the importance of neighborhoods to the quality of black American life, little empirical research has been conducted. Their findings suggest the critical role that voluntary associations play in improving the quality of neighborhood life for blacks.

In Chapter 4 Hatchett, Cochran, and Jackson turn to an examination of another critical environmental context, the family, to explore
the nature of changes in family structure on reports of extended family behavior and contact, and how these reports influence the availability and utilization of informal family resources. The fifth Chapter, by Hatchett, examines the nature of tensions and resources that
influence successful and unsuccessful marital patterns among black
men and women.

Chapter 6 takes up an important theme in the historical and contemporary life of African Americans, church involvement and religiosity. Taylor and Chatters explore the meaning and nature of religious commitment among demographic subgroups (e.g., age, gender, education) in the population. Their findings suggest that there
are important subgroup variations in religious commitment and
that, contrary to some speculation, religious involvement enhances
social and political commitment and collective efforts to better the
lives of African Americans.

In the employment area, the broader life implications of a history
of dead-end jobs, a breakdown in the nuclear family, or a disabling
illness can be very different for blacks in the rural South than for
those in the inner cities of the North or for younger versus older
blacks (Bowman, Jackson, Hatchett, & Gurin, 1982). Bowman examines the nature of work life in Chapters 7 and 8, followed by a related focus on retirement by Gibson in Chapter 9. In Chapter 7
Bowman explores the nature of perceived inequality in work life in
the population and the impact of placement on primary and secondary job sectors of the economy. Bowman concludes that policies to
ameliorate the downward spiral in employment opportunities must
focus on both external barriers and individual skill improvement.

Chapter 8 explores the increasingly important role that joblessness plays in the lives of black men and women. The historical patterns and reasons for the lack of work are presented. Bowman concludes that the distinction between official and hidden unemployment is critical in understanding individual and group reactions to
joblessness. Systemic, familial, and individual factors are found to
be important in accounting for joblessness.

In Chapter 9 Gibson presents a global picture of the nature of retirement among blacks, conceiving of the retirement process as an
event, a role, and a precipitator of other important life events. Her findings suggest the need to examine retirement as a process, perhaps
having different meanings than conventional conceptions, in rela-

tionship to labor force history (e.g., in Chapters 7 and 8) and the availability of health and financial resources. These findings call into question traditional approaches to retirement research.

In Chapter 10 Chatters examines the physical health status of black Americans. She suggests that survey data of this type provide an important complement to national health statistics that point to the high level of illness in black America. The findings suggest that health is a very important resource, and one that is differentially distributed among subgroups. Based on these findings she raises questions about the adequacy of current conceptions of health and illness and the effectiveness of existing public policy in providing service delivery.

Existing data suggest that black Americans make less use of formal psychological help resources than do white Americans. It has been hypothesized that one reason for this is that black Americans place greater reliance on family and friends for help with their personal problems. Others have suggested, to the contrary, that those who use fewer formal resources also turn less often to friends and family. Any assessment of "unmet need" obviously would depend on whether or not people who do not use formal help resources have available alternative informal resources (Neighbors, 1984b; Neighbors & Jackson, 1984, 1986, 1987). In Chapter 11 Neighbors examines mental health status among the populations from a stress and coping model. His findings point to important demographic differences, widespread inappropriate use of services among poor groups, and the important role that ministers play as professional sources of care.

Chapter 12 by Jackson, McCullough, Gurin, and Broman examines the nature and distribution of racial identification and consciousness in the populations. These constructs of collective attachment to the group are conceptualized as important resources in the coping and survival of African Americans. The findings reveal widespread high attachment among all segments of the population and important socialization influences on collective positions in adulthood. Following up on this chapter, Brown in Chapter 13 examines one form of political expression, voting, and finds widespread interest and participation among the black electorate. Although some differences appear (e.g., age and gender), collective membership and group resources also show significant relationships.

The final chapter provides a synthesis and summary of the substantive findings. The importance of a resource-based model of black behavior and the interaction among systemic constraints, in-

dividual characteristics, and group resources is used as an explanatory model. Some of the main themes that emerged from the analyses are examined and the nature of subsequent volumes is outlined.

2

METHODOLOGICAL APPROACH

James S. Jackson

The purpose of this chapter is to provide an overview of the methodological procedures and approaches used in conducting the National Survey of Black Americans (NSBA). In this chapter the establishment of the National Advisory Panel and its major role in the design and execution of the national survey is reviewed. The development of the questionnaire and the meticulous procedures used to achieve cultural sensitivity are discussed, and the procedures designed to ensure a representative national sample are described. Finally, the quality control methods and coding schemes devised to guarantee high quality interviews and meaningful interpretations of the open- and closed-ended material are discussed. In addition to its methodological emphasis, the chapter also provides a brief summary of the major substantive themes of the sections of the questionnaire.

Questionnaire Development and Substantive Themes
in the National Survey of Black Americans

The NSBA Cross-Section Study was the first of the six national studies conducted by the Program for Research on Black Americans (PRBA). Its development laid the foundation for subsequent research and training activities. During 1977, the first year of the project, attention focused exclusively on the conceptual and methodological analysis of previous scientific work on Americans of African descent, the development of meaningful data collection strategies, and the creation of a pretest instrument sensitive to specific racial-ethnic issues in the substantive topics of the research. Work groups were established, comprised of students and professionals from a broad range of disciplines including organizational and social psychology, economics, education, medicine, nursing, political science, and social work. At different points in this first-year process, over 20 black graduate students and a dozen black social scientists at the University of Michigan were involved.

Generally, the work groups paralleled the major substantive divisions of the project that had evolved out of the preliminary conceptual discussions held by the staff. These were identity; consciousness and self-esteem; employment and unemployment; social support, including family, religion, coping, help seeking, and mental health resource utilization; social background and demographics; and methodological issues related to interviewer-respondent interaction. Each work group was charged with the responsibility of covering the relevant literature, abstracting it, and describing broad interest areas suitable for empirical investigation.

A multidisciplinary National Advisory Panel was also established. This group was convened in Ann Arbor for two 2-day sessions, one prior to the first pretest and the second between the first and second pretests. The panel was composed of individuals, selected to represent many different disciplines, with broad experience and backgrounds in areas relevant to the project. Members included: Drs. Edgar Epps, Lena Meyers, Dorothy Pearson, Walter Allen, June Christmas, Reginald Jones, Lewis King, Henry Tomes, A. J. Franklin, Halford Fairchild, Esther Jenkins, Diana Slaughter, and Mr. Louis Ramey. Combined with the input from local black professionals and students, every relevant social and behavioral science discipline was consulted.

Modified Black-Translation Procedures and Pretests

The outcome of the first meeting of the advisory panel was the further delineation of important areas of concern and refinement of topics that should be explored in a national survey of black Americans. Following the identification and specification of these broad areas, open-ended questions were developed. Local community members representing varying socioeconomic levels in the surrounding black communities were contacted and those interested in participating were placed in homogeneous groups. Attempts were made to make the different groups as heterogeneous as possible (old and young, southern and northern born, men and women). Group members' responses to the open-ended questions were tape recorded and later transcribed. These transcriptions served as the basis of the development of the first pretest instrument. The sessions supplied very rich and detailed information regarding the meaning of many different concepts. We felt that it was important to have our concepts defined and verified by members of black communities similar to those who would later serve as respondents in the actual surveys. Questions were written using words whose shared meanings were obtained from the sessions, and informal pretests with other indigenous community members were held to ascertain that these questions were working and meaningful to black people (Bowman, 1983; Jackson, Tucker, & Bowman, 1982; Word, 1977).

Two large formal pretests were held in Detroit and Montgomery, Alabama. During May and June, 1978, black interviewers in these areas were recruited and trained. In the first pretest, local black interviewers were particularly helpful in assisting in wording changes and the flow of the questions. During the first pretest, black respondents in Detroit and Montgomery were selected in a nonscientific procedure. Both rural and urban areas were designated and interviewers were instructed to select a variety of sex, age, and socioeconomic status individuals. Nearly 200 interviews were collected in this manner in June 1978. Following data collection, rough preliminary analyses were conducted. A second meeting of the advisory panel was held, and the results of the analyses and open-ended code development were made available to them in their respective substantive work groups. Based on this interaction and input from the staff and other local professionals, a subset of the original questions was retained for the second pretest.

A second preliminary instrument was developed, and indigenous members of local black communities were again approached for input regarding the meaningfulness of the concepts. Scientific sampling procedures were used this time to generate new samples of blacks in both Detroit and Montgomery. A second set of meetings and training sessions was held with the local interviewers, and modifications were made in the instrument based on this input. During August 1978, nearly 200 black respondents were interviewed. Similar to the first formal pretest, these questionnaires were coded and basic analyses were conducted on the closed-ended items. Open-ended codes were developed and checked, and work began on the development of the final interview instrument. After a preliminary version of this instrument was made, copies were distributed to work groups, interested local professionals, and the advisory panel. Comments, suggestions, and changes were solicited, collated, and used in making modifications. Additional informal pretests were conducted with members from the larger black communities in surrounding areas. In this period pretesting also began on a number of new sampling procedures. These procedures, which are discussed later in the chapter, permitted the first truly sophisticated national probability samples of black Americans to be drawn.

In summary, in the first year pretest instruments and new procedures were devised through intensive staff interaction, concentrated reviews of the relevant literature, and meetings with a national, multidisciplinary panel of academicians and practitioners. Additional input regarding the preliminary cross-section instrument was obtained from local community residents, interviewers, and two major pretests. Extensive attention also was focused on the appropriateness of methods and procedures for sampling, contacting, and interviewing black respondents.

During the first half of 1978 another small, formal pretest and informal interviews were conducted, and refinements in the cross-section instrument were completed. In keeping with the national focus of the study and the general objectives of this project as a national resource, contact was maintained by mail and telephone with members of the advisory panel; they were integrally involved with assessing the final instrument. Much of the work on the questionnaire, as described earlier, was devoted to making it culturally sensitive and responsive to the concerns of the black population. The final cross-section instrument contained several traditional measures, as well as many new and unique measures gleamed from the year of extensive conceptual, theoretical, and empirical work.

Substantive Overview of NSBA Questionnaires

The final instrument was comprehensive, encompassing several broad areas related to the mental health and general life situation of Americans of African origins. These areas included:

1. *Neighborhood,* including topics of community integration, services, crime, and related issues.
2. *Religion* and its impact on the black community. Topics such as the role

of the church and religion in the development of the individual and the community are covered.

3. *Health and problems,* focusing on physical health, self perceptions, and specific life events.

4. *Employment and unemployment,* focusing on the impact of job-related problems, underemployment issues, effects of chronic unemployment, and attempts to investigate some aspects of the "irregular economy."

5. *Family and friendships,* assessing the degree of individual contact with family and friends and their social support role. Special topics of loneliness and role relationships are also covered.

6. *Mental health utilization,* focusing directly on the problem-recognition and help-seeking processes related to self- and other definitions of mental health functioning. A special problem-centered (nonchronic) approach is followed in this section, and multiple indicators of positive functioning are included. Attitudinal items related to mental health policies are also included.

7. *Identity,* containing items related to the integration and separation of personal and group identity. Multiple indicators of identity and consciousness are included, as well as measures of socialization related to these concerns. Also included in this section are items that assess racial attitudes and attitudes related to education, busing, civil rights, and racism.

8. *Background,* including items related to traditional demographics of the individual and family as well as measures of political affiliation and participation. Education and job training experiences are also assessed.

9. *Roots,* relating to the three-generation lineage study and providing information concerning the family history of the respondent. Important information was gained concerning the extent and distribution of three-generation lineage black American families in the United States. This last section also provided the important bridge to the three-generation, youth, and elderly parts of the project.

Overall, the cross-section questionnaire is extensive and has been shown subsequently to permit a detailed examination of black American life. Particularly noteworthy is the inclusion of novel and culturally sensitive material.

In addition to the cross-section instrument, two other questionnaires, the three-generation and reinterview, were also developed as part of the National Survey of Black Americans. The three-generation instrument was administered to members of the Three-Generation Family Study—the two other family lineage members identified by the original cross-section respondent. The reinterview instrument was developed for the second interview of the original respondent. The items in the three-generation instrument overlap extensively with those in the cross-section questionnaire, providing data on health, mental health, and other important areas on national samples of three-generation families, youth, and elderly blacks.

In order to maximize the overlap between the work on the Cross-Section and the Three-Generation Family Studies, much of the material developed for the cross-section instrument was included in the three-generation instrument. In fact, the three-generation questionnaire was primarily a subset of the cross-section instrument, with the addition of new material in the youth, elderly, and three-generation sections. This questionnaire contains items in sections 1 through 7, discussed above, plus three-generation issues: for the elderly, age identification, life review, attitudes toward age-based housing discrimination, institutionalization, and role of the federal government, collective action strategies of older Americans, functional disability, health problems, medical regimen adherence, home remedies, family interaction patterns, and work-related and retirement issues; and for the young, school, work, and adolescent-related issues. The instrument also includes personal data—traditional background items, political affiliations and activity, racial composition of place of rearing, and church, school, neighborhood, and household membership.

The items in the last sections of the three-generation survey were developed by two special task groups. The conceptual work on the aging section was completed in conjunction with specialists on aging and from pretests done on two separate occasions. A similar approach was followed in the development of the youth portion of the section. The result is an integrated, rich instrument with a great deal of new material not previously asked of black Americans. As explained later in the Field Procedures section, this questionnaire was administered to the two family members generated by cross-section respondents who were identified as members of three-generation families. As also explained later, the cross-section respondent who generated two additional family members was reinterviewed in order to gain additional information obtained in the three-generation questionnaire from that respondent's two family members.

In addition to the information detailed above, the reinterview instrument contained several additional sections, including items originally developed for the cross-section instrument but removed because of time considerations and a special section designed to obtain the data for the multiplicity sampling probabilities (Jackson & Hatchett, 1986). Specifically, the reinterview instrument included the following sections:

A. *Family Relationships* with items covering areas of reciprocal aid with children and family, value of children and evaluation of parenthood, sex role items, and perceived closeness to family.

B. *Family Composition* with questions designed specifically to provide information on the multiplicity sampling probabilities. This series of questions, for the appropriate three-generation family types, was designed to ascertain all possible ways, given our inclusion rules, that a particular three-generation respondent could have been included in the sample. Following the inclusion rules, respondents were asked questions regarding other family members who could have generated the three-generation family members that were selected. In addition, extensive questions were asked about the household composition of the family members and the amount of contact that the respondent/informant had with each family member.

C. *Three-Generational Issues,* which duplicates the special section of the three-generation questionnaire.

D. *Work and Family Economic Well-Being* with items designed to assess additional information about work, job, and economic discrimination, job quality, race attitudes, black culture, and involvement in the irregular economy.

The intent, then, of the reinterview was primarily to provide information regarding the multiplicity sampling probabilities and additional data on family contact, economic well-being, and three-generational issues. Effectively, this resulted in over three hours of interview material on all cross-section family members (866) who were part of three-generation families.

These two questionnaires, the reinterview and three-generation, combined with the cross-section questionnaire, provide the basis for data on the youth, elderly, and three-generation lineage samples. The questions in these instruments were extensively pretested with special procedures to insure cultural relevance and sensitivity. As described in the next section of this chapter, additional field procedures were also introduced to minimize interviewer bias and other problems that may have affected the quality and meaningfulness of the completed questionnaires.

Interviewer Recruitment and Training

The bulk of time in the second year of the project (1978) was spent in locating, recruiting, and training a national interviewing staff. In order to minimize the problems of interviewer-respondent interaction due to race and language, a team of entirely black interviewers had to be located and trained in the methods and procedures of survey sampling and interviewing.

In an attempt to reduce problems of social class and geographical differences, indigenous community interviewers were sought. Thus, it was necessary to recruit nationwide for interviewers in the 76 separate locations that constituted primary sampling areas of the NSBA. Some thought was given to recruiting and training a smaller group of interviewers and having them travel in turn to all of the areas. This procedure, however, was rejected because of the potentially uncontrollable costs (call-backs, hotels, transportation, etc.) and, even more importantly, because indigenous interviewers would know their own areas intimately and therefore be much more efficient at their work and better ambassadors for the study.

Before initiating search procedures for interviewers, field coordinators were selected from several areas of the country (Detroit, New Orleans, Boston, New York, Dallas, Los Angeles, and Atlanta). Both personal and professional contacts were used in locating these individuals. In all cases these women had extensive interviewing experience. A Field Coordinators' Conference was held in Ann Arbor on February 12–16, 1979, and the coordinators were trained in the details of the study, particularly sampling.

Several research units in addition to the Survey Research Center were contacted in the search for interviewers. Contacts were made with black colleges, consulting firms, and individuals across the United States. In addition, organizations like the National Urban League and the National Association for the Advancement of Colored People (NAACP) were also helpful. One of the most successful techniques, in addition to the field coordinators, however, proved to be newspaper and radio advertisements (both general and black oriented). Application forms were developed, and in certain cases personal interviews were conducted by staff members, coordinators, and professional colleagues. In the final analysis, the very best interviewers proved to be public school teachers, who had the time and necessary educational backgrounds to conduct the sampling and interviewing. Local school systems and teachers' unions were pleased to participate in the recruitment efforts.

In most cases, telephone conversations were held with potential candidates to assess their eligibility. In some instances Ann Arbor staff people were sent to personally recruit potential trainees. The goal was to obtain individuals who were outstanding representatives of their local communities and who could serve as positive translators of the project to local people (Myers, 1977). In addition, we felt that interviewers who were aware of particular local problems (e.g., high crime rates) would function better than interviewers who were brought in from other parts of the country. This procedure was also seen as less expensive, given the extensive number of call-backs and sampling problems that were expected. Because of difficulties in locating and maintaining interviewers in certain primary areas, however, approximately 40 interviewers were required to travel beyond the bounds of their own areas.

Eight training sessions were originally planned in different geographical sites, located to minimize the travel costs of interviewers living in the 76 primary areas. Because of the difficulties of always finding individuals coincident with our interviewing needs (the sample was prepared in stages, beginning in the South, then in the Northeast, West, and North Central), two additional training sessions were held in Ann Arbor for the North Central region and to train interviewers from other areas who had not been previously available. In addition, retraining sessions had to be held in New York and Chicago because of interviewer attrition.

The first training session was held in Detroit. The next session was held in Atlanta with many trainees drawn from neighboring states. The Dallas training was held next, followed by training sessions in New Orleans, Washington, D.C., New York, Chicago, Los Angeles, and the two in Ann Arbor. In addition to holding more training and retraining sessions than originally planned, the length of the training sessions had to be extended because of the complicated interviewing instructions, intricate sampling procedures, and relative inexperience of the trainees. Instead of the original five days generally allotted for training at the Survey Research Center, we found that nine days were barely adequate to provide the knowledge necessary for these new people to function and deliver high quality sampling and interviewing. As a result of these recruitment efforts, approximately 450 individuals were trained and supervised during the course of the study.

In summary, in the absence of an adequate existing network, the necessity of recruiting indigenous interviewers to work in 76 different geographical areas scattered across the United States proved extremely time-consuming and difficult. However, our basic commitment to community involvement and the belief that a better scientific product would ensue from using local people for the interviewing necessitated this approach (Myers, 1977; Weiss, 1977). As in other survey research projects, certain methods of recruitment and training proved more fruitful than others. Because of the complicated sampling and interviewing required of an essentially new staff, fairly high educational attainments of interviewer recruits became a necessity. Thus, the best interviewers proved to be college-trained individuals who held professional positions and who were able to work during the summers and part time. The very best were current and retired public school teachers. In addition, certain demographic and personal characteristics were relevant. As in previous survey research (Jackson, 1989; Jackson et al., 1982), black men, particularly young black men, found it difficult to carry out the assignments. The task of entering neighborhoods without previous introduction, knocking on doors, selecting respondents, and obtaining completed interviews was a difficult chore in many of the neighborhoods selected for study. For related reasons, young female interviewers also were nearly as problematic. Middle-aged and older women and couples were the most reliable and efficient interviewers. Retired couples were particularly good, having dedication, an abiding interest in the study, and ample time for participation.

Our interviewing experiences suggest that the selection and training procedures worked well. Although an inordinate amount of time was needed to locate, select, and train interviewers, it was necessary given the critical role they played in the community and the emphasis on careful control of interview quality.

National Samples of Black Americans

NSBA Cross-Section Sampling and Sample

New procedures developed during the course of the project provided a substantial savings over ordinary self-weighting probability sampling methods. The need to base the sample on the distribution of the black population, rather than the total population, however, necessitated much more work in the Ann Arbor office than had been anticipated. In addition to new materials (tapes, maps, etc.), 21 additional people were hired to conduct the basic work of identifying the primary sampling areas, doing the secondary selections, and preparing maps and other detailed information for the block-level cluster records from which the selection of households would be made. If blacks had been merely overselected from existing primary areas used in the Survey Research Center's (SRC) national population sample, a practice common in many previous national studies, many of these costs would have been avoided. It was determined, however, that this procedure would not produce a sample with acceptable precision (Hess, 1985).

A major impediment in previous attempts to conduct national research on representative samples of black Americans has been the unacceptable costs associated with scientifically locating blacks in high density, white geographical areas (Jackson & Hatchett, 1983, 1986). The first year of the grant period explored alternative methods of screening for black households in largely white residential areas. Work also began on the construction of a sample design, including the number of primary areas to be selected. Through an examination of black subsamples of previous national surveys, estimates of the precision of survey results were made with various numbers of primary areas. In view of the cost and precision estimates, a sample design of 76 primary areas was decided on. This sample design is similar in number of primary areas to most samples of the total population but has other features (e.g., probabilities of selection of areas, stratification) tailored to the black population. This design proved to be much more sophisticated than the one originally proposed and provided a sample with greater precision. This was accomplished, as explained later, through the creation and implementation of two novel screening procedures (Hess, 1985).

The development of a completely new national sample required more work than is usually needed in the:

1. Definition of primary sampling units
2. Construction of estimates of black households in each area
3. Allocation of primary areas to regions of the country
4. Stratification by other variables
5. Selection of primary areas
6. Identification of secondary sampling units
7. Estimation of black households in each secondary area

8. Stratification of secondary units
9. Selection of secondary areas
10. Mapping of areas selected
11. Subdivision of areas into smaller units
12. Sampling those smaller units
13. Listing and screening housing units

Whenever possible, the design profited from the previous Survey Research Center sampling work on the national sample of households (Hess, 1985).

The multistage, national probability sample was based on the distribution of the black population indicated in the 1970 Census, and subsequent updates. The selection of the 76 certainty and noncertainty primary areas was done to maximize the utilization of current SRC sample areas that attained minimum size requirements for black households. The overall rate of selection was 1:2,300. Approximately 58% of the black sample areas were also in the 1970 SRC national sample. The sample was self-weighting, and every black American household in the continental United States had the same probability of being selected. The sampling of housing units within primary areas was done in an effort to yield approximately the same level of clustering and precision of estimates as SRC household samples of comparable size. This outcome was accomplished through extensive work in the Institute for Social Research Sampling Section and the development of several new screening methods.

The Standard Listing and Screening Procedures (SLASP), applied in both mixed and mostly black areas, provided a unique method of identifying black households by using reference housing units. The Wide Area Screening Procedure (WASP) was developed for use in areas with suspected few or no black-occupied households. This procedure employed the reference housing unit approach but in a less systematic manner. In the SLASP procedure the interviewer was told explicitly which housing units to contact. In WASP, the number or location of these reference units depended on the interviewers' assessment of the number and distribution of housing units in the area. Whereas the SLASP interviewers listed and classified each housing unit in a cluster, the WASP interviewers asked the reference housing units about blacks in the area and listed only the black units. This procedural difference minimized the cost of screening in geographical areas of low density black and was highly effective in reducing the cost and time in locating and listing black housing units. Within sample households one person was randomly chosen from the list of eligible respondents (18 years of age, self-identified black, and U.S. citizens) using the Kish selection procedure (Kish, 1965).

Twenty percent of the WASP clusters were selected for intensive screening of households to estimate the extent, if any, of undercoverage. Analyses indicated that the procedure was far more effective than originally anticipated. Only eight black households in the sample WASP clusters were missed, the majority of these in one cluster. Because of the selection procedures, none of the overlooked black housing units would have been selected for the study. The WASP procedure permitted the NSBA sample to be obtained with clustering and precision comparable to SRC household samples of comparable size for a fraction of the cost. It also appears to be an effective and generally useful screening method for future sample surveys of blacks and other rare population groups. (See Hess, 1985, for further details on the development and evaluation of the NSBA sample.)

The sampling procedures reported here resulted in 2,107 completed interviews. The overall response rate was 67%. The black population is disproportionately distributed within urban areas, where historically response rates have been low. An average of 3.4 callbacks, with a range of 1 to 22 per selected household, were required to complete the interviews.

Overall, the national sample is fairly representative of the black population as reported by the 1980 Census. There is, however, a disparity in the proportion of women to men and a slight tendency to underrepresent younger people of both sexes and to overrepresent older women. Analyses reveal no sex differences between respondents and identified nonrespondents. The sex differences may be due to the disproportionate representation of black female-headed households in the United States (Jackson, 1989). Finally, there is a slight tendency to overrepresent low-income groups and for a slightly higher proportion of individuals to come from the South than their distribution in the population would indicate. These differences from expected Census distributions are relatively slight (particularly if Census undercount and enumeration problems in the black population are considered) in comparison with other large studies of the black population (Jackson, 1989; Jackson & Hatchett, 1986; Smith, 1987).

General Field-Work and Quality Control of Interviews

In certain geographical areas, field coordinators served as super-visors over a number of interviewers (Boston, Baltimore, Los Angeles, New York, Atlanta, and Washington, D.C.). We tried to avoid asking interviewers to travel to other areas. Since white SRC interviewers were employed for the WASP procedure, black interviewers from nearby areas were dispatched to attempt these interviews when no local black interviewer was available.

Elaborate procedures for computer checking-in of the interviews and coversheets as well as a continuing record of the sample were adapted and used. When each interview arrived in the Ann Arbor office, it was checked for accuracy and mistakes. A record was kept for each interviewer, and if consistent mistakes were found, the person was contacted and the mistakes corrected. The interview was logged in and assigned an identification number, the recontact sheet and coversheet were removed (and logged in separately), and University payroll was instructed to send the respondent a $10 or $5 check for participation in the cross-section or the three-generation study, respectively. Finally, a verification procedure to ascertain that an interview had actually taken place was initiated for the first, fifth, and tenth interviews of each interviewer. Thus, it could be ascertained very early in the field process which interviews were being done legitimately, and corrective steps could be taken, if necessary, before serious damage had occurred. Using these extensive procedures, verification did not find a single case of inappropriate interviewer behavior. Overall, the logging in, checking, and verification procedures provided a high level of quality control on the accuracy and authenticity of the field work.

As described in detail by Jackson and Hatchett (1986), approximately 53.3% (1,124) of the cross-section respondents proved to be members of eligible (youngest lineage generation member 14 years of age or older) three-generation families (approximately 60% were members of three-generation families of any age). Given the design, this proportion of eligible families generated an additional 3,372 interviews to be taken (1,124 reinterviews and 2,248 three-generation family interviews). By any estimation this was a prodigious number of supplementary interviews. Because these numbers far exceeded the original estimates (2,080 additional interviews), it was not possible to conduct all the three-generation interviews in the face-to-face mode, because interviewees were scattered across the continental United

States. It was considered imperative, however, that all potential three-generation interviews at least be attempted.

Given scientific and financial considerations, it was decided to attempt contact and completion with the approximately 1,000 three-generation and reinterview subjects who had not been contacted face to face. The instruments were shortened to 45 minutes, and a team of 10 black telephone interviewers was located, hired, and trained at the SRC's Telephone Interviewing Facility. During a 2-month period approximately 570 additional interviews (370 three-generation interviews and 200 reinterviews) were completed.

Thus, during the course of the entire NSBA study a grand total of 4,350 interviews was completed (2,107 face-to-face cross-section interviews, 667 face-to-face and 200 telephone reinterviews, and 1,006 face-to-face and 370 telephone interviews). Given the distribution of three-generation, reinterview and cross-section interviews, a total of 510 (1,530 interviews) intact three-generation lineage triads were completed.

Coding

The nature of the research questions demanded a higher than usual ratio of open- to closed-ended questions (Jackson et al., 1982). Work groups similar to those used in the creation of the original instruments were convened to work on the open-ended coding schemes. The professional coding staff in the SRC's Coding Section was heavily consulted during this process. Responses from 100 randomly drawn cross-section, three-generation, and reinterview questionnaires were used to develop the conceptually based codes. Code development was particularly tedious and time consuming because of the special care that was taken to make the codes as exhaustive as possible, meaningful to conceptual orientations in extant theory, and culturally sensitive. Issues of language and culturally related response sets were considered in the development of both the open- and closed-ended coding conventions.

Coding was completed under the auspices of the Coding Section, although the PRBA staff was heavily involved in the recruitment, selection, training, and supervision of the individuals hired to do the actual coding of the 4,350 cross-section, three-generation and reinterview questionnaires. To address issues of cultural sensitivity of the items and responses, more than half of the coders used were black. All coding work was regularly checked by PRBA staff throughout the duration of the coding process. The preliminary codes developed from the subsample of 100 open-ended responses had to be continually expanded to incorporate additional responses that emerged during the production coding. This necessitated the review of thousands of individual responses by the professional staff. Although these procedures were time consuming and tedious, we believe they resulted in higher quality and more exhaustive codes. The more closed-ended sections in all questionnaires were coded with computerized Direct Data Entry (DDE). Because of its complexity, each of the reinterview questionnaires was hand coded.

In many cases it was necessary to precode many of the culturally sensitive items. This precoding was required particularly in the Identity sections and in the Family Relations section of the reinterview instrument. During this process it was discovered that approximately 130 of the reinterviews had been completed with some extent of inadequate information. In order to correct these problems, each of the 130 respondents was called and asked to provide the missing or incomplete data. The desired information was obtained from over 90% of the respondents.

Finally, because of concern with the shared meaning between research staff and respondents of even our closed-ended items (Jackson, Tucker, & Bowman, 1982), the "random probe," a unique methodological process pioneered by Howard Schuman (1966) of the Survey Research Center was used. This technique uses predetermined random assignment of selected items that are given standard probes during the interview. Thus, for each of the 10 closed-ended items selected, nearly 1,000 responses were obtained that have been coded by project staff. In keeping with our qualitative/quantitative research approach (Jackson, Tucker, & Bowman, 1982), analyses of these responses will provide some indication of the shared perspective between respondents and research staff (Chatters, 1986).

Summary

The area and telephone sampling methods that we have contributed in the course of our work provide the first opportunity to generalize survey research findings to the entire adult black population, the black elderly population, and black three-generation lineage families. To our knowledge, the latter represents the first national probability survey of three-generation lineage families in any population group. These surveys were made possible by four novel developments in screening techniques: the Wide Area Sampling Procedure (WASP), the Standard Listing and Screening Procedure (SLASP) (Hess, 1985; Jackson, Taylor, & Bowman, 1982), the Multiplicity Sampling Procedure (Jackson & Hatchett, 1983, 1986), and the disproportionate random-digit-dial telephone sampling procedure (Inglis, Groves, & Heeringa, 1985). Each makes important general methodological contributions to the social and behavioral sciences.

The methodological techniques used in constructing the questionnaires, designing and obtaining the samples, and training interviewers provide new information on survey research generally and particularly on the problems of studying racial-ethnic groups (Jackson, 1986). The work that we have done will provide the basis for feasible drawing of national household samples of black Americans in future studies. The existence of these high quality samples has also made follow-up studies on these individuals very cost effective. In addition to the panel studies already completed (NPSBA and NBESP), a longitudinal study of three-generation families, for example, would provide unparalleled data on black family and individual development across the next decade or more (Jackson & Hatchett, 1986).

The content of the questionnaires, the quality of the national samples, and the data collection techniques give promise that these studies will stand for many years as sources of high quality data for scientists and policy makers in the broad areas of physical health, employment, family relationships, political behavior, personal adjustment, and mental health. Although the costs of conducting these novel national sample surveys were relatively high, the results will have important, immediate scientific and practical consequences and the potential to influence the nature of future social and behavioral science research on Americans of African descent.

During the course of the project three new questionnaires and related materials were completed; recruitment and training procedures were developed; and a national team of black interviewers was located and trained. It is important to note that the establishment of this well-trained team of black interviewers facilitated subsequent PRBA research efforts and what was learned in the process of this training could be important for other research organizations and groups as well.

Three new sampling methods and related materials that will have important contributions to subsequent procedures used for sampling low density population groups were developed. Both WASP and SLASP are methods that can be readily applied in different racial-ethnic groups as well as for more traditional sampling problems. Additionally, inclusion rules, three-generation field procedures, and a simplified sampling process to obtain random samples of contiguous generation family members were developed by the staff so that selections could be made based on information from the original cross-section respondent. Section B of the reinterview provides information on the multiplicity sampling process so that appropriate probability weights can be applied to the members of the resulting three-generation and elderly samples.

The scope of the NSBA data is represented by the summary of the questions asked in the interviews. The questionnaires cover many aspects of the lives of Americans of African descent. It was noted earlier in this chapter that several unique research opportunities derive from the fact that these data are based on large and nationally representative samples of black Americans. Prior social scientific knowledge, as well as public policies based on this knowledge, have been limited by a lack of appreciation for the heterogeneity of black American life. The need to examine this heterogeneity is also relevant for subgroups within the African American population, particularly those that are seen as experiencing special problems. For example, much has been written about the special problems of the black elderly (Taylor & Taylor, 1982). Because of the three-generation study, a very large national probability sample of the black elderly now exists, which permits complex multivariate analyses of their problems, strengths, and coping strategies (Jackson, Chatters, & Neighbors, 1982; Jackson & Gibson, 1985; Gibson, 1986; Gibson & Jackson, 1988).

3

NEIGHBORHOOD LIFE

Norweeta G. Milburn
Phillip J. Bowman

The role that neighborhoods play in the overall quality of life among Americans of African descent has not been adequately explored in the psychological or social science literature. As black neighborhoods become increasingly prominent in the fabric of urban America, voluntary organizations within these neighborhoods become crucial for societal, community, and individual functioning. To be sure, a widely held theoretical assumption is that active participation in voluntary associations reflects psychological well-being, community integration, and involvement in the broader social structure of society (Tomeh, 1974). Voluntary associations have become pivotal social agencies that not only help fulfill individual goals but also facilitate collective action and empower communities in the democratic process. Indeed, black neighborhood organizations are major resources for reducing alienation and improving the overall quality of life in our post-industrial and increasingly urbanized society. As we approach the 21st century, active participation in neighborhood organizations may well become a major weapon in the escalating struggle against crime, drugs, and other problems that seriously threaten the quality of life in black communities (Smith & Freedman, 1972).

Existing literature suggests that African Americans participate quite extensively in voluntary associations (McPherson, 1977; Olson, 1970). However, the major function that voluntary associations serve among African Americans has been the subject of considerable controversy. From a psychological perspective, drawing in part from social psychiatry and psychiatric epidemiology, participation in a broader social network may have a major impact on the mental health of African Americans. Previous studies have suggested that participation is correlated with positive psychological characteristics, such as global happiness, self-esteem, and personal efficacy (Bradburn, 1969; see Milburn, 1982, for a review of the literature). Studies have also shown that African Americans who are involved in voluntary associations have fewer symptoms of psychological distress than those who are not involved (Gary, Brown, Milburn, Ahmed, & Booth, 1989; Gary, Brown, Milburn, Thomas, & Lockley, 1983).

Studies have also pointed out the instrumental or collective goal-oriented purposes of many of these organizations, such as economic cooperation, community problem-solving, and political/social action (e.g., Barnes, 1979). Much of the previous research, though, has emphasized the expressive or sociocultural-oriented functions of black voluntary associations. These include opportunities for self-expression, achievement, and self-fulfillment (e.g., Babchuck & Thompson, 1963). Nonetheless, black voluntary organizations within the neighborhood environment have served as informal resources for a wide range of social support and community action (Jones, 1977; McPherson, 1977; Tomeh, 1974). Black voluntary organizations, especially women's clubs, have been very active in providing social services to low-income black communities (Billingsley & Giovannoni, 1972). Moreover, in addition to voting, active involvement in neighborhood organizations may become an important mode of political participation at the local level. We currently know far too little about the antecedents of active involvement in voluntary associations among African Americans, despite their crucial psychological, community, and societal functions.

Critical Issue: Predictors of Involvement

Previous studies on participation in neighborhood and community organizations suggest that demographics and neighborhood-related factors are important determinants of participation (e.g., Wandersman, 1981). However, very little research has been done on the relative effects of these two sets of factors. The purpose of this chapter is to examine the relationship of demographics and community embedment to involvement in neighborhood groups among African Americans.

Involvement will be defined as participation in any type of voluntary neighborhood group such as a block club, community association, social club, and/or helping group in the neighborhood. The demographic characteristics that will be examined include age, education, homeownership, family income, "urbanicity" or the degree of urban development in an individual's geographic area, and the region of the country an individual lives in. Social or community *embedment* will be defined as the enmeshment of an individual in the social environment of the neighborhood. Specifically, the focus is on rootedness and bondedness within the immediate community that includes neighboring activities such as visiting with other neighborhood residents (Riger & Lavrakas, 1981).

The following research questions are addressed: What demographic variables are associated with involvement in neighborhood organizations? How strong is the relationship between various demographic predictors and involvement? Do community embedment variables increase the tendency for involvement? What are the relative effects of demographic and community embedment predictors on involvement? How much overall variance in involvement can be explained with the most salient set of demographic and community embedment predictors? Previous findings from the general literature are highlighted in the next section to provide a better context for understanding our national findings on predictors of neighborhood organizational involvement among African Americans. The chapter concludes with a broader discussion of the major findings and issues.

Demographics and Participation

Researchers typically have tried to identify the individuals who are most likely to participate in voluntary associations using various demographic characteristics such as socioeconomic status, sex, and age (e.g., Tomeh, 1974). Briefly, these findings can be summarized as follows: individuals of higher socioeconomic status participate more than individuals of lower socioeconomic status; men participate more than women, except in expressive voluntary associations; and the relationship between age and participation tends to approximate a normal distribution with middle-aged individuals participating more than younger or older individuals.

Other demographics have also been found to be related to participation. Wirth's (1938) work, among others, suggests that the degree of urbanicity will affect involvement in voluntary associations; participation will be higher in urban areas than nonurban areas. This hypothesis has been supported somewhat by empirical research, but it may be moderated by socioeconomic status. For example, Houghland, Kyong–Dong, and Christenson (1979) found higher levels of participation in voluntary associations in urban areas, but this finding appeared to be accounted for primarily by socioeconomic status; that is, individuals of lower-socioeconomic status in urban areas had higher levels of participation than their middle- and upper-socioeconomic counterparts.

Research that focuses on demographic correlates of participation in voluntary associations that are specifically neighborhood organizations is still somewhat sparse (e.g., Jameson, 1973; Kaul, 1976; Muller, 1971; Warren, 1975). Overall, demographic patterns similar to those found in other voluntary associations, with the exception of sex differences, are seen in neighborhood group participation patterns. For example, Hunter (1975) found that participation in the local community association was related to education, number of years one has lived in the neighborhood, age, and homeownership. Residents who were older, newcomers, more educated, and homeowners were more likely to participate in the organization than were their counterparts. Women have been found to be more likely than men to participate in some neighborhood groups, even though these are instrumental rather than expressive organizations (Jameson, 1973).

Demographic characteristics have been the primary focus in previous research because they provide profiles of who is likely to participate and who is not. These findings suggest that African Americans who are middle-aged, more educated, have higher incomes, and own homes will be more likely to be involved in neighborhood groups than will their counterparts. However, other variables, such as community-based ecological factors, also need to be considered to understand more fully the tendency to participate in neighborhood organizations.

Community Embedment and Participation in Neighborhood Groups

One set of such variables includes neighboring activities and social interaction within the local community. Participation and neighboring have been used as both independent and dependent measures in research that has been done in this area. In a reciprocal manner, neighboring seems to encourage participation and vice versa.

Participation in voluntary organizations has been found to be related to two specific dimensions of neighboring, in both the intensity and extensiveness of the interaction: People who participated in voluntary organizations had higher levels of intensity and extensiveness in their neighboring than those who did not participate (McGahan, 1972). Moreover, Hunter (1975) found that participation in a community organization was positively related to informal neighboring and a sense of community. Residents who participated in the community organization were more likely to engage in neighboring activities, such as chatting with the neighbors and exchanging things, than those who did not participate. In addition, those who participated expressed a higher sense of community than those who did not participate.

As an independent variable, there is also some evidence that neighboring may be an important antecedent, as well as a consequence, of participation in successful community organizations. Where block organizations were successfully organized, Unger and Wandersman (1983) found that residents reported engaging in more neighboring activities before the block organization was developed than residents on blocks that were not successfully organized. However, contrary to their expectations, there was no clear evidence that members of block organizations had engaged in more neighboring activities than nonmembers prior to joining the block organization. They did find, though, that over time neighboring activities increased among members of block organizations. Neighboring included recognizing and/ or knowing the names of, visiting, and borrowing from people in the neighborhood. Therefore, neighboring may influence and be influenced by involvement in neighborhood organizations.

Neighboring can be viewed as an indicator of embedment in the community—how much an individual is rooted and bonded within his or her neighborhood (Riger & Lavrakas, 1981). Riger and Lavrakas (1981) observed that social embedment, bondedness, and rootedness in the neighborhood was linked to involvement in neighborhood groups. In this instance, bondedness included forming "social bonds" within the neighborhood, such as recognizing nonresidents, feeling like a part of the neighborhood, or knowing kids in the neighborhood by name. Rootedness included being "settled" within the neighborhood, such as living in the neighborhood for a while or being a homeowner. Two profiles emerged for people who were likely to be involved in neighborhood groups: working class, young adults with children, and older adults with children at home who lived in a single-family dwelling. The latter had the highest levels of participation. The former were high bonded, low rooted, and the latter were high bonded, high rooted.

In addition to demographic antecedents, community embedment variables further help to distinguish people who will participate in neighborhood organizations. These findings suggest that African Americans who are more socially embedded in their neighborhoods are more likely to be involved in neighborhood groups than those who are less socially embedded. Therefore, both demographics and community embedment will be simultaneously considered in this national study of African Americans. In a sample that was two-thirds black, Wandersman and his colleagues (1981) found that sociodemographic variables (age, marital status, tenure in the neighborhood, and sex) and community embedment factors (perceiving that there were problems on the block, being involved in community activities, neighboring activities, and personal influence on the block) were both related to people becoming members of neighborhood organizations. Guided by these findings, we now turn to data from a nationally representative sample of African Americans.

National Findings

Relevant Subsample

Over one-third (38%) of the respondents from the National Survey of Black Americans reported that they had and were involved in neighborhood organizations in their communities. Only these 799 respondents with access to membership comprised the sample for this investigation. As can be seen in Table 3.1, the respondents in communities with neighborhood organizations were similar to the general national sample. Approximately 63% of the respondents were female, primarily young and middle-aged adults, with an average age of 42.9 years (SD = 16.9 years). They were not a highly educated group, but typically were high school graduates (64.3%). Over half of the sample (57.8%) had family incomes of $10,000 per year or above. These respondents were mostly from large cities (61.6%). Very few (less than 7%) were from the western part of the United States; most were from the northern (53.2%) and southern (40.3%) regions of the country.

Table 3.1
Description of the Sample (*N* = 799)

Demographics	Percent of Sample
Sex	
Male	37.2
Female	62.8
Age	
18 to 34 years	38.9
35 to 54 years	35.1
55 years or older	26.0
Education	
0 to 11 years	35.7
High school graduate	31.8
Some college	19.1
College graduate	13.4
Family Income	
< $5,000	19.2
$5,000 to $10,000	23.0
$10,000 to $20,000	28.7
> $20,000	29.1
Urbanicity	
Large city	61.6
Small city	24.0
Rural	14.4
Region	
South	40.3
North	53.2
West	6.5

Measures

Dependent variable

Involvement was defined as participation in the neighborhood organization in one's own local community. It was a dichotomous variable. Involvement was scored "5" if a respondent was not involved in a neighborhood group and "1" if he or she was involved. Of respondents with access to neighborhood organizations, 312 (39.1%) were involved, and 486 (60.9%) were not.

Independent Variables

The *demographic characteristics* that were used included age, education, family income, homeownership, urbanicity, and region. *Age* was broken into three groups: 18 to 34 years, 35 to 54 years, and 55 years or older. *Education* was coded as: 0 to 11 years of schooling, high school graduate, some college, and college graduate. *Family income* was coded as: under $5,000, $5,000 to $10,000, $10,000 to $20,000, and over $20,000. *Homeownership* categories included: homeowner, renter, and other, such as receiving a house as a job benefit or living at home with one's parents. *Urbanicity* was a measure of the degree of urban development in the respondent's geographic location. Primary study areas from which respondents were selected were classified either as a large city, a small city, or a rural area. *Region,* like urbanicity, was based on the primary study areas and was coded as northern, southern, or western sections of the country.

The community embedment measures that were used included the number of neighbors that respondents visited, the frequency of visits to neighbors, respondents' feelings about their neighborhoods, the length of time people had lived in the respondents' neighborhoods, and respondents' impression of interpersonal relations in their neighborhoods. The *number of neighbors* that respondents visited was categorized as: many, some, a few, and none. The *frequency of respondents' visits* to neighbors was coded as: nearly every day (4 or more times a week), at least once a week (1 to 3 times a week), a few times a month (2 to 3 times a month), once a month, a few times a year, and never. Respondents' *feelings about the neighborhood* were categorized as: very good, fairly good, fairly bad, and very bad. The length of time people had lived in respondents' neighborhoods was coded as: more than 10 years, 5 to 10 years, 2 to 5 years, and less than 2 years. The *number of relatives* in the neighborhood was coded as: many, some, a few, and none. The last social embedment variable, *social climate,* or respondents' impressions of the interpersonal relationships in their neighborhood, was coded as: most people keep to themselves and don't talk or visit much with other people who live here; some people keep to themselves but others talk or visit a lot with the other people who live here; and most people talk or visit a lot with the other people who live here.

Analysis Strategy

Bivariate and multivariate relationships were examined with Multiple Classification Analysis (MCA). This technique estimated the independent (Eta), controlled for all other (Beta), and overall multiple (R^2) effects of the various demographic and social embedment predictors of involvement. Initially, separate analyses were done within each category of predictors; subsequent analyses combined both categories to determine an overall set of salient predictors.

Findings

Table 3.2 shows that, despite differences in the power of specific predictors, the set of demographic characteristics accounted for only 5% of the variance in explaining involvement in neighborhood groups. Homeownership, age, and education were the demographic variables that had the strongest relationship with involvement (*Eta* = .21, .14, .11, respectively). Homeowners were more involved than respondents who did not own homes, that is, those who were renters or had other living arrangements. Individuals aged 55 years or older were more involved than younger or middle-aged individuals. Finally, individuals who were college graduates were more involved than those who had less education.

Table 3.3 shows that, overall, the community embedment characteristics also had some effect on involvement in neighborhood groups. However, similar to the demographic predictors, community embedment variables accounted for only 6% of the variance. The Eta statistic reveals that the number of neighbors visited (*Eta* = .17), feelings about the neighborhood (*Eta* = .14), and the length of residence in the neighborhood (*Eta* = .12) were the most powerful community embedment predictors. Individuals who visited many of their neighbors were more involved than individuals who visited fewer of their neighbors. Individuals who felt good about the neighborhood were more involved than those who felt bad about the neighborhood. There also appears to be some tendency for those who had many relatives in the neighborhood to be *less* involved ($X = 2.66, N = 41$) than those who reported only some ($X = 3.44, N = 77$), a few ($X = 3.31, N = 161$), or none ($X = 3.30, N = 334$). Involvement in neighborhood organizations has no clear relationship to frequency of visits to neighbors or

Table 3.2

Influence of Demographics on Involvement: Multiple Classification Analysis

	Class Mean	Adjusted Mean	Beta	Beta²	Eta	Eta²	N
Homeownership							
Own	3.06	3.18	.14	.02	.21	.04	384
Rent	3.88	3.74					294
Other	3.67	3.57					18
Age							
18 to 34 years	3.75	3.66	.11	.01	.14	.02	281
35 to 54 years	3.24	3.30					245
55 years or older	3.16	3.13					170
Education							
0 to 11 years	3.47	3.52	.09	.01	.11	.01	235
High school graduate	3.60	3.53					228
Some college	3.43	3.36					188
College graduate	2.89	3.03					95
Urbanicity							
Large city	3.45	3.48	.08	.01	.06	.00	730
Small city	3.55	3.51					165
Rural	3.14	3.03					101
Family Income							
< $5,000	3.65	3.62	.08	.01	.12	.01	136
$5,000 to $10,000	3.68	3.56					158
$10,000 to $20,000	3.39	3.39					199
> $20,000	3.11	3.23					203
Region							
South	3.46	3.56	.07	.01	.04	.00	281
North	3.37	3.29					371
West	3.64	3.68					44

NOTE: R^2 (unadjusted) = .07; R^2 (adjusted) = .05; N = 696.

subjective descriptions of the neighborhood. However, surprisingly, those who visited their neighbors infrequently (a few times a month or a few times during the year) were more likely to be involved than those who visited their neighbors every day.

Tables 3.4 and 3.5 suggest that demographic factors, in combination with community embedment variables, may be necessary but are not sufficient for predicting involvement in neighborhood organizations among African Americans. As shown in Table 3.4, despite

Table 3.3
Influence of Social Embedment on Involvement: Multiple Classification Analysis

	Class Mean	Adjusted Mean	Beta	Beta²	Eta	Eta²	N
Number of neighbors visited							
Many	2.76	2.84	.14	.02	.17	.03	166
Some	3.37	3.37					152
A few	3.54	3.50					327
Frequency of visits to neighbors							
Every day	3.50	3.63	.11	.01	.10	.01	72
Weekly	3.32	3.40					138
Few times a month	3.10	3.10					139
Once a month	3.33	3.24					67
Few times a year	3.15	3.11					147
Never	3.68	3.58					82
Feelings about the neighbors							
Very good	2.98	3.07	.10	.01	.14	.02	220
Fairly good	3.42	3.41					263
Fairly bad	3.42	3.27					73
Very bad	4.37	4.03					19
Time people have lived in the neighborhood							
> 10 years	3.07	3.15	.08	.01	.12	.01	324
5 to 10 years	3.50	3.45					235
2 to 5 years	3.63	3.47					67
< 2 years	3.53	3.37					19
Relatives in neighborhood							
Many	2.66	2.87	.06	.00	.09	.00	41
Some	3.44	3.49					77
A few	3.31	3.33					161
None	3.34	3.30					366
Description of the neighborhood							
Most people keep to themselves	3.36	3.29	.03	.00	.02	.00	217
Some people keep to themselves	3.27	3.26					314
Most people visit a lot	3.28	3.43					114

NOTE: R^2 (unadjusted) = .06; R^2 (adjusted) = .03; N = 645.

Table 3.4
Additional Variance Explained by Social Embedment

Respondent Characteristics	R^2 (unadjusted)	R^2 (adjusted)
Demographic	.07	.05
Homeownership		
Age		
Education		
Demographic and social embedment	.12	.07
Number of neighbors visited		
Region		
Homeownership		
Age		
Family income		
Education		
Frequency of visits to neighbors		
Feelings about the neighborhood		
Time people have lived in the neighborhood		
Relatives in the neighborhood		
Urbanicity		
Description of the neighborhood		

the fact that bivariate effects of community embedment variables were comparable to those of demographic variables, their inclusion increased the explained variance by only 2%. This raises the possibility that effects of the more distal sociodemographic variables may be mediated, to some degree, by the more proximal community embedment variables in predictions of neighborhood organizational involvement.

For the sake of parsimony, only the effects of the most salient demographic and social embedment predictors of neighborhood group involvement were estimated in Table 3.5. In order of their relative effects, the most powerful predictors were homeownership, the number of neighbors visited, and feelings about the neighborhood. These three community-based variables accounted for relatively more variance in neighborhood organization involvement than did age or education. These findings suggest that future inquiries should go beyond traditional demographic models to consider how community embedment and other relevant variables combine to increase the involvement of African Americans in neighborhood organizations.

Table 3.5

Relative Effects of the Most Salient Demographic and Social Embedment Variables

Variables	Beta
Homeownership	.14
Number of neighbors visited	.13
Feelings about the neighborhood	.10
Age	.08
Education	.08
Frequency of visits to neighbors	.07

NOTE: R^2 (unadjusted) = .09; R^2 (adjusted) = .06; N = 639.

Discussion

As African Americans become increasingly prominent in the fabric of urban life, their participation in local block clubs and other neighborhood organizations takes on greater significance. Active involvement in such voluntary associations has important individual, community, and societal functions. To be sure, such neighborhood involvement may be not only an important source of psychological well-being but also a critical instrument for community empowerment and a major sociopolitical resource in the national struggle against racial inequalities, drugs, and crime. Despite these crucial functions, we know far too little about factors associated with involvement in neighborhood organizations among African Americans. To begin to address this issue, the present chapter presents empirical findings from a national probability sample. Findings reveal that over one-third of all African Americans have access to some type of neighborhood organization with about two out of every five actually involved. As expected, demographic and social embedment characteristics were significant predictors of involvement in these neighborhood organizations.

The demographic characteristics that were the strongest predictors of involvement were homeownership, age, and education. The relationship of homeownership and education to involvement was as expected and supported the findings of previous research (Tomeh, 1974). Black Americans who were homeowners and college graduates were more involved in neighborhood groups than those who were not homeowners or had less education. Age also was related to involvement but not as anticipated. Older black Americans, not those who were middle-aged, were more involved than those who were younger or middle-aged. Among black adults, participation in neighborhood groups does not seem to follow a bell curve as it does among other Americans (Tomeh, 1974).

The community embedment characteristics that were the strongest predictors of involvement were visiting neighbors, both the number of neighbors visited and the frequency of visits to neighbors, and feelings about the neighborhood. Previous research has suggested that community-based variables such as neighboring are positively related to participation (Hunter, 1975; Unger & Wandersman, 1983). Generally, people who are involved in neighborhood groups are more likely to engage in neighboring activities such as visiting with neighbors, and neighboring seems to increase among those who are involved in neighborhood groups. Among African Americans, this was only partially true. Black adults who were involved in neighborhood groups did visit more neighbors than those who were not involved. However, the frequency of visits to neighbors was lower among those who were more involved in neighborhood groups than it was among those who were less involved.

The overall strength of demographic and social embedment predictors, as a parsimonious set of variables to explain involvement, was relatively small. Nonetheless, as suggested by others (Wandersman, Jakubs, & Giamartino, 1981), these findings demonstrate that social embedment characteristics enhance our understanding of African Americans' involvement in neighborhood groups. Interestingly, although not surprisingly, the strongest predictors of involvement—homeownership and the number of neighbors visited—are both linked to community embedment (Riger & Lavrakas, 1981). However, homeownership was treated as a demographic characteristic in this investigation because residents who are homeowners are physically rooted in their neighborhoods, whereas residents who visit their neighbors are socially bonded to their neighborhoods. Nevertheless, African Americans who are socially and psychologically embedded in their neighborhoods tended to be more involved in neighborhood organizations. The findings in this chapter provide accurate national data on involvement in neighborhood organizations among African American adults, a more externally valid basis to explore critical predictors of such organizational involvement, and a basis to monitor future changes in neighborhood organizations within African American communities.

Future inquiries should build on the present findings to further clarify the nature, antecedents, and consequences of involvement in neighborhood organizations. Given the growing urbanization of African Americans, a better understanding of the sociopolitical and other functions served by neighborhood organizations in urban America is needed.

FAMILY LIFE

Shirley J. Hatchett
Donna L. Cochran
James S. Jackson

The American family is changing and at the forefront of this "revolution" in family living patterns is the African American family (Farley & Allen, 1987). There has been an increase in the number of people living alone and in the number of families headed by women. Accompanying this trend is a decrease in the number of men who live in husband-wife households and head families. Although the trend is evident among all families, these changes have been more substantial for black families (Glick, 1988). The increase in single-person households stems from young people delaying marriage but still establishing their own households as well as from marital dissolution.

The increase in female-headed households is rooted primarily in the increases in marital dissolution but also may have as a contributing factor the continuing fertility of unmarried women in contrast to married women (Bianchi & Spain, 1986; Farley & Allen, 1987; Jaynes & Williams, 1989). Women with children who find themselves alone because of separation, divorce, or the death of a spouse, as well as those who do not marry more and more are living on their own (Bianchi & Farley, 1979; Bianchi & Spain, 1986; Glick, 1988; Macklin, 1980).

The trend in female headship is causing some concern among both family scholars and policy makers (Jaynes & Williams, 1989; Moynihan, 1986). Most of the concern centers around possible negative psychosocial adjustment and impaired achievement of children, although reviews of work in this area have argued that research has failed to find conclusive evidence for these effects of single parenting (Blechman, 1982; Elder, 1985; Herzog & Sudia, 1968). Other factors, some situational and others socioeconomic, are now thought to be more responsible for supposed differences between children reared in two-parent versus single-parent homes (Jones & Demaree, 1975; Ogbu, 1988).

As these changes in living patterns unfold among white families, family dissolution and nonformation (as the case may be for mothers who decide not to marry) are perhaps being viewed in a slightly different light than previously when the phenomenon was thought to be chiefly a problem of black families (Elder, 1985). Whereas these living patterns among blacks were often seen in past literature on black families as "deviant" or "pathological" (Allen, 1978; Billingsley, 1968; Farley & Allen, 1987; Staples & Mirande, 1980; Taylor, Chatters, Tucker, & Lewis, 1990), among white families, they are being examined more as legitimate family forms growing out of the realities of modern American life (Scanzoni & Scanzoni, 1981; Sweet & Bumpass, 1987).

Although differences between black and white families, and whether or not black families are "culturally deviant, equivalent, or variant" (Allen, 1978; Farley & Allen, 1987) in respect to dominant culture families, are still being reviewed and debated, the emphasis has turned to advancing both the study of black families (Glick, 1988; McAdoo, 1988; Slaughter & McWorter, 1985) and families in general as new family forms change conceptions of the American family (Elder, 1985). Socialization issues will continue to plague family scholars. Of particular concern in the 1990s, however, is the impact of economic opportunity on families headed by women. For blacks, this is a particularly important issue given the disproportionate representation of these types of families among blacks. Not only are these families different from each other in terms of economic well-being but the continuing political mood and economic situation portend even more economic jeopardy (Hill, 1983; Jaynes & Williams, 1989; Taylor et al., 1990). Underscoring the economic implications of increasing female headship, some writers have called these trends the "feminization of poverty" (Bartlett & Poulton–Callahan, 1982; Bianchi, 1981; Bianchi & Farley, 1979; Bianchi & Spain, 1986; McAdoo, 1988).

Another important concern stemming from recent demographic trends is the increase in older blacks, particularly women, who are

living alone. Like those in female single-parent households, they differ in their economic well-being from those in other types of households (Mitchell & Register, 1986; Taylor, 1985; Troll, 1986).

As sources of formal support for these households are threatened
by cutbacks, informal sources of support become very important. This
chapter addresses the situation of these households in the context of
describing black family structures and extended family behavior in
a national survey of black households. These "at-risk" households
will be compared to other households in terms of availability of social support from the family.

Family Structure and Support

Family structure typically has been assessed by an examination of
household composition. Billingsley's (1968) typology of black families went beyond traditional unidimensional views of family structure by adding extended (nuclear plus other relatives) and augmented
(nuclear plus nonrelated persons) families and by expanding the
definition of nuclear families with such modifiers as incipient (a
couple without children), simple (a couple with children), and attenuated (a single parent with children). As Staples (1971) noted, however, this perception of black families still emphasized the household
and neglected a special characteristic of black families, namely "extendedness." Besides being more likely to be extended at the household level by the inclusion of family members beyond the nuclear
family, black families are extended beyond individual household
boundaries. The black kinship network, although purported to be
particularly salient in situations where resources are limited to the
nuclear family, is also an important aspect of black American family life, fulfilling many of the functions traditionally ascribed to the
nuclear family (Aschenbrenner, 1978; Hill, 1988; Martin & Martin,
1978; McAdoo, 1988; Shimpkin, Shimpkin, & Frate, 1978; Stack, 1974).
The black extended family has been viewed both as an adaptive response to situational constraints in America (Billingsley, 1968;
Stack, 1974; Staples & Mirande, 1980) and as a vestige of West African culture (Sudarkasa, 1988).

Martin and Martin (1978) view the extended family as being multigenerational, interdependent, organized around a dominant figure,
and structurally made up of individual households serving as sub-
families connected to a base household or households of the family

of origin. From her work in "The Flats," Stack (1974) derived the following definition of family: "the smallest organized, durable network of kin and non-kin who interact daily, providing domestic needs of children and assuring their survival. The family network is diffused over several households and fluctuations in household composition do not significantly affect familial arrangements" (p. 31). Evidence of the extendedness of black families has brought into doubt perspectives on the black family that question its viability based on household composition. Underscored is the need to examine the family, particularly the black family, as an extended family (McAdoo, 1988).

This chapter uses the extended family perspective in describing black American families. It is particularly suited for addressing what we consider important issues in the 1990s related to black families—those concerning black single parents and elderly blacks (Farley & Allen, 1987; Taylor, 1986b). Different types of black households will be examined with respect to their potential and actual kin networks. *Potential kin networks* are defined here as the availability (existence) and location of kin. *Actual kin networks* are defined in terms of subjective feelings of connectedness or closeness, interaction, and helping patterns among kin. The extended family can be viewed both as a family network in the physical-spatial sense and in terms of family relations or contact and exchanges. In this view of extendedness, family structure and function are interdependent concepts.

Chapter Overview

This chapter employs a family developmental approach because family structure and function tend to reflect responses to life-cycle situations of family members. Age of head of household is used as a simple indicator of life cycle; more complex indicators include marital and job statuses. To some extent marital status is reflected in the household composition variable that was developed for the analyses. Job status is assessed only indirectly by using family income along with age of head in the subgroup analysis of family structure and support.

The first section examines the household composition of all households in this national black sample and those of the subgroups noted above. All analyses in this section are at the household level; that is, all variables are descriptive of the household unit. The next major section describes and discusses the potential kinship networks of households in the National Survey of Black Americans (NSBA) sample. Finally, the support aspect of black extended families is examined by exploring the actual kin networks of different types of black families. The analyses in the later sections are on the individual respondent level. Only respondents who were heads of household or spouses or partners of heads are included in these analyses, because it is felt these respondents are the best sources of information on the kinship structure and interaction of households. Heads and spouses constituted more than 85% of all respondents in the study sample.

The household composition and potential and actual kin networks of black Americans are described generally by age of the designated household head (in some cases, also by age of the respondent), family or household income, and region and degree of urban development of place of residence. The potential and actual family networks of black households also are described by household composition in addition to the other demographic variables in an attempt to describe the supportive resources of households we have suggested are at risk in the 1990s and further document extended family behavior among black Americans.

Household Membership

The U.S. Census defines the *family unit* as two or more persons living together and related by blood, marriage, or adoption. This is a definition also shared by many family researchers. As mentioned earlier, this emphasis on household living arrangements has led to the operationalization of family structure as household composition (Sweet & Bumpass, 1987). By this definition, persons living alone or with nonrelated persons are not families. However, as suggested by Martin and Martin (1978) and others, these persons may be embedded in extra-household kin networks of contacts and exchanges. Given the concern here for the situations of persons in all types of households, these households will be included in this examination of family structure and function.

For these analyses household structure was derived by the identification of all individuals residing in the sample households.[1] Table 4.1 shows the distribution of the 2,107 households in this national study across 12 categories describing household composition. Categories 5 through 12 capture roughly the dimensions of household

Table 4.1
Composition of Households in the National Survey of Black Americans

Household Composition	Percent of Sample
Male head only	8.5
Female head only	12.3
Male head, other relatives and/or nonrelated persons	3.3
Female head, other relatives and/or nonrelated persons	3.4
Male head, spouse or partner	12.2
Male head, spouse or partner, other relatives and/or nonrelated persons	2.9
Male head, spouse or partner, children	26.9
Male head, spouse or partner, children, other relatives and/or nonrelated persons	6.0
Male head, children	1.4
Male head, children, other relatives and/or nonrelated persons	0.5
Female head, children	16.9
Female head, children, other relatives and/or nonrelated persons	5.7
Total	100.0

NOTE: Total respondents = 2,107

family structure identified in Billingsley's typology of black families (1968)—the incipient nuclear family, the incipient nuclear extended and/or augmented nuclear family, the simple nuclear family, the simple extended and/or augmented nuclear family, the attenuated nuclear family, and the attenuated extended and/or augmented family, respectively.[2] Members of households are classified according to their relationship to a designated "head".[3] As shown in Table 4.1, 12.2% of the households in our sample contained just a male head and spouse or partner;[4] 2.9%, a male head, spouse or partner, and other relatives or nonrelated persons; 26.9%, a couple with their own offspring; and 6.0% a couple with their own offspring and other relatives and/or other persons. In this study, *other relatives* are persons related by blood or marriage outside of the nuclear family (a couple or a couple and their own children). One and a half percent or so of the households contained a male head only with children, and another 0.5% contained a male head with children and other relatives or nonrelated persons. Female headed households with the head's own children constituted 16.9% of the households in our sample, and those with their own children and other relatives and/or other persons, 5.7% of all households. Households with other relatives are not distinguished from those with nonrelated persons in Table 4.1 because of the low percentage of nonrelated persons in all households (3.3%).[5] Of the households in our sample not traditionally treated in family literature, 8.5% contained a male head only, 12.3% a female head only, 3.3% a male head with other relatives and/or other persons, and 3.4% a female head and other relatives and/or other persons.

In all, 15.1% of the sampled households were basically nuclear without children, 33% nuclear with children, 1.9% male-headed with children, and 22.6% female-headed with children. Twenty-one percent of the households contained one person; 6.7% contained related persons or nonrelated roommates or boarders.

The distribution of headship of households classified as families by census definition is very similar to 1975 Bureau of the Census figures. Roughly 61% of the households in our study were male-headed with spouse, 33% female-headed without spouse, and 6% male-headed without spouse. The comparable census figures were 60%, 35%, and 4% respectively. Our sample had slightly fewer female-headed households and more male-headed households without spouses.[6]

Age of Head

Sixty-eight percent of the households in this study were headed by persons less than 55 years of age, 15% by persons between the ages of 55 and 64, and 17% by persons 65 years old or older. Table 4.2 presents household composition by age of head. Older persons, in general, and older women, in particular, are more likely than young and middle-aged persons in the sample to live alone. Of the households with heads aged 18 to 34, only 12.4% (7.8% male, 4.6% female) live alone, in contrast to 41.4% (11.5% male, 29.9% female) of households with heads 65 to 74 years old, and 50.8% (10.8% male, 40.0% female) of the households with heads over 74 years of age. Also, households with older heads were more likely to have a couple without children than those with younger heads. Only 9.8% of households with heads aged 18 to 34 and 9.3% of households with heads aged 35 to 54 contained a male head and spouse or partner, in contrast to 20.9% of households with heads aged 55 to 64, 33.7% with heads aged 65 to 74, and 24.2% of those with heads over 75.

Conversely, younger households were more likely to contain a couple with their own children than older households. Thirty-seven percent of households with heads aged 18 to 34 and 42.6% of those with heads aged 35 to 54 were of this type, whereas only 26.9% of house-

Table 4.2

Household Composition by Age of Designated Head

Household Composition	Age of Designated Head (% of Total)				
	18–34	*35–54*	*55–64*	*65–74*	*75 +*
Male head only	7.8	7.9	8.5	11.5	10.8
Female head only	4.6	6.7	19.3	29.9	40.0
Male head, others [a]	5.6	1.7	3.5	0.9	5.8
Female head, others	2.4	2.0	7.0	6.0	2.5
Male head, spouse, others [b]	9.8	9.3	20.9	33.7	24.2
Male head, spouse, children, others	36.5	42.6	26.9	9.4	9.2
Male head, children, others	0.8	2.4	3.2	1.3	3.3
Female head, children, others	32.5	27.4	10.7	7.3	4.2
Total	100.0	100.0	100.0	100.0	100.0
Total respondents	625	781	316	234	120

a. "Others" refers to other relatives and/or nonrelated persons. b. These categories were obtained by combining the basic family category (for example, male head + spouse only) with the extended family version of the category as shown in Table 4.1. The majority of households in these categories contain only the basic family unit.

holds with heads aged 55 to 64, 9.4% of those aged 64 to 74, and 9.2% of those with heads 75 years of age and older contained couples with their own children. The pivotal cohort for the divergences between households containing couples with and without children is the 55- to 64-year-old group. This is no doubt reflective of the family life cycle phenomenon of the emptying nest.

Households with single parents are more likely to be young households. However, as shown, this is much more apparent for female heads with children than for male heads in similar circumstances. Female single parents are more concentrated in the younger households. Nearly 33% of the households with heads aged 18 to 34 and 27.4% of those with heads aged 35 to 54 were female-headed. Only 10.7, 7.3, and 4.2% respectively, of households with heads aged 55 to 64, 65 to 74, and over 74 years old were headed by females. In contrast, the proportion of male single-parent households is roughly more equally distributed across all age-of-head categories.

As one might expect given the life cycle of families, households with younger heads are more likely to contain a couple with children or a single parent with children than households with older heads. Households with older heads are more likely to contain a single adult, particularly a woman because of the differential mortality rate between men and women, which is more pronounced among blacks than in the general population. They are also more likely than younger households to contain a couple without resident children.

Family Income

More than 50% of the households in this study had a family income[7] less than $10,000 a year. Households with incomes of less than $4,000, $4,000 to $9,999, $10,000 to $14,999, $15,000 to $24,999, $25,000 to $29,999, and over $30,000 composed, respectively, 19.6, 31.1, 14.8, 20.5, 6.3, and 7.7% of households for which family income data were available. (Information was missing for 13% of all households.) Of households with incomes of more than $10,000, 37.3% had one contributor, 50.2% two contributors, and 12.5% three or more contributors.[8]

Table 4.3 shows the distribution of family income across the different types of households. As indicated in this table, households with incomes of less than $4,000 are more likely to be headed by females, either with or without children. Conversely, single-parent male households are more concentrated among the higher income households. Households with a male head, spouse or partner, and children comprise the largest proportion of households with higher family incomes. These large differences between male- and female-headed households can perhaps be attributed primarily to two factors: the large income differences for males and females generally and the increase in multiple earners in male-headed households (Bartlett & Poulton–Callahan, 1982; Farley & Allen, 1987).

The number of contributors to family income differs by type of household. Female-headed households are more likely to have only one contributor than other family households. (Single-person households and those with related or nonrelated roommates are excluded from this table.) Fifty-two percent of households with one contributor to family income are female-headed, whereas 16% are male-headed with spouse, 29% male-headed with spouse and children, and 3.2% male-headed with children. Of households with two contributors, 29% contain a couple without children, 53% a couple with children, 2% a male single parent, and 16% a female single parent. Surprisingly, among households with three or more contributors, the largest proportion were those with a couple and children and the next largest

Table 4.3
Household Composition by Family Income

Household Composition	< $4,000	$4,000–9,999	$10,000–14,999	$15,000–24,999	$25,000–29,999	$30,000+
			Family Income (% of Total)			
Male head only	8.9	9.6	8.5	7.5	6.1	7.8
Female head only	30.3	11.5	8.8	3.7	0.9	1.4
Male head, others	5.0	3.5	3.3	2.1	1.7	3.5
Female head, others	6.1	2.8	2.6	1.6	0.9	2.1
Male head, spouse, others	9.7	17.5	16.9	14.3	13.0	18.4
Male head, spouse, children, others	7.5	22.4	33.8	54.4	67.8	58.9
Male head, children, others	1.4	1.8	2.6	3.4	0.9	2.2
Female head, children, others	31.1	30.9	23.5	13.0	8.7	5.7
Total	100.0	100.0	100.0	100.0	100.0	100.0
Total respondents	360	570	272	377	115	141

proportion were female-headed households. Sixty-three percent of households with three or more contributors were those with a male head, spouse, and children, 28% with a female head and children, 7% a male head and spouse, and 4% a male head and children.

The relatively large proportion of households with three or more contributors that are female-headed could be reflective of the fact that the collapsed version of the household composition variable (see Table 4.1) included the extended version for all types of households (other relatives and other persons, if present). However, except for households that contain a couple and other relatives and persons, the number of households with three or more earners is not entirely determined by the extended households. Contributors besides the head might also include older children as well as other relatives or boarders.

Some writers have suggested that family extendedness at the household level may result from economic problems, while others, as noted earlier, argue that extendedness is a cultural characteristic of black families that mediates economic distress. Angel and Tienda (1982) investigated whether the extended household is culturally determined or determined by other factors, specifically economic distress, by examining extendedness and relative income contributions of persons outside of the nuclear family (in this case, head, spouse, and children and single heads and children). They found some evidence that extendedness may alleviate economic problems. The income contributions of other relatives had a strong positive effect on total household income, although these contributions were not enough to ameliorate the overall poverty level of households sampled in the 1976 Survey of Income and Education (Angel & Tienda, 1982). However, they were unable to dismiss extendedness as culturally determined and prove that economic distress causes extendedness. Minority households, particularly black households, and female-headed households, were more likely to be extended and to evidence positive income contributions from non-nuclear family members. Differences in extendedness between female-headed households and other households were not found in this study. Households headed by women in our sample were as likely to be extended as male-headed households and less likely to have more than one earner. Because of the limitations of the data in this area, we are not able to examine in relative terms whether or not non-nuclear members in female-headed households contributed more to the household income than similar earners in other households.

Overall, for all four basic types of households, 4% had only one contributor to family income, 47% had two, and 12% had three or more. Although nearly a third of female-headed households with children had two or more persons contributing to the family income, they did not fare as well economically as households headed by males. There was also a significant income difference between households with a single female or male head. Part of this difference may be the result of the large proportion of older women living alone who may be on fixed incomes (Table 4.2). Table 4.4 shows family income by age of head and household composition. As shown, controlling for age of head does not narrow the differences between households headed by men and those headed by women. There is still a big income differential between these households.

Region and Degree of Urban Development

There are no reliable differences in household composition by region and degree of urban development. Nuclear households with children are slightly less likely to be found in the Northeast and in rural

Table 4.4
Household Composition by Family Income and Age of Designated Head

Household Composition	18–34 Years		35–54 Years		55–64 Years		65 + Years	
	< $10,000 (%)	$10,000 + (%)	< $10,000 (%)	$10,000 + (%)	< $10,000 (%)	$10,000 + (%)	< $10,000 (%)	$10,000 + (%)
Male head only	8.4	8.9	10.8	8.5	9.3	12.8	14.9	4.3
Female head only	4.8	5.7	14.1	3.4	36.4	7.4	41.2	13.1
Male head, others	2.0	2.5	1.9	0.9	3.4	1.1	1.4	0.0
Female head, others	0.4	1.4	3.3	0.9	9.3	3.2	3.7	0.0
Male head, spouse, others	8.8	12.4	8.9	12.0	20.3	31.9	28.2	58.7
Male head, spouse, children, others	23.5	52.4	21.6	57.8	10.3	38.3	4.6	21.7
Male head, children, others	0.0	1.8	0.9	2.0	0.8	2.1	0.9	2.2
Female head, children, others	52.1	14.9	38.5	14.5	10.2	3.2	5.1	0.0
Total	100.0	100.0	100.0	100.0	100.0	100.0	100.0	100.0
Total respondents	251	282	213	351	118	94	216	46

NOTE: Includes heads of households.

areas. On the other hand, households headed by females are slightly more likely to be found in the Northeast and North Central and urban areas. Neither trend, however, is statistically significant.

Households With Children

The average number of persons per household in this study was 3.15 persons. The range was 1 to 13 persons. This is slightly larger than that reported by the Bureau of the Census in 1980, 3.08 (Sweet & Bumpass, 1987). Overall, households in this study sample had a mean number of 1.96 adults and 2.24 minors. The mean number of adults in households in the Northeast and the West was larger than for those in the North Central and southern regions, whereas the mean number of minors per household was higher in the latter two regions.

More than 60% of all households in this study contained children—both younger than 18 years old and 18 years old and older. Of all households with children, 55.2% had head's minor children only, 11.9% head's older children only, and 13.6% both head's older and minor children. Nineteen percent of the households with children had minors who were not the head's. Most of the children in this category were grandchildren, nieces, or nephews of the head. These are instances of informal fostering or adoption—absorption of minor children by kin networks. Informal adoption, an important function of extended families, is seen by Hill (1977) as evolving during slavery and continuing into present times as a mechanism for family survival (Hill, 1977; Stack, 1974).[9] Most of these households with children other than head's (13.6%) also contained head's own minor and/or older children; however, 5.8% had only minor children who were not the head's.

Table 4.5 shows the distribution of other minors across the different types of extended households. By definition (the coding scheme used in Table 4.1), households with male or female heads and other relatives and those with a male head and spouse and other relatives can only have minor children who are not head's own. Among these households, other minors are concentrated in households with a female head and other relatives, and households with a male head and spouse and other relatives. As discussed earlier, these households tend to have older heads of households than other types of households. This suggests that these households are those with a grandmother and grandchildren or with grandparents and grandchildren. Extended nuclear and female-headed households are much more

Table 4.5
Extended Households by Combinations of Head's Own and Other Children

Household Composition	Head's Own Minors, Other Minors (%)	Head's Older Children, Other Minors (%)	Head's Minor & Older Children, Other Minors (%)	Other Minors Only (%)
Male head, others	—*	—	—	9.5
Female head, others	—	—	—	36.5
Male head, spouse, others	—	—	—	50.8
Male head, spouse, children, others	46.2	48.7	66.7	3.2
Male head, children, others	0.0	2.6	0.0	0.0
Female head, children, others	53.8	48.7	33.3	0.0
Total	100.0	100.0	100.0	100.0
Total respondents	39	39	21	63

NOTE: Includes respondents living in extended and/or augmented families only.
* These are structurally null cells defined by coding scheme used for household composition (see Table 4.1).

likely than single-parent male extended households to have a mix of the head's own and other minors. Female-headed extended households are more likely to have both the head's own minor children and other minors. More than 55% of the households with children in this study were basically nuclear, while 44% were single-parent households.

Extended Households

Approximately one in every five households in this study were extended households; that is, they contained what we have called in this chapter "other relatives." These other relatives are persons other than spouse or children who are related to the designated head. The majority of these extended households contained grandchildren of the head. A number of writers have noted that for blacks an extended household is most likely one that contains grandchildren either with or without the parents of the grandchildren (children of the head). Indeed, in households where other minors are present, 70.6% also include head's own children (18.1% head's minor children, 3.9% head's older children, and 20.6% both head's minor and older children).

Parents and siblings constituted the next highest proportion of other relatives in extended households. Fifteen percent of extended households contained parents and siblings, 13% other relatives (other than parents, grandparents, siblings, and grandchildren), 9% parents, and 9% nonrelated persons. Only 1% contained grandparents. The rest contained various other combinations of relatives and nonrelated persons.

The type of other relatives in households differed by age of head of household. Households with heads less than 55 years of age tended to have grandparents and parents more often than older households. Siblings are present more often in households with heads aged 18 to 34 as are other nonrelated persons. Households with heads 35 years old and older are more likely than younger households to have grandchildren in residence. Roommates or boarders tend to be in households with heads less than 35 years old and relatives other than grandparents, parents, siblings, or grandchildren (i.e., aunts, uncles, cousins, siblings-in-law) are located slightly more often in households with heads 35 years and older.

There is no significant difference by family income, region, or urbanicity in the distribution of the different types of other relatives. However, the distribution of other relatives does differ significantly by type of extended household. Table 4.6 presents type of other relative by type of extended family. Households containing a male head and others have a much larger proportion of nonrelated persons than other extended or augmented households. So, in households where the

Table 4.6
Type of Other Relative by Type of Extended Family

Household Composition	Male Head, Others (%)	Female Head, Others (%)	Male Head, Spouse, Others (%)	Male Head, Spouse, Children, Others (%)	Male Head, Children, Others (%)	Female Head, Children, Others (%)
Grandparents, parents	10.0	16.9	11.1	12.1	16.7	8.3
Siblings	26.0	25.6	16.7	11.2	16.7	12.5
Grandchildren	4.0	32.1	44.4	59.6	50.0	64.6
Other relatives	14.0	18.6	19.5	14.1	16.6	11.5
Other persons	46.0	6.8	8.3	3.0	0.0	3.1
Total	100.0	100.0	100.0	100.0	100.0	100.0
Total respondents	50	59	36	99	6	96

NOTE: Includes respondents living in extended and/or augmented families only.

designation of head is made using a criteria of economic activity or age closest to 45, nonrelated persons constituted 46.0% of others in households with a male head and only 6.8% of households headed by a female. Nearly a third of households with a female head and others contain siblings, and another third of these households contain grandchildren.

The largest proportion of other relatives in the other extended households are grandchildren, 44.4% in households with male head, spouse, and others; 59.6% in households with male head, spouse, children, and others; 50.0% in households with male head, children, and others; and 64.6% in households with a female head, children, and others.

These data further document the diversity of households in which black Americans reside. The majority of these households are nuclear, containing one or both parents with their own children. Roughly equal proportions of extended households and households with persons living alone are found in our sample. The type of household with the lowest frequency was households with couples only. Male-headed households outnumbered female-headed households slightly less than 2:1, with proportions similar to those reported by 1975 Bureau of the Census figures.

Overall, household structure varied in response to life-cycle dictates. Households with children were more likely to be headed by younger persons. Households headed by older persons were more likely to be those with only one person or a couple.

One in five black American households contained persons outside of the nuclear family. However, there were no significant differences in the tendency to be extended at the household level by sex of head as documented elsewhere. Owing to the tendency of black families to absorb dependent children through informal adoption, most of the extended households in these data were those with grandchildren.

This section also further documented what is perhaps the most dramatic and disturbing consequence of female-headship—economic disadvantage. All types of female-headed households had family incomes lower than those of male-headed households and were less likely to have multiple earners. The female heads of these households are mostly young with dependent children, or elderly women living alone. These are the at-risk households that are the focal point of this chapter. The next section describes and examines the supportive networks of these households in comparison to other households by exploring potential and actual kin networks.

Potential Kin Networks

A given family or household can be extended at the household level with the inclusion of other relatives outside of the nuclear core or extended beyond the household to include all relatives in a kin network. As mentioned earlier, an actual kin network or family extendedness involves a feeling of closeness among relatives, contact and interaction, and mutual aid (Aschenbrenner, 1978; Martin & Martin, 1978; McAdoo, 1988; Stack, 1974). Family structure, both intra- and extra-household, is only a precursor of this functional aspect of kin network. The spatial arrangement of relatives in, around, and beyond the base household determines the potential kin network.

Noting geographical mobility as a requisite for occupational mobility in developing societies, Parsons (1944) posited that, because of its need for physical propinquity, the extended family was not as functional in modern societies as the nuclear family. Disagreeing with this indictment of the extended family, Litwak (1965) suggested that, whereas the "classical extended family" demanded such propinquity, advances in travel and communications technology allow "modified extended family" relations. Modified extended families, according to Litwak, not only are *not* dysfunctional in modern society, but can aid both occupational and geographical mobility of members. Proximity or propinquity of relatives is important only in determining the type and frequency of kin relations (Lee, 1980; Litwak, 1965). Its absence does not negate extended family functioning.

In this section we examine the correlates of the potential kin networks of black households. Two indicators of potential kin systems are used: the proximity of immediate family members and the proximity and density of relatives. The importance of proximity in determining the extent of actual kin networks is examined in the next section.

Immediate Family

The proximity of immediate family members was measured in this study by the following question: "Where do most, that is, more than half, of your immediate family members live? By immediate family members we mean your parents, children, brothers, and sisters." The response categories were: "in this household," "in this neighborhood," "in this city," "in this county," "in this state," "in another state," and "outside the country." More than half of the respondents (heads and spouses only) reported that most of their immediate family members were located in their city of residence: household, neighborhood, or city. Only 7% of the respondents said that most of their immediate family lived in their own household; 6.9% said most of their family lived in the same neighborhood; 38.6% said the same city, 5.7% the same county, 15% the same state, and 25.8% another state. Less than 1% of the respondents indicated that most of their immediate family members lived outside of the United States.

Age of the respondent, region, urbanicity, and household composition all are related to the proximity of immediate family members. No association was found for family income and proximity of immediate family members. Table 4.7 shows the reported location of respondents' immediate family members by age, region, urbanicity, and household composition. The strongest relationship, although modest, was found for age. Older respondents were more likely than younger respondents to report that their immediate family members lived further from their household. When the few respondents who reported that most family members live in their household are excluded, 59, 51, 52, and 42%, respectively, of respondents aged 18 to 34, 35 to 54, 55 to 64, and 65 years old and older report that more than half of their immediate family members are located at least within their county of residence.

The associations for region, urbanicity, and household were slight but statistically reliable. Respondents in the north central region were the most likely to have the majority of family members within a close range and those in the South the least likely. Also, respondents in urban areas had immediate family members at a closer range than those in less urban or rural areas. Proximity to immediate family members also varies by type of household. Respondents in female-headed households with children were more likely to report being geographically closer to immediate family members than those in other types of households. Respondents in single-person households and those in head and spouse households were more likely to report immediate family members as more distant from their household.

Proximity and Density of Relatives

Seven separate questions were asked to assess the density and proximity of relatives outside of immediate family members. Each question asked how many relatives—"many," "some," or "a few"—lived in the respondent's household, city, county, state, another state, or outside of the country. These items were combined to form an ad-

Table 4.7
Where More Than Half of the Respondents' Immediate Family Members Live by Age, Region, Urbanicity, and Household Composition

	Household (%)	Neighborhood (%)	City (%)	County (%)	State (%)	Other/State (%)	Other/Country (%)	Percent (N)
Age								
18 to 34 years	2.0	7.6	46.7	4.9	16.2	22.4	0.2	100 (594)
35 to 54 years	4.2	6.2	37.1	7.3	16.0	27.7	1.5	100 (614)
55 to 64 years	1.9	6.1	38.5	7.5	16.0	30.0	0.0	100 (213)
65 years or older	2.3	6.4	30.2	5.4	16.1	39.3	0.3	100 (298)
Region								
Northeast	3.1	7.1	40.5	5.6	14.6	27.2	1.9	100 (323)
North Central	3.9	4.9	54.5	2.3	7.8	26.1	0.5	100 (384)
South	2.1	7.9	32.8	8.0	20.6	28.3	0.3	100 (916)
West	4.8	1.9	39.4	5.8	10.6	37.5	0.0	100 (104)
Urbanicity								
Large urban	3.6	6.8	46.2	4.0	10.9	27.6	0.9	100 (805)
Other urban	2.0	3.5	42.5	6.1	18.2	27.0	0.7	100 (560)
Rural	2.5	11.3	19.9	11.1	24.0	31.2	0.0	100 (362)
Household Composition								
Head only	0.0	7.0	37.6	4.2	13.4	37.1	0.7	100 (402)
Head, others	0.0	8.5	40.8	1.4	21.1	28.2	0.0	100 (71)
Male head, spouse, others	1.3	4.3	34.3	8.7	17.7	32.7	1.0	100 (300)
Male head, spouse, children, others	4.9	6.4	39.2	8.3	15.9	24.8	0.5	100 (577)
Female head, children, others	3.9	9.0	45.7	3.4	16.9	20.5	0.6	100 (356)

NOTE: Includes heads of households and spouses only.

ditive index of the proximity and density of relatives, with each item weighted by its relative proximity to the respondent's household. Because of the interest here in comparing different types of households, the item about the number of relatives in the respondent's household was not included in this index. The index was then collapsed into three categories—low, medium, and high—indicating, respectively, a low concentration of relatives at a more distant range, an intermediate concentration of relatives at a closer range, and a high concentration of relatives at a closer range.

Table 4.8 shows the proportion of respondents reporting many, some, a few, or no relatives in their neighborhood, city, county, state, another state, and another country. On the whole, respondents in our study tended to have more relatives living in their city, county, or state than in their neighborhood and another country. For the collapsed proximity and density index, 42% of the respondents had a low score, 32.6% a medium score, and 25.4% a high score.

As found for the other indicator of potential kin network, age of respondent, region, urbanicity, and household composition were related to the proximity and density of relatives, while family income was not. Table 4.8 shows this measure of potential kin network by age, region, urbanicity, and household composition. The relationship of this measure with age and household composition was the same as for proximity of immediate family members. However, different relationships were found for region and urbanicity. Older respondents were more likely to have a lower density and proximity of relatives than younger respondents, and respondents in female-headed households with children were more likely to have higher concentrations of relatives at a closer range than those in other types of households. In contrast to the findings for proximity of immediate family members, respondents in the southern and the north central regions and those in rural areas had higher concentrations of relatives at a closer range than those in other regions and those in urban areas.

The availability of potential kin networks then varies by age of respondent, by the region and degree of urban development of the respondent's place of residence, and by the type of household in which the respondent resides. Thus far, we have found that the households or types of families in which we are particularly interested, those with older respondents and those with a single female parent and children, are similar in economic disadvantage but differ in availability of potential kin networks. The older households, those with

Table 4.8

Density and Proximity of Relatives by Age, Region, Urbanicity, and Household Composition

	Low (%)	Medium (%)	High (%)	Percent (N)
Age				
18 to 34 years	33.3	35.0	31.7	100 (810)
35 to 54 years	44.6	33.3	22.1	100 (610)
55 to 64 years	46.5	28.2	25.3	100 (213)
65 years or older	55.7	27.4	16.9	100 (296)
Region				
Northeast	48.6	30.9	20.5	100 (356)
North Central	39.8	29.8	30.4	100 (440)
South	39.2	34.3	26.5	100 (1,022)
West	50.8	33.1	16.1	100 (118)
Urbanicity				
Large urban	43.6	32.7	23.7	100 (895)
Other urban	44.0	32.3	23.7	100 (632)
Rural	34.5	32.5	33.0	100 (409)
Household Composition				
One person	53.0	27.9	19.1	100 (377)
Head, others	45.4	31.1	23.5	100 (132)
Male head, spouse, others	46.4	33.6	20.0	100 (295)
Male head, spouse, children, others	37.4	33.6	29.0	100 (652)
Female head, children, others	35.2	35.1	29.7	100 (441)

older heads and spouses, are more isolated from kin than are younger households headed by single female parents. The latter also tend to have greater potential kin networks than those of persons in nuclear households.

Actual Kin Networks

The importance of the availability and location of kin to extended family functioning is well documented in the literature (Lee, 1980; Taylor, 1988; Taylor et al., 1990). The mere presence of kin, however, is a necessary but not sufficient condition for functional family extendedness. According to the theoretical formulations of black family extendedness presented earlier, other conditions must be met, among them a feeling of emotional closeness to family members, contact with family members, and a mutual aid system. This section examines the relationship of these conditions to the type of household, age, family income, urbanicity, and availability of potential kin networks of black Americans.

Subjective Closeness

Subjective closeness was assessed in this study by asking respondents the following question: "Would you say your family members are very close in their feelings toward each other, fairly close, not too close, or not close at all?" Although this question does not address the issue of obligation, which is thought to be important in functional extended families, it does seem to tap feelings of general connectedness. The responses on this variable were very skewed with more than 90% of all respondents reporting that their family members were "very" or "fairly" close in their feelings toward each other. So in the general black population, as the literature has suggested, there is an overwhelming perception of family solidarity.

Table 4.9 shows perceived family closeness by age, family income, household composition, and the proximity and density of relatives. There were no reliable differences in perceived family closeness across regions or areas with different degrees of urban development. Significant differences did emerge for age. Older persons were more likely to say their families were "very close" in their feelings toward each other, whereas younger respondents were more likely to say their families were "fairly close." When family income is considered, we find that as income increases so do feelings of family solidarity. Persons with family incomes less than $5,000 were less likely than those with higher incomes to report family closeness. When the type of household the respondent lives in is considered, we find that on the whole persons in female-headed households with children and respondents who live alone are more likely to say their families are "not too close" or "not close at all" than persons in other types of households.

Perceived closeness of family members is also related to the density and proximity of family members. Those with higher concentra-

Table 4.9
Perceived "Closeness" of Family Members by Age, Family Income,
and Household Composition

	Very Close (%)	Fairly Close (%)	Not Too Close/ Not Close At All (%)	Percent (N)
Age				
18 to 34 years	54.5	33.9	11.6	100 (611)
35 to 54 years	60.0	32.1	7.9	100 (632)
55 to 64 years	60.1	31.1	8.8	100 (228)
65 years or older	69.6	21.8	8.6	100 (313)
Family Income				
< $5,000	56.2	31.7	12.1	100 (406)
$5,000 to $9,999	59.4	29.3	11.3	100 (399)
$10,000 to $19,999	58.6	32.8	8.6	100 (432)
> $20,000	62.0	33.4	4.6	100 (347)
Household Composition				
Head only	58.0	31.3	10.7	100 (429)
Head, others	61.0	32.5	6.5	100 (77)
Male head, spouse, others	67.5	25.4	7.1	100 (308)
Male head, spouse, children, others	58.2	34.8	7.0	100 (586)
Female head, children, others	57.5	27.7	14.8	100 (372)
Density/Proximity of Relatives				
Low	54.5	33.4	12.1	100 (784)
Medium	63.0	28.8	8.2	100 (576)
High	66.2	27.9	5.9	100 (408)

NOTE: Includes heads of households, and spouses or partners of heads of households.

tions of relatives at a closer range are more likely to perceive family members are "close" than those who have less dense and more distant kin networks. Although not statistically reliable, similar trends are found for our other measure of potential kin networks, the proximity of immediate family members.

Frequency of Contact

Respondents were asked how often they saw, wrote, or talked on the telephone with family members and relatives not in their household to determine the frequency of contact among family members. Response categories of this question ranged from "nearly every day (at least four times a week)" to "never." Thirty-eight percent of all respondents reported contacting their relatives nearly every day; 28% said at least once a week; 17% said a few times a month; 7% said at least once a month; 6% reported contacting relatives a few times a year; 5% said once a year; and less than 2% said they never contacted their relatives.

Table 4.10 presents frequency of contact with relatives by family income, household composition, degree of urban development, and both measures of potential kin networks. There were no reliable differences in reported frequency of contact by age or by region. There were differences across income groups, however. Persons in households with family incomes less than $10,000 reported less frequent contact than those with larger family incomes. Although there were no differences by region, there were differences by degree of urban development. Persons in urban areas reported more frequent contact than those in rural areas.

When the type of household is considered, we find that respondents in female-headed households with children and persons who live alone or in other non-nuclear family situations reported more contact with relatives than those in other types of households.

As suggested in the literature, the proximity of relatives is related to the frequency of contact with relatives. For both measures used in this analysis, the closer one's family members and relatives (and the greater the density of these relatives), the more frequent the contact.

Frequency of Help Received From Family

Mutual aid, perhaps the most important function of the extended family, was assessed in this study in a limited manner. Respondents only were asked how often people in their family helped them out and not how often they helped members of their family out. Also no distinction was made between immediate family members and other relatives as help givers. However, it can be argued that this lack of specificity is not important for our purposes. The literature suggests that norms of reciprocity may exist that obligate family members to repay family members in kind or related goods and services or support when they are in need (Martin & Martin, 1978; Stack, 1974). In this light, this item can be seen a an indicator of mutual aid, although admittedly one-sided.

Less than half of all respondents reported that family and relatives helped them out "very" or "fairly" often. Twenty-one percent said they received help "very often;" 21% said "fairly often;" 28% said "not too

Table 4.10
Frequency of Contact With Relatives by Age, Family Income, and Household Composition

	Nearly Every Day (%)	Once Weekly (%)	Few Times Monthly (%)	Once Monthly (%)	Few Times Yearly (%)	Once Yearly/ Never (%)	Percent (N)
Age							
18 to 34 years	40.5	27.9	15.2	7.4	3.4	5.6	100 (612)
35 to 54 years	37.4	28.7	17.0	7.6	4.9	4.4	100 (631)
55 to 64 years	41.2	25.9	15.4	4.8	7.0	5.7	100 (228)
65 years or older	32.9	24.7	17.7	8.5	7.0	9.2	100 (316)
Family Income							
< $5,000	39.8	22.1	14.7	8.1	4.4	10.9	100 (407)
$5,000 to $9,999	35.3	25.6	18.3	8.5	6.3	6.0	100 (399)
$10,000 to $19,999	38.5	30.0	15.6	8.1	3.4	4.4	100 (434)
> $20,000	37.3	33.5	16.5	5.5	5.8	1.4	100 (346)
Household Composition							
Head only	36.8	26.5	15.7	7.6	5.1	8.3	100 (434)
Head, others	41.6	23.3	10.4	9.1	9.1	6.5	100 (77)
Male head, spouse, others	36.5	27.4	19.5	7.8	3.6	5.2	100 (307)
Male head, spouse, children, others	31.9	31.6	17.3	7.7	6.7	4.8	100 (586)
Female head, children, others	50.4	22.4	13.5	5.9	2.7	5.1	100 (371)

Proximity of Immediate Family							
Neighborhood	50.8	19.0	7.8	8.6	6.9	6.9	100 (116)
City	49.7	29.3	10.8	3.7	3.4	3.1	100 (678)
County	47.2	32.1	11.3	1.9	0.9	6.6	100 (106)
State	36.2	26.4	18.8	6.2	6.2	6.2	100 (276)
Other state	21.6	27.4	24.6	13.0	5.6	7.8	100 (486)
Other country	18.2	18.2	9.1	27.2	18.2	9.1	100 (11)
Proximity/Density of Relatives							
Low	27.8	29.0	20.6	9.4	6.1	7.1	100 (720)
Medium	43.6	28.7	14.4	6.6	3.0	3.7	100 (534)
High	49.8	25.5	11.5	5.2	3.5	4.5	100 (400)

often;" and 29% reported never receiving help. More than two thirds of our sample reported receiving some help from family members.

Table 4.11 presents frequency of help by age, family income, household composition, and proximity of family/relatives. As can be seen in the first section of this table, older respondents are much more likely to

Table 4.11

Frequency of Help From Relatives by Age, Family Income, Household Composition, and Proximity of Family Relatives

	Very Often (%)	Fairly Often (%)	Not Too Often (%)	Never (%)	Percent (N)
Age					
18 to 34 years	26.9	28.9	32.7	11.5	100 (581)
35 to 54 years	23.7	22.6	34.8	18.9	100 (561)
55 to 64 years	19.7	20.2	28.6	31.5	100 (203)
65 years or older	20.7	19.4	25.8	34.1	100 (252)
Family Income					
< $5,000	19.0	21.3	31.7	28.0	100 (379)
$5,000 to $9,999	25.1	21.7	32.3	20.9	100 (359)
$10,000 to $19,999	23.6	27.5	34.8	14.1	100 (382)
> $20,000	27.6	28.6	29.2	14.6	100 (301)
Household Composition					
Head only	16.9	20.9	31.1	31.1	100 (373)
Head, others	26.4	16.7	34.7	22.2	100 (72)
Male head, spouse, others	25.0	21.4	27.4	26.2	100 (252)
Male head, spouse, children, others	26.4	28.8	31.5	13.3	100 (542)
Female head, children, others	25.0	23.6	35.9	15.5	100 (348)
Proximity of Immediate Family					
Neighborhood	10.0	20.0	20.0	50.0	100 (10)
City	22.8	20.5	32.0	24.7	100 (425)
County	25.5	21.9	30.7	21.9	100 (247)
State	24.7	20.4	35.5	19.4	100 (93)
Other state	24.7	27.3	31.8	16.2	100 (616)
Other country	28.3	27.4	32.1	12.2	100 (106)
Proximity/Density of Relatives					
Low	21.9	21.2	30.3	26.6	100 (623)
Medium	23.4	26.4	34.6	15.6	100 (482)
High	26.3	27.9	32.4	13.4	100 (373)

NOTE: Includes heads of household, or spouses/partners of heads only.

"never" receive help than younger respondents. Thirty-four percent of older blacks said they never received help from family members in contrast to only 11.5% of younger blacks. The pattern over the age categories is fairly linear, with the reported frequency of help decreasing as age increases.

Income is only moderately related to frequency of help. Lower-income respondents are more likely both to report receiving help less frequently than other income groups and to say they never receive help. On the other hand, middle-income respondents, those with incomes between $10,000 and $20,000, are more likely to say they received help very or fairly frequently and less likely to say they never received help. This lends some support to McAdoo's (1978) contention that upward mobility and higher socioeconomic status do not significantly impede or diminish extended family relations.

The relationship between the type of household the respondent resides in and frequency of help is a bit stronger. Single persons who live alone report receiving help less often than persons in other types of households. Also, households with a male head and spouse only were more likely to say they "never" received help. Female single parents were just as likely as persons in other nuclear family situations to say they received help "very" or "fairly" often. There were no differences in the reported frequency of help from family members by region or urbanicity.

Frequency of help received from relatives is also related to the geographical closeness of relatives. For both measures of geographical closeness, the frequency of help increased as proximity increased. Respondents whose relatives were closer (and in greater concentration) reported receiving help from family members more often than other respondents.

Type of Help Received

Respondents were also asked what type of help they received from family members. Responses were coded into six categories of help: advice and comfort, goods and services, money or financial help, child care, general help ("anything I need"), and help during sickness or family death.

Table 4.12 presents type of help received by age, family income, and household composition. Older respondents reported receiving goods and services more often than younger respondents, whereas younger respondents reported receiving money and childcare more often

Table 4.12

Type of Help Received by Age, Family Income, and Household Composition

	Advice/Comfort (%)	Goods/Services (%)	Money (%)	Child Care (%)	General Help (%)	Help with Sickness/Death (%)	Percent (N)
Age							
18 to 34 years	30.8	10.3	25.8	21.5	8.9	2.7	100 (503)
35 to 54 years	28.5	20.7	23.9	10.0	13.5	3.4	100 (439)
55 to 64 years	25.5	35.0	19.7	1.6	13.1	5.1	100 (137)
65 years or older	28.8	35.6	17.2	0.0	9.2	9.2	100 (163)
Family Income							
< $5,000	21.9	24.9	29.8	7.8	8.2	7.4	100 (269)
$5,000 to $9,999	28.9	18.6	27.1	7.9	13.9	3.6	100 (280)
$10,000 to $19,999	30.6	18.0	22.1	17.0	10.1	2.2	100 (317)
> $20,000	33.3	19.3	16.1	18.1	10.8	2.4	100 (249)
Household Composition							
Head only	34.3	24.2	25.5	0.4	10.0	5.6	100 (251)
Head, others	36.4	25.5	20.0	1.8	12.7	3.6	100 (55)
Male head, spouse, others	35.3	22.1	23.8	0.6	12.7	5.5	100 (181)
Male head, spouse, children, others	27.4	17.3	21.7	19.9	10.7	3.0	100 (457)
Female head, children, others	23.0	18.1	25.4	19.2	10.8	3.5	100 (287)

NOTE: Includes heads of households and spouses/partners of heads only.

than older respondents. This relationship suggests that the type of support people receive from their families is dictated to some extent by needs defined by family life cycle.

Family income is related to type of help in a similar fashion. Respondents with incomes greater than $5,000 are more likely to report receiving advice and comfort than those with family incomes less than $5,000, whereas lower income respondents are more likely to report receiving goods and services and financial aid.

The relationship of type of help and household composition (which captures dimensions of family life cycle other than age) also suggests that help received is influenced by family life-cycle needs. Households with children, those with both parents or single parents, receive child care more than other households. There is little difference in reports of receiving money among respondents in the different households. However, persons in households with children (at least head's own) report receiving advice and comfort and goods and services less than those in other households.

There were no reliable differences in the type of help received by region, urbanicity, proximity of immediate relatives, and proximity and density of relatives. These results suggest that for different subgroups of black Americans, potential kin networks do not translate directly into actual kin networks. Indeed the relationships are quite complex. Striking differences are found across age, income, and type of household. Older persons are more geographically isolated from kin but are more likely to feel their families are very close in their feelings toward one another. On the other hand, older persons have less frequent contact with their relatives and are less likely to say they receive any type of aid from family members. Painted is a picture of black elderly with high psychological connectedness to family in the midst of relative geographical and interactional isolation. Recent work (Chatters, Taylor, & Jackson, 1985, 1986; Taylor, 1985, 1986a) drawing from these same data documents in greater detail the strengths as well as the limitations of the supportive networks of the elderly.

Different complexities emerge for income. Whereas no differences were found between income groups in terms of potential kin networks, differences were found for the different indicators of actual kin networks. Persons with lower family incomes reported less family solidarity, contact, and help than persons with higher family incomes. This conflicts greatly with previous research on extended family behavior among lower income black Americans (Stack, 1974), but it is consistent with some work by McAdoo (1988) and others (Taylor et al., 1990).

Female-headed households may have greater potential kin networks and report more frequent contact with relatives than other types of households. Female heads (and persons who live alone), however, are more likely to say they feel "not too close" or "not close at all" to family members. On the other hand, they report receiving aid almost as frequently as male-headed households. Female-headed households with children also receive the same type of aid as male-headed households with children.

The complexities observed above derive both from the actual complexities in extended families' behavior across groups and to some degree from the limitations of the level of analyses employed thus far. The relationships among the variables—particularly age and household type; age and help; and age, headship, and income—confound the overall interpretations of these results. Although we have examined the relationships between age, income, household type, and potential and actual kin networks, we do not have a clear picture of the support available to female-headed households relative to that available to other households and the relative importance of all the variables examined in determining supportive networks.

Predictors of Familial Support

One explicit objective of this chapter was to evaluate the availability of informal support for different types of households within an extended family perspective. Implicitly explored in this chapter has been a model of social support where life-cycle indicators (here, age of head or the respondent and, to some extent, household composition) as well as other demographic variables are thought to influence potential kin networks, which in turn influence actual kin networks or extended family functioning. Potential kin networks were defined as the density and proximity of relatives and actual kin networks as psychological and behavioral connectedness (i.e., closeness, contact, and aid). Although this model will not be treated formally here, we should, through the following limited analysis, gain some insight into its dimensions and appropriateness for explaining informal social support through family extendedness.

Up to this point, the data presented have been principally descriptive or on the bivariate level. As mentioned above, although informative, these analyses fail to illuminate differences among households in terms of both support available and the relative importance of all the variables examined in determining the level of support available. The following multivariate analyses address both of these questions.

Determinants of Support

For these analyses support is operationalized as frequency of help from family members. Although included thus far in our discussion as an indicator of actual kin networks or extended family functioning, in the model sketched above, help from family members can be seen as an outcome predicted by the various life-cycle indicators, other demographic variables, indicators of potential kin networks, and the other aspects of actual kin networks. In order to explore the efficacy of this model, age, income, household type, degree of urban development, region, proximity of immediate family, proximity and density of other relatives, subjective closeness to family, and frequency of contact with relatives were included as predictors of the frequency of help from family members in a Multiple Classification Analysis.[10]

Up to now, sex has not been given much attention in this chapter except in reference to household headship. However, because we are relying on both heads and spouses as informants about extended family behavior in our sample, there is a need to control for the sex of respondents when considering both potential and actual networks. Women are more likely to report relatives at a closer distance, report more frequent contact with relatives, and report more frequency of help. Men are more likely to say they never need help.

Age and subjective closeness emerge in this analysis as the two most important predictors of the frequency of help from family members. The next two important variables are contact and the type of household in which the respondent resides. The relationships reported between these variables and help on the bivariate level hold when other predictors are controlled. These relationships are as follows:

1. Age is negatively related to the frequency of help. As age increases the frequency of help reported decreases.
2. Subjective closeness is positively related to the frequency of help. As the perception of familial closeness increases so do reports of familial help.
3. Like subjective closeness, contact is positively related to the frequency of familial help. The more frequent the contact, the more frequent the help from family members.

4. Households differed in the frequency of support reported by heads or spouses. They ranged from male head, spouse, and children households, which had the highest mean frequency of familial help, to households with single heads and other relatives and/or persons and those with female single parents, which had a frequency of help below that of classical nuclear families, to households with the lowest frequency of help—those with a couple only and persons living alone.

All of these variables are significantly associated with each other as well as with some of the other predictors. It is possible that interactions exist. Because they are not explicitly included in this analysis they may be depressing the overall explanatory power of individual variables and the entire model. However, we feel these effects are probably negligible.

Although most of the other predictors—the two indicators of potential kin networks, family income, region, urbanicity, and sex—were significantly individually related to familial help on the bivariate level, they have little overall impact upon family support in the multivariate model.

Are There Different Models of Support by Household Type?

Although the frequency of support differs significantly by household type, when other variables are considered, household type is not as important a predictor of support as age, subjective closeness, and contact. However, the differences in the frequency of support between households increase in the multivariate model. Because of their small numbers male single-parent households were deleted from these analyses. Help was coded 1 to 4 with 4 indicating very frequent help from relatives. The difference in the frequency of help between households with a male head, spouse, and children and those with a female single parent and children increases when the other predictors are controlled.

Given the relationship of household type and the other variables examined here, particularly age, it is possible that determinants of support may be different for different types of households. In order to investigate this possibility separate analyses were done for four types of households: single person, couple only, couple with children, and female single parent.

Age is the most important predictor of support only for the two households that have high proportions of older respondents or heads of households, single-person households and households with a couple only. Subjective closeness, on the other hand, is the most important predictor of help for households with a male head, spouse, and children and those with female single parents. The most important predictors of help for each type of household are age, contact, and income for single-person households; age, contact, subjective closeness, and proximity of immediate family for couple-only households; closeness for households with a male head, spouse, and children; and closeness and contact for female single-parent households. The model for households with a male head, spouse, and children— the classical nuclear family—explained only half as much variance as was explained by the model for the other households.

Summary

Within the context of examining extended family behavior among black Americans, this chapter described the informal support resources of black American households. Of particular interest to us was the availability of informal support for households we think are particularly at continuing risk in the 1990s—female-headed households and households in which the elderly, mostly female, reside. The numbers of these households are increasing. They constitute approximately two-fifths of all African American households. This trend, which given broader cultural changes shows no sign of reversing, is the impetus for what some writers have called the "feminization of poverty" (e.g., Bianchi & Spain, 1986). The conservative political and economic mood that characterized the 1980s and shows little abatement in the beginning of the 1990s portends even more jeopardy for individuals in these households. As more formal sources of aid and support are threatened by cutbacks, informal support networks become more important for survival.

These informal support resources can lie in family, friends, neighbors, church, or community. This chapter focused on support from family members. (See Chatters, Taylor, & Neighbors, 1989; Chatters, Taylor, & Jackson, 1986; and Taylor & Chatters, 1986b, for work on these same data that examines both kin and non-kin sources of social support.) Theoretical formulations on extended family behavior provided a framework for examining familial support networks within our national sample of black adults. Households were compared in terms of both their potential and actual kin networks. We defined potential kin networks as the density and proximity of kin and actual kin networks as psychological and behavioral connectedness (i.e., subjective closeness, contact, and mutual aid). The former is a necessary although not sufficient condition for the second, which is, in essence, extended family functioning.

Our analyses further documented the economic disadvantage of households headed by women. Female-headed households of all types—those with a single person, those with a single head and other relatives, and those with a female single parent and children—had lower family or household incomes than male-headed households and were less likely to have multiple earners. These female heads were for the most part either young with dependent children or elderly and living alone. One in every five of the households in this study was extended at the household level. Most of the extendedness at the household level resulted from the absorption of minor children, most of whom were grandchildren.

We found no differences between female- and male-headed households in the tendency to incorporate relatives outside the nuclear family. Although some writers have suggested that economic hardship is possibly an impetus for incorporating other family members, there is little evidence to suggest this leads to substantial improvement in the overall economic situation of the household (Angel & Tienda, 1982). Working wives make greater contributions to household income than other earners. Thus, multiple earners in female-headed families may do little to alter the economic differential between female- and male-headed households.

Although extended households may offer the possibility of multiple earners, there are other advantages and some possible disadvantages to extended households. Whether an extended household is supportive or stressful may depend on the age of the other relatives; either age extreme could be stressful for core family members. As we found in the households of our study, the majority of other relatives were minor children, primarily grandchildren of heads who co-resided with the head's own minor and adult children. The next largest category of other relatives was that of parents and siblings. McAdoo (1988) and others have suggested that parental authority and spousal relationships may be impaired in some multigenerational or extended households. Although extended households may be supportive in terms of providing the possibility of multiple earners, help with household tasks and childcare, and socioemotional support, they can also be stressful because of dependency of very young or very old relatives and possible personal conflict.

Given the lack of headship differentials in the rate of extendedness at the household level, we must conclude that such advantages that might derive from the presence of other persons in a household do not seem to favor male- over female-headed households.

Respondents who were heads or spouses of heads were used as informants on the kin structure and behavior of households. The availability of kin, both in terms of proximity and number or density, is an important precursor to extended family functioning. In our study we found that the elderly are relatively isolated from kin; households in which older persons reside show less dense and close kin networks. The other type of household of particular interest, female-headed households with children, has kin networks at least as dense and close as those of "classical" nuclear households.

Potential kin networks did not translate directly into actual kin networks. Complex relationships were found across age, income, and type of household. From these data came a picture of the black elderly with high psychological connectedness to family in the midst of relative geographical and interactional isolation from them. The image of female single-parent households is, on the other hand, the reverse or negative of this picture. Female heads were geographically closer to kin, had more contact with them, and received more help from family but did not perceive as much family solidarity or psychological connectedness.

The results for income were not consistent with some previous findings for extended family behavior. Whereas Stack (1974) found intense kin behavior among lower income black households in her study of "The Flats," these data found less perceived family solidarity, contact, and help among families with incomes less than $10,000 than for those with higher incomes. Although extended family behavior as indicated by the measures in our study was less for lower income families, it was not absent. Household extendedness at both household and extra-household levels appears to be a characteristic of black families, regardless of socio-economic level.

This chapter explored a model of extended family behavior or support in which life-cycle indicators and socioeconomic variables were seen to influence potential kin networks, which in turn influenced extended family behavior. Age and subjective closeness were found to be the most important variables influencing familial support. The type of household a person resides in and the frequency of contact with relatives were also important.

Because of the intercorrelation of age and household type, separate analyses were performed for four types of households. Different models of support emerged for each. Age was important in predicting help only for the households that were more likely to have older heads or spouses, single-person households and those with a couple only. Subjective closeness to family, on the other hand, was the most important predictor of help for male-headed households with spouse and children and female single-parent households.

Age, contact, and income were the three most important predictors for single-person households; and age, contact, subjective closeness, and proximity of immediate family were important variables for couple-only households. Traditional nuclear households and female single-parent households also had different models of familial support. Subjective closeness to family members was the most important variable for predicting support for nuclear households, whereas subjective closeness and contact had the most influence on help from family members for female-parent households.

In summary, the households we suggested were at risk because of current political conservatism and an ailing economy are indeed in a more precarious position than other black households in regard to informal support. Admittedly there are sources of support outside of the family. However, it is doubtful that these other support networks can sufficiently counteract the economic disadvantage faced by these households (Wilson & Neckerman, 1987). There is a need for more formal support by either public or private agencies (Edelman, 1987). The continuing cutbacks in social programs currently underway can only worsen the conditions of these African American families (Edelman, 1987; Jaynes & Williams, 1989; Wilson & Neckerman, 1987).

Notes

1. This information was taken from household listings obtained by interviewers before the actual interviews.

2. The nuclear family in Billingsley's typology, as in other typologies, is a couple with or without their own children. An incipient nuclear family is one without children; a simple nuclear family, one with children; an attenuated family, one with one parent and children. Each of these basic family types can be modified by "extended"

or "augmented" or both. The former means including "other relatives" and the latter "other nonrelated persons" (Billingsley, 1968).

3. For this study, head was determined as follows: If a household contained a couple (man and wife or man and partner), the man was designated the head. If there was no couple, the most economically dominant person was designated as head. If no one was economically dominant, the person closest to age 45 was designated as head.

4. There were only 56 households with partners. This is 6% of all households identified with spouse or partner.

5. There were in total 64 other persons identified in households in this study. Fifty-four were roommates or friends, and 10 were boarders or roomers.

6. These figures are from the Current Population Reports, Special Studies, Series P-23, No. 80 entitled "The Social Economic Status of the Black Population in the United States: An Historical View, 1790–1978," Table 74, p. 103. Differences in percentages may be due to differences in classifying households that contain more than one person but do not have the head's children.

7. Family income here is household income derived from responses to the following question: "What was the total income of all persons living in your household in 1978, that is, considering all sources such as salaries, profits, wages, interest, and so on, for *all* family members?"

8. Number of contributors was assessed by: "How many people in your household, *including yourself,* give money to support your household?"

9. According to Hill (1977), "informally adopted" children are those who "live in households headed by relatives or non-relatives with and without the presence of one or both natural parents" (p. 9).

10. Multiple Classification Analysis is similar to multiple regression but permits the examination of both the independent and relative importance of a set of categorical variables in predicting a criterion of interest. For the sake of brevity these tables are not presented here but are available from the authors upon request.

5

WOMEN AND MEN

Shirley J. Hatchett

The trends in marriage and family living arrangements—increased marital dissolution, female headship, delayed first marriages—which are slowly sketching new images of the American family are being inked by the changing relationship of women and men (Taylor, Chatters, Tucker, & Lewis, 1990; Tucker & Taylor, 1989). Noting that divorce is increasing although most of the socioeconomic indicators linked to marital instability have been changing in directions that would lessen their impact, Norton and Glick (1979) wrote:

> "The current period of adaptation and resocialization regarding the roles of women . . . will not be passed through easily . . . In the long run, the broadening of work-and-marriage experience seems likely to encourage women to develop a greater self-perception as players of multiple roles and to result in familial and societal gains; however, the short-term effects may be somewhat disruptive." (p. 12)

They, among others, see current trends in marriage and marital stability as deriving from the changing sex role preferences and behavior of American women and men. Scanzoni (1976), Scanzoni and Scanzoni (1981), as well as Norton and Glick, contend that these trends are not evidence of the decline of marriage and the family. Rather, these fundamental institutions are going through a period of adaptation and change as the options of both women and men within these institutions are broadened.

It is ironic that the same indicators have been cited in past research as evidence of both the pathology and decline of the black

84

family (see reviews by Allen, 1978a; English, 1974; Staples & Mirande, 1980). The particular history and experiences of blacks in America have resulted in constrained familial role options for men and broadened options for women which have had particular consequences for the relationship between men and women, marriage, and the family. Although these adaptive responses have resulted in male-female, spousal, and parental relationships that have foreshadowed current patterns in the general population, they can not be seen as benign "alternative life-styles."

The changes in families along these lines have been much greater for blacks than for whites. Female headship has increased dramatically in black households in the past two decades. In 1985, 44% of black families were headed by women compared to only 12% of white families (Farley & Allen, 1987). These changes in headship are generally seen as a consequence of a complex set of factors tied to black Americans' reactions to their social and economic status in this country. The most serious consequence of female headship for all families, both black and white, is economic well-being. Female-headed families are more likely to be in poverty than those with male heads. In 1985, 53% of black female-headed households compared to 15% of black male-headed households fell below the official poverty line (Farley & Allen, 1987). Because female-headed households are more likely to contain children under 18 years of age, black children are three times more likely than white children to live out their lives in poverty.

The complexity of the factors underlying these trends suggests that female headship will be an enduring feature of black communities for some time to come. These factors have been exacting their toll, both separate and joint, on black male and female relations and black families over a long period of time. The system of slavery endured by Americans of African descent in the first 200 years of this country effectively constrained the formation and maintenance of stable families. However, it did not permanently alter family organization among blacks. Husband and wife centered families became the prevalent form among blacks after slavery, and this pattern, like that among whites, persisted until World War II. From that point on, a trend of increasing female headship emerged, gaining momentum in the 1960s and the 1970s. The proportion of black households headed by women went from a baseline in 1940 of around 17% to 22% in 1960, 28% in 1970, and 42% in 1983 (Wilson, 1987). Farley and Allen (1987) estimate that 44% of black households in 1985 were headed by women. Female headship has also increased among whites. These households decreased from 10% in 1940 to 8% in 1960 and have since increased to more than 12% of white households. Changes in family organization, however, have been more dramatic for blacks, and the underlying dynamics of this trend suggests that the ceiling has yet to be reached.

While widowhood was the primary contributor to female headship rates in earlier periods, marital dissolution and out-of-wedlock child bearing have become the driving forces in the changing structure of American families. This is particularly true for blacks, whose rates of divorce and separation as well as out-of-wedlock births are much larger than those for whites (Farley & Allen, 1987). Another contributor to the increase in female heads is the growing number of adult women who report being "never married." The proportion of such women increased from 30% in 1960 to 69% in 1980 among blacks and from 29% to 47% among whites (Wilson, 1987).

The documentation of these trends in the early 1960s sparked questions about the viability of black families (Moynihan, 1986). The chicken and egg debate, which began then about the causes of contemporary black family structure and functioning, and about the relationship between these family characteristics and blacks' continued economic disadvantage, has been revived in the 1980s. Murray's (1986) analysis of factors contributing to poverty complemented the ascendancy of neo-conservative political and economic policy makers. This analysis, reminiscent of "culture of poverty" or "blaming the victim" perspectives of the earlier period, implicated the interaction of individual traits and motivations with a particular feature of the social structure, the welfare system, as the source of continued economic disadvantage of certain groups. The welfare system was seen as encouraging the very patterns linked to female headship and poverty—out-of-wedlock births, marital dissolution, and joblessness among black men and women.

Structural Constraints and the Decline of Marriage Among Blacks

Responding to this neo-conservative perspective, Wilson (1987) presented an analysis that located the source of these trends and poverty in the social structure rather than the individual. According to Wilson, black male joblessness, which has increased since the 1960s especially among young blacks, is not only related to the economic well-being of male-headed households, but to the increases in female-headed families as well. Wilson and Neckerman (1986) suggest that disparate sex ratios deriving from disproportional black male mortality and incarceration rates have combined with unemployment among black males to create a limited pool of "marriageable" men. Although once seen as a "tangle of pathology," the organization and functioning of black families is now recognized as being intimately tied to blacks' history of oppression and discrimination. While Wilson (1987) used this perspective to address problems of the urban underclass, it, as has always been argued by black scholars, speaks to the present situation of black Americans as a whole.

This theoretical framework flows out of an intersection of two dominant sociological theoretical traditions—economic materialism (Marxism) and structural functionalism (Merton, 1957). It is one that views racial inequality as mainly deriving from social structural constraints, from macro-level phenomena rather than micro-level individual motivations and behaviors. Thus, the patterns of behaviors that appear to contribute to continued black disadvantage are seen as adaptations to an interaction of general social organization and racial stratification.

According to Wilson (1987), group variation in behavior, norms, and values will reflect variation in their access to benefits, privilege, and power from the existing social order. Because of stratification, mostly on the basis of class and race, which constrains this access for certain groups, Wilson notes that disadvantaged groups may question the legitimacy of the current working arrangements. Addressing underclass issues, he underscores the fact that the combination of race and class increases the structural constraints of blacks and that "ghetto-specific culture is a response to these structural constraints and limited opportunities" (1987, p. 137). Wilson distinguished this perspective from the "Culture of Poverty," espoused mostly by conservatives, by noting that the latter stresses that the adaptive (and as some may say, pathological) cultural traits have been internalized by individuals and guide their behaviors and assumes these traits are pretty immutable. Wilson's perspective, on the other hand, sees these cultural responses as arising out of historical social constraints and as being continually fed by changes in the economic and technological aspects of the social order. Within this view, these cultural traits are not necessarily internalized but are functional in certain circumstances when groups and individuals are unable to benefit from the general social order. Although Wilson deemphasizes the impact of

contemporary racial discrimination, the overall perspective emphasizes continued black disadvantage as a legacy of the cumulative effect of historical discrimination.

Black men and women have long been at odds with traditional sex
roles. For years, black men's sense of power and masculinity has
been undermined by racial oppression. At the same time, black wom-
en were more likely to work outside the home than their white counterparts, forced first by slavery and later, by economic necessity (Dill,
1988). For some black men (and fewer black women), being able to
assume traditional gender roles may be seen as part of the larger
struggle for equal opportunity. However, because most researchers
fail to view gender roles among blacks within a historical and structural opportunity perspective, they have concluded that blacks are
less traditional than whites on most dimensions of gender relations.
The fact that these more egalitarian patterns are now becoming acceptable has not lessened this gender issue among blacks.

In this chapter we examine the general norms, values, and attitudes of black men and women surrounding familial roles, conjugal
living, and the institution of marriage. It is our purpose to get a better
understanding of how the disjuncture between structural opportunity and family norms can lead to the trends in family formation
currently observed among black Americans. The data presented are
from the full national Cross-Section Study of the National Survey of
Black Americans (NSBA) and the reinterview of a subsample of this
study.[1] Indicators of sex role norms, values of conjugal living, and
the efficacy of marriage will be discussed in terms of the total population and by their relationship to gender; two life-cycle indicators,
age and marital status; and an indicator of socioeconomic status, education. All of these variables have been implicated in the literature
as possible determinants of norms, values, and attitudes in the area
of male-female relationships and the family.

Sex Role Norms

The contemporary sex role attitudes of black women and men
must be examined in the context of their particular history and experiences and the changes in the perception of women's roles in the
broader society. The interaction of racial and sexual stratification
complicates the unraveling of both the dimensions and determinants
of black sex role attitudes. Several scholars have raised questions

about the value of trying to understand black sex role attitudes with a framework of white sex role ideology and have suggested that such constructs as "traditional" and "modern" may not be appropriate for blacks (Gump, 1977). Given this, the sex role attitudes of black women and men will be evaluated here in terms of the flexibility and interchangeability of roles. Attitudes that constrain the possible roles of men or women will be described as "conservative" and those that support flexibility and interchangeability as "liberal."

Much of the existing research on black sex roles has been limited to studies of racial differences. The focus has been on whether or not blacks have more egalitarian or flexible sex role attitudes than whites. The data in this area are very conflicting. Some studies have found blacks to have more egalitarian attitudes (Scanzoni, 1976); others have found them to have more traditional or conservative attitudes (Gump, 1975; Hershey, 1978; Rosen, 1978). A third group of studies noting the conflicting evidence suggests that black sex role attitudes may be more complex than white sex role attitudes. Blacks are more conservative than whites in some domains and more liberal in others (Gump, 1975; Millham & Smith, 1981; Scanzoni, 1978). Recently, Sutherland (1989) has further documented the more liberal stance among blacks than among whites in a sample of newlywed couples.

In addition to findings of racial differences, gender and socioeconomic differences have also been found. Although men generally have been found to be more conservative than women, there is some indication that these sex differences are less pronounced among blacks (Crovits & Steinmann, 1980; Hershey, 1978). The findings for socioeconomic variables have been consistent with those found for whites. Educated persons, as well as those with high incomes, tend to be more egalitarian and liberal in their sex role attitudes than persons with lower incomes and less education.

In general the available research on black sex roles is much less developed than that on whites. In addition, there have been a number of conceptual and methodological limitations. The conceptual limitations were noted above. The methodological limitations stem from the fact that most analysis on black sex roles has been based on small and often nonrepresentative black samples. Our data comes from a large national survey of black adults and of a subsample of respondents in this cross-sectional study.

The data presented here are from five sex role attitude questions. Two items tapping attitudes toward the sharing of familial roles are from the larger cross-section study. Four other items addressing the role of black men in child rearing, the role of motherhood for women, and the effect of female employment on the family were asked only in the reinterview. Table 5.1 shows the wording of each item and the name used for each in this chapter.

Sex Differences

Overall there was a great deal of support for an egalitarian division of family tasks and responsibilities among the respondents in our study. More than 88% of women and men agreed (both "strongly agree" and "agree") that men and women should share in child care and household tasks and more than 98% agreed that blacks should spend more time raising their children. Three out of every four black Americans also feel that both men and women should have jobs to support the family. In addition to these egalitarian views of familial roles, the majority of our respondents did not feel that having a job took away from a woman's relationships with her husband or children. However, more than 85% agreed that motherhood is the most fulfilling role for women.

Table 5.1 shows each item by sex. Significant sex differences are found for only three of the five items. Women were more likely than men to agree that both men and women should share household tasks and child care and that both should have jobs to support the family. The biggest difference between the sexes is found for the Share Provider Role item. Interestingly, on the other item that showed significant sex differences, women had more conservative responses than men. More women than men agreed that motherhood is the most fulfilling role for women. Sex differences were not found for Women's Job Hurts or black Fathers.

Socioeconomic Correlates

Hatchett and Quick (1982) have examined the relationship of age, marital status, and education to black sex role attitudes using these data. Their results will only be summarized here. Generally, they found the correlates of sex role norms of black men and women to be different. Age was found to be related to attitudes toward the division of family tasks and roles only for women. Younger women were more likely to hold liberal attitudes toward role and task sharing than older women. No age relationship was found for either sex for perceptions of the effects of women working. However, age was related to

Table 5.1
Five Sex Role Attitude Items by Sex

Sex Role Attitude Items	Strongly Agree (%)	Agree (%)	Disagree (%)	Strongly Disagree (%)	Percent (N)
	Cross-Section Only				
Share Tasks "Both men and women should share equally in childcare and housework."					
Men	42.8	42.9	11.4	2.9	100.0 (788)
Women	51.4	39.3	8.2	1.1	100.0 (1,284)
Share Provider Role "Both men and women should have jobs to support the family."					
Men	21.2	44.0	30.2	4.6	100.0 (775)
Women	31.0	49.6	17.8	1.6	100.0 (1,277)
	Reinterview Only				
Black Fathers "Most black fathers should spend more time raising their children than they do now."					
Men	58.5	39.1	1.7	0.7	100.0 (294)
Women	66.8	30.8	1.8	0.6	100.0 (561)
Women's Job Hurts "Having a job takes away from a woman's relationship with her husband or children."					
Men	13.0	35.9	46.9	4.2	100.0 (284)
Women	8.7	37.0	48.7	5.6	100.0 (552)
Motherhood "Being a mother and raising children is the most fulfilling experience a woman can have."					
Men	29.7	53.6	13.1	3.6	100.0 (276)
Women	39.1	47.9	11.7	1.3	100.0 (553)

attitudes about motherhood only for black men. Interestingly, both men 18 to 34 years old and those over 55 had more conservative attitudes toward motherhood than men 35 to 54 years old. This relationship is contrary to what one might expect given the exposure of younger men to new emergent role norms. Because parental and marital status (along with a number of socioeconomic variables) were controlled in these analyses, it is doubtful these life-cycle issues influenced this relationship. Hopefully, further analyses will illuminate these results.

Marital status was related only to women's attitudes toward sharing the provider role. Married women were more conservative than previously married and never married women.

Support for the egalitarian division of labor within the family did not differ by socioeconomic level for men. However, education as an indicator of socioeconomic status was related to attitudes toward the sharing of familial roles and tasks for black women. Women with at least 16 years of education were more liberal in their attitudes than women with less education. Conversely, education was related to the perception of harmful effects stemming from female employment among men but not among women. Men who had some education beyond high school but were not college graduates were the most conservative. Those with more education were the most liberal. Education was related to evaluations of motherhood as the most fulfilling role for women among both sexes. Liberal attitudes increased with years of education.

In sum, these data further document the existence of a great deal of support for egalitarianism among black Americans—both men and women. Generally, these data show support for liberal sex role norms in all areas save one—motherhood. Motherhood is seen as the most fulfilling role for women by a large majority of both sexes. Although there are sex differences on three of these norms, they are perhaps not as large as one might expect. These findings are consistent with the literature in which sex differences have been found to be less evident for blacks and blacks have been found to be more liberal than whites on some sex role norms and more conservative on others. Scanzoni (1975) found blacks were more conservative on norms pertaining to the appropriate behavior of the sexes but more liberal on those addressing the rights and individualism of women. Also, black women have been found to have more nurturant attitudes than other women. Motherhood and family responsibilities have not been seen as antithetical to working or to being "liberated" in the modern sense of the word (Gump, 1977). Indeed, these dimensions of sex role norms were not correlated for women in this study.

The sex role norms and behavior of blacks are confounded by the unique experiences of being black in America and by the influence of the larger white society. The limited subgroup analyses reported here and the more extensive analyses presented in Hatchett and Quick (1982) were pursued in an effort to gain insight into the influence of both. It is possible that the large amount of support of egalitarianism among black Americans is attributable to their unique experiences in this country. The differences found for sex, age, marital status, and education may stem from influences from the broader society.

Value of Conjugal Living

While the research on black sex role attitudes has been limited, the study of values in marriage or what blacks hope to gain by marriage or the establishment of similar conjugal relationships is almost non-existent. What has been done has been limited in most cases by a focus only on married women (Duncan, Schuman, & Duncan, 1973). Indeed until recently this focus has been the shortcoming of most research on marriage (Bernard, 1966). A related area of inquiry which has included both sexes is the study of values in mate selection. These studies, however, have been limited for the most part by small, nonrepresentative samples (often college students).

With a few exceptions (e.g. Ladner, 1971), most of the work in this area has involved comparisons between blacks and whites. Melton and Thomas (1976) in their study of mate selection among college students found evidence to support their contention that black women and men value the instrumental characteristics of potential mates more than white men and women. This emphasis on instrumental goals or values, they suggest, derives from the relative economic insecurity of blacks. According to them, black men are more supportive of their wives working, and indeed some may actually expect wives to work. Therefore, a wife who has the potential of enhancing the overall socioeconomic status of the family is more desirable. In a similar vein, from her work with black female adolescents, Ladner (1971) suggests that black women may marry for more instrumental reasons than white women. Both studies suggest that reasons for marriage among blacks derive more from instrumental values than socioemotional ones.

Because men and women traditionally have been expected to fulfill different roles within the family and the marital dyad, one would expect differences in values or goals within marriage to emerge. Since the role of provider traditionally has been relegated to males, men would be expected to place less emphasis on the economic advantages of marriage than women. However, the long history of wife employment among black families and the attitudes of black men toward wives working suggests this may not be true for black men.

In this part of the chapter we examine the influence of gender, life cycle, and socioeconomic status on the values in marriages or conjugal living for black Americans. Age and marital status will be used separately as indicators of life cycle and education and family income as indicators of socioeconomic status.

Sex Differences

Our respondents were asked to evaluate six reasons for living with a person of the opposite sex in terms of their importance to them.[2] We decided not to limit our inquiry to reasons for marriage because of recent trends in the general population of couples living together outside of marriage. The majority of respondents felt conjugal living was very important for raising children (69%), financial security (48%), jobs around the house (49%), good love life (61%), and companionship (67%). Women also were asked about the importance of having a man in the house for safety. Only a little more than a third of them felt safety was an important reason for conjugal living.

We also asked respondents which was the "most" and the "least" important reason for living with a person of the opposite sex. More than 36% felt raising children was the most important reason and another 27% felt companionship was the most important reason for conjugal living. The majority felt that getting jobs done around the house was the least important reason for living with someone of the opposite sex.

Because of the different roles and responsibilities historically assumed by men and women in conjugal living situations, one would expect the values expressed by each sex to be different. Indeed there are significant sex differences on all but one of the reasons for conjugal living. Men were more likely than women to feel that conjugal living was important for raising children, for a good love life, and for companionship. Women, on the other hand, were more likely to say that financial security was an important reason for living with a person of the opposite sex. There were no differences between men and women on the importance of conjugal living for jobs around the house.

Men and women also differed on which reasons they felt were the "most" and the "least" important. Twice as many men as women (41% vs. 19%) said that companionship was the most important reason for living together. The difference was smaller between men and women for those saying raising children was the most important reason for conjugal living (30% vs. 40%). A good love life was the third most frequently cited reason for men and financial security was the third most frequent response for women.

Men and women also differed on what they felt was the least important reason for living with the opposite sex. Thirty-nine percent of the men compared to 7.5% of the female respondents felt that financial security was the least important reason for conjugal living, whereas 40% of the women felt household tasks were the least important reason for conjugal living compared to 35% of the men. Men listed jobs around the house as the next least important reason for conjugal living, while women listed love life.

Other Correlates

In order to examine the impact of age, marital status, and education on the perceived value of conjugal living, two indices were constructed—one tapping the socioemotional dimension of conjugal living and the other, the instrumental dimension.[3] The Socioemotional Procreative Value Index is made up of Children, Love Life, and Companionship and ranges from 1 to 10, with 10 indicating high importance or value. Housework and Financial Security are included in the Instrumental Value of Conjugal Living Index, which ranges from 1 to 7. Separate Multiple Classification Analyses were run for men and women with each index as the dependent variable.

The results for the Socioemotional Procreative Value Index are shown in Table 5.2. There were significant bivariate relationships for all three independent variables for both sexes. In the multivariate model, marital status (for men, Beta = .35; for women, Beta = .32) had the most impact. Next came age (for men, Beta = .15; for women, Beta = .14), and then education (for men, Beta = .10; for women, Beta = .11). Overall the three variables explained 13% of the variance in the index for men and 15% for women.

Married men and women tended to value the socioemotional and procreative dimension more than previously married and never mar-

Table 5.2

Age, Education, and Marital Status as Predictors of the Socioemotional Procreative Value of Conjugal Living Index

	Mean	Adjusted Mean [a]	S.D.	Eta	Beta	N
Men Only						
Marital Status						
Married	9.34	9.39	1.50	.30	.35	412
Separated/Divorced	8.50	8.55	2.19			121
Widowed	8.09	8.48	2.63			44
Never married	7.91	7.67	2.51			190
Age						
18 to 34 years	8.78	9.08	1.88	.08	.15	328
35 to 54 years	9.00	8.75	1.96			236
55 years or older	8.53	8.34	2.44			202
Education						
0 to 11 years	8.68	8.79	2.22	.10	.10	333
12 years	8.86	8.86	1.97			221
13 to 15 years	9.10	8.85	1.43			143
16 + years	8.36	8.33	2.65			70
Women Only						
Marital Status						
Married	8.90	8.85	1.88	.35	.32	440
Separated/Divorced	7.17	7.12	2.68			315
Widowed	6.38	6.77	3.26			233
Never married	7.44	7.24	2.56			264
Age						
18 to 34 years	7.96	7.94	2.34	.19	.14	513
35 to 54 years	8.07	7.90	2.45			399
55 years or older	6.84	7.07	3.28			340
Education						
0 to 11 years	7.47	7.76	2.98	.08	.11	550
12 years	7.89	7.69	2.52			411
13 to 15 years	7.72	7.42	2.37			181
16 + years	7.98	7.78	2.39			110

a. Class means for each predictor are adjusted for effects of all other predictors in the model. Regions and time of interview were other predictors included in analyses but not shown in above table.

ried men and women. A negative linear pattern emerges for age. As age increases the socioemotional and procreative value of conjugal living decreases. Similarly for men, the value of this dimension of conjugal living decreases as education increases. A curvilinear pattern, however, emerges for education among women. Women with both high and low levels of education valued the socioemotional/procreative aspect of living with the opposite sex more than those with high school or only a few years of education beyond high school (13–15 years).

Table 5.3 shows the results for the Instrumental Value of Conjugal Living Index. All three variables have significant bivariate relationships with the index. However, the variables have different relative impacts on the index in the models for men and women. The variables in order of their importance for determining instrumental value of conjugal living for men are education (Beta = .23), marital status (Beta = .23), and age (Beta = .05). For women, the order is marital status (Beta = .25), education (Beta = .11), and age (Beta = .09). While marital status and education have almost equal impact for men, education is much less important than marital status in determining the instrumental value of conjugal living for women. Overall, the models explained 12% of the variance for men and 10% for women. Married men scored higher on the Instrumental Value of Conjugal Living Index than previously married and never married men. The same pattern holds for women.

The relationship found for the Socioemotional Procreative Value Index and education for men is the same as that found for the Instrumental Value of Conjugal Living Index. Men with 16 or more years of education on the average tended to value both dimensions of conjugal living less than men with less education. Different patterns, however, emerge for women across the indices. A negative linear relationship was found for the Instrumental Value of Conjugal Living Index while a curvilinear pattern was found for the Socioemotional Procreative Value Index. As education increases the mean value or importance of the instrumental dimension of conjugal living decreases. On the other hand, the mean value of the socioemotional dimension is lower for women with 13 to 15 years of education and higher both for those with 0 to 12 years and 16 or more years of education.

A curvilinear pattern emerges for age for both sexes. The pattern is more pronounced for women than men. Middle-aged men and women place more value on instrumental aspects of marriage than both

Table 5.3

Age, Education, and Marital Status as Predictors of the Instrumental Value of Conjugal Living Index

	Mean	Adjusted Mean [a]	S.D.	Eta	Beta	N
		Men Only				
Education						
0 to 11 years	5.19	5.18	1.91	.22	.23	340
12 years	4.83	4.89	1.91			224
13 to 15 years	4.58	4.55	1.70			141
16 + years	3.69	3.63	1.97			72
Marital Status						
Married	5.24	5.24	1.73	.22	.23	413
Separated/Divorced	4.34	4.26	2.06			125
Widowed	4.54	4.26	2.06			48
Never married	4.38	4.50	2.03			191
Age						
18 to 34 years	4.59	4.74	1.84	.11	.05	330
35 to 54 years	5.01	4.96	1.99			238
55 years or older	5.03	4.86	1.97			209
		Women Only				
Education						
0 to 11 years	5.30	5.34	2.06	.11	.11	565
12 years	5.32	5.30	1.78			419
13 to 15 years	4.84	4.82	1.85			182
16 + years	4.80	4.77	1.87			110
Marital Status						
Married	5.87	5.84	1.52	.25	.25	445
Separated/Divorced	4.85	4.84	2.02			320
Widowed	4.88	4.75	2.19			243
Never married	4.80	4.97	1.19			268
Age						
18 to 34 years	5.00	5.03	1.81	.11	.09	518
35 to 54 years	5.49	5.42	1.83			407
55 years or older	5.16	5.19	2.18			351

a. Class means for each predictor are adjusted for effects of all other predictors in the model. Regions and time of interview were other predictors included in analyses but not shown in above table.

younger and older persons. This age relationship is different from negative linear patterns found for the Socioemotional Procreative Value Index for both sexes.

All in all, black women seem to value the instrumental aspects of marriage—particularly financial security—more than black men. Black men, according to our data, place more emphasis on the socioemotional aspects of living with the opposite sex. In some ways, these differences reflect aspects of complementarity implied by traditional sex roles. There are subgroup differences, however, for both sexes. As one would expect, marital status is a good predictor of the amount of value one places on all aspects of conjugal living. Married men and women place more value on both dimensions than previously married or never married men and women. Age, as another indicator of life cycle, also distinguishes the amount of importance placed on socioemotional and instrumental dimensions of marriage or other conjugal relationships. The socioemotional aspects become less important as people age. This is understandable in light of real life-cycle constraints on children. It is less understandable for love life and companionship. Because social myths persist about aging and sexuality, it is possible that companionship might be more important for older persons than younger persons. However, the relationship between age and the separate companionship item is the same as that found for the socioemotional index. It is possible that this result is partially due to an interaction between marital status, sex, and age. Most of the older persons in our sample are female and most of the widowed are female. Indeed, when we look at the results for marital status and this index for women, we find that widowed women score significantly lower than women in other marital status groups. These women may value being on their own after years of parental and marital responsibilities and tend to rely on kin and friend networks as well as religion for solid emotional support (Lopata, 1969, 1986).

Of the two indicators of socioeconomic status, only education proved to be a significant predictor of values of conjugal living. The relationship between education and the socioemotional index was different for men and women. As education increased, men were less likely to place high value on the socioemotional dimension. For women, both those with high school or less and with four or more years of college placed more emphasis on this dimension than women with only some training beyond high school. Less emphasis is placed on the instrumental aspect of conjugal living as education increases for both men and women.

Attitude Toward Marriage

The incidence of marital dissolution is higher among blacks than any other group in this country. Although recent census data show the gap is narrowing as divorce increases for the general population, the rates are uniformly higher for blacks at all socioeconomic levels. In light of current trends in nonmarital family formation, divorce, and separation, it has been questioned whether blacks still value marriage as an institution. Our data allow us to answer this question for blacks in general and for various subgroups of the black population.

Black men and women in the reinterview sample were asked whether they strongly agreed, agreed, disagreed, or strongly disagreed with the following statement: "There are so few good marriages these days that I don't know if I want to be married." A plurality of respondents (50%) disagreed with this statement. However, more than two out of every five black Americans agreed that there were so few good marriages that they didn't know if they wanted to be married. There were no significant differences between men and women in their attitudes toward marriage.

Significant subgroup differences, however, were found for marital status and education. Table 5.4 shows marital status and education as predictors of attitude toward marriage. As one would expect, married and never married persons, both male and female, were more likely to disagree with negative evaluations of marriage. On the other hand, previously married men and women were more likely to argue that marriage may not be a worthwhile venture for them. Experience seems to have a negative impact on the evaluation of the institution of marriage for black Americans. All in all, the fact that never married and married individuals are less likely to reject marriage as a desired institution indicates that marriage is still a value among large numbers of black Americans.

Summary and Discussion

Chapter 4 examined black families in all their diversity—from those formed around married couples to those headed by women only. In that chapter, we were interested in the ability of the black family's

Table 5.4
Marital Status and Education as Predictors of Attitude Toward Marriage

	Mean	Adjusted Mean [a]	S.D.	Eta	Beta	N
		Men Only				
Marital Status						
Married	2.91	2.91	0.77	.30	.29	152
Separated/Divorced	2.25	2.24	0.78			44
Widowed	2.31	2.43	0.95			16
Never married	2.64	2.64	0.88			70
Education						
0 to 11 years	2.57	2.54	0.89	.19	.19	120
12 years	2.70	2.75	0.82			89
13 to 15 years	2.93	2.90	0.69			45
16 + years	3.00	2.98	0.90			28
		Women Only				
Marital Status						
Married	2.86	2.85	0.78	.30	.28	209
Separated/Divorced	2.33	2.33	0.88			130
Widowed	2.19	2.26	0.83			86
Never married	2.57	2.53	0.87			118
Education						
0 to 11 years	2.46	2.52	0.85	.14	.08	236
12 years	2.58	2.56	0.87			187
13 to 15 years	2.63	2.59	0.89			79
16 + years	2.93	2.79	0.88			41

a. Class means for each predictor are adjusted for effects of all other predictors in the model. Regions and time of interview were other predictors included in analyses but not shown in above table.

cultural adaptation of strong family networks, at both the household and community level, to buffer economic adversity and to complement aspects of family functioning lacking in mother-only families. We found that while there is considerable evidence that these networks are still prominent, they are not evenly distributed among all black families. Those that are particularly at risk, low-income and female-headed families, appear to have less access to these kin networks and their potential benefits. In this chapter, we stepped back to examine some of the factors underlying the trends in family organization that some analysts call the "decline of marriage" among black Americans.

Within a theoretical perspective used by Wilson (1987) to address these issues, we presented analyses from our national survey of attitudes regarding gender roles and marriage. Wilson and others (e.g., Tucker & Taylor, 1989) have presumed relatively strong values toward the institution of marriage while arguing that current trends in black family structure are cultural adaptations to more than social structural constraints. Using data from our national survey, we were able to assess the value of marriage as well as adaptive norms that govern marriage, family formation, and gender roles among a representative sample of black Americans.

We summarize and discuss these results by first looking at attitudes toward marriage, and then the norms regarding entering into a conjugal relationship such as marriage. Finally, we discuss what we believe are adaptive cultural norms regarding gender roles and how these norms may facilitate or threaten black marriages.

Attitudes Toward and Values in Marriage

Marriage is still a strong value among black Americans regardless of the current rates in which this union is entered and dissolved. Never-married men and women were less likely to reject marriage for themselves in spite of its negative reputation for success among blacks. Also, those currently in marriages seem more committed to this institution than those who have experienced it and lost out against the challenges that confront black couples in this country. However, the reasons for getting married among blacks appear to predispose many to never marrying, or to separation or divorce if they do marry.

Black men and women differ on what they feel are reasons for getting married. Black men are more likely to say that such conjugal relationships should be entered into for socioemotional reasons (love and companionship, children) than black women. The latter are more likely to express instrumental reasons for getting married. Foremost among these reasons is financial security. Herein lies the contradiction or lack of fit between values and opportunity that have generated the adaptations in family formation we have discussed in this chapter and in Chapter 4. The size of the pool of "marriageable men," given black women's criteria, has decreased dramatically in the past 30 years or so, according to Wilson and Neckerman (1986). The cumulative effects of racial stratification in this country, as well as the current restructuring of the economic sector, have resulted in large numbers of jobless, low paid, and incarcerated black men. Although black women with higher education place less emphasis on marrying for financial security than those with less education, the pool of employed black men with similar education is much less than that for other black women. All in all, the future looks bleak for black women finding marriage partners, if the economic marginalization of black men does not decrease. The probability of this happening in the near future is slim, given the prominence of neo-conservative racial and economic politics and the complexity of the problem.

Attitudes About Gender Roles

Our analyses further documented evidence that a significant proportion of black men and women are fairly egalitarian in their attitudes about gender roles. While the literature suggests that whites are more traditional than blacks, this does not necessarily mean that black Americans are closer to the views advanced in the modern Women's Movement. The flexibility in gender roles and power among blacks was an adaptation to social structural factors that kept most blacks from achieving the gender relations evident in the majority population. Hatchett, Veroff, and Douvan (in press), in a study of marital instability in the first marriages of black and white couples, found that gender issues around marital power and role flexibility figure prominently in black marital instability. Regardless of their income, black husbands who worried about their ability to perform the role of provider were more likely to be in unstable marriages. Black marriages were also unstable if black men felt their wives had equal power in the family, and if black wives felt there was not enough role sharing in regard to family tasks and responsibilities. Black men and women seem to be at odds about the current gender roles in black families. Most black women appear to feel that keeping the arrangement as it is is not only desirable but a necessity. A large number of black men, on the other hand, feel that assuming the long-denied traditional gender roles of whites is part of the general struggle to achieve racial equality. Resolution of these differences is imperative if black marriages are to survive or even start. Using relationship narratives from the same study as Hatchett and colleagues (in press), Chadiha (1989) found the male provider issue figures prominently in courtship and the decision to marry.

We conclude that prospects for black family formation and stability will remain perilous until the general society and the black community directly address all of the issues arising from cultural adaptations to more than 200 years of oppression. The situation is at a crisis level. Progress must be made in this decade if we are to improve the quality of family and married life for black Americans.

Notes

1. The result samples for the cross-section and the reinterview, which was a special subsample of the cross-section, were very similar. There were no significant differences by study in the distribution of all of the background variables included in these analyses for men and women, before, during, and after marriage.

2. "How important is it for you to have a (man/woman) live in the house with you for the things I'm going to read? . . ."

3. Two dimensions emerge from simple cluster analyses of these items. Cronbach's alphas were .83 and .68 respectively, for the Socioemotional/Procreative Index and the Instrumental Value of Conjugal Living Index.

RELIGIOUS LIFE

Robert Joseph Taylor
Linda M. Chatters

The religious experience of American blacks has been of continuing
interest to academic and religious audiences, attested to by the broad
and rich literature on black theology (Cone, 1969, 1985), as well as
work on the social and political functions of churches in black communities. Religion and churches occupy an important position in
the lives of black Americans. Their impact on the development and
preservation of black communities has been documented in previous work (Drake & Cayton, 1945; Frazier, 1974; Woodson, 1939).
Black churches are a unique social entity in that they were developed
by an oppressed group that was refused access to the institutional life
of broader American society (Morris, 1984). In that role, they assumed many social organization functions (e.g., education, social
welfare, civic duties, business enterprises).

The significance of black churches to community life may be attributed, in part, to their position as one of the few indigenous institutions in black communities that are built, financed, and controlled
by blacks (Drake & Cayton, 1945; Frazier, 1974). In addition to providing spiritual sustenance and a temporary refuge from the discrimination and racism found in broader society, black churches fulfill
a variety of functions. Black churches serve as the organizational
hub of community life. In this capacity, black churches furnish outlets for social expression, provide a forum for the discussion of political and social issues, and serve as a training ground for potential
community leaders (Morris, 1984). The continuing significance of

religion and churches in black American life is evident in recent research indicating that religion constitutes a coping resource for handling stressful life events (Krause & Tran, 1989; Neighbors, Jackson, Bowman, & Gurin, 1982), and that black churches provided the organizational foundation and human resources for the Civil Rights Movement (McAdam, 1982; Morris, 1984).

Theories of black religious experience in the sociology of religion share an appreciation of the notion that the religious orientation and behaviors of black Americans emerged as a reaction to blocked opportunities for full participation in the American mainstream. In effect, black religious expression and behavior reflected an attempt to compensate for the political, social, and economic exclusion from broader society. But reflecting a very different emphasis on the significance of this situation, these theorists speculated that, because of black Americans' limited opportunities to transform an oppressive social structure, black churches claimed the spiritual life of black people as their undisputed province and exclusive sphere of influence. Consequently, black religion was characterized as being escapist and concerned with "other-worldly" matters. Black religion's remedy for the deleterious effects of pervasive discrimination and racism, and the resulting psychological alienation and demoralization, was to emphasize the transitory nature of the physical world and the enduring nature of the spiritual realm.

This conceptualization of black religious experience suggests that position within the social structure has an immediate and direct impact on the form and character of religious attitudes and behaviors. Adopting this perspective, one would expect that the nature of black religious experience would vary as a function of differences in other social status position indicators apparent within the general black population. Specifically, socioeconomic differences should shape the form and content of religious behaviors and commitment, with higher status position (and presumably greater social, economic, and political power) associated with a diminution of the escapist and other-worldly qualities of black religious experience.

The issues and questions related to the nature and spectrum of black religious experience and expression are numerous, yet there is scant concrete information on these phenomena. There is a paucity of data on basic religious behaviors of black Americans, such as religious affiliation, church attendance and membership, and private religious behaviors such as prayer. The scarcity of quantitative literature on the religious experience of blacks is particularly conspicuous on examination of the publication histories for leading journals of religious behavior. From 1961 to 1988, the *Journal for the Scientific Study of Religion* published over 600 articles, less than 15 of which addressed the religious experiences of blacks. In addition, the majority of these articles did not involve quantitative data analysis. Special issues in another prominent religious journal, *Review of Religious Research* (October and December, 1988), have sought to rectify this situation. Although the articles in this journal are generally quantitative in nature, the majority of work in these special issues was not based on empirical data. Clearly, empirical research on the religious experience of blacks is needed in order to gain a better appreciation of the nature of black religious experiences and the role of religion and black churches in the lives of individuals and communities.

This chapter specifically investigates attitudes towards religion and the nature and extent of religious behaviors and involvement as reported by black Americans. The chapter is divided into five sections which address different aspects of religious experience: (a) a profile of religious affiliation, (b) rates of participation and involvement in religious services and activities (e.g., frequency of attendance, church membership, frequency of prayer, subjective religiosity), (c) perceptions of the socio-historical role of the black church, (d) the role of church members in the informal social support networks of black Americans, and (e) religion and mental health among blacks.

Religious Affiliation

There have been only a few profiles of religious affiliation among black Americans. One compilation, conducted by the Census Bureau in 1957 (Jackson, 1983; Nelsen, Yokley, & Nelsen, 1971), is limited in that blacks and other nonwhites are combined into a single category. In this Census, nine out of ten nonwhites report that their religious affiliation is Protestant. The two largest religious affiliations were Baptist (59.1% of men and 62% of women) and Methodist (17% of men and 17.5% of women). Roman Catholicism was the next most reported religious affiliation (6.4% of men, 6.6% of women). Only 5.4% of nonwhite men and 1.7% of nonwhite women reported that they were not affiliated with any religion. Using data from the General Social Surveys of the National Opinion Research Center (NORC), Greeley's profile (1979) of religious affiliation among blacks revealed a situation comparable to earlier work. Fifty-nine percent of black respondents in the NORC data reported being Baptist, 13% were Methodist, 8% Roman Catholic, and 5% indicated having no religious preference.

The NSBA data provide a current profile of religious affiliation among black Americans. Table 6.1 presents the univariate distribution of respondents' current religious affiliation. Forty different religious affiliations were reported, demonstrating the breadth and diversity of religious preference among black Americans. One half of the respondents indicated that they were Baptist (52.1%), 11.7% reported being Methodist, and 6.3% stated that they were Roman Catholic. Also, 3.2% of respondents indicated that they were Holiness, and 2.1% reported being Jehovah's Witnesses. Fifteen percent of respondents identified one of the 35 remaining denominations or groups as their current religious affiliation. One out of ten respondents indicated that they had no religious preference, and eight respondents indicated that they were either atheist or agnostic.

The percentage distribution for NSBA respondents' current religious affiliation is comparable to affiliation profiles reported in earlier research (Jackson, 1983; Greeley, 1979). Overwhelmingly, respondents were Protestant, the majority of whom identify their religious affiliation as being either Baptist or Methodist. The NSBA data is, however, limited by the fact that information is not gathered on affiliation with specific subdivisions or subgroups within larger denominations. Respondents who reported that they were Methodists were not probed as to whether they were African Methodist Episcopal (AME), African Methodist Episcopal Zion (AME Zion), or Colored Methodist Episcopal (CME). By and large, respondents spontaneously provided this specific information on religious affiliation. However, because some respondents simply reported that they were Methodists, the data can only provide an overall percentage for that larger category of religious affiliation; it can not provide accurate percentages of respondents in each subdenominational affiliation comprising the larger group of Methodists. However, in contrast to the 1957 Census (Jackson, 1983) and the NORC data (Greeley, 1979), the NSBA data provides a greater sense of the heterogeneity of religious affiliation among black Americans.

A comparison of respondents' current and childhood religious affiliation and religious affiliations (trichotomized into Baptist, Methodist, and other) of respondents' parents reveals that respondents overwhelmingly report that their own affiliation (current and child-

Table 6.1
Religious Affiliation of Black Americans

Religious Affiliation	Percent of Sample	N
Congregational	0.2	4
Episcopalian	1.2	25
Lutheran	0.4	9
Presbyterian	0.9	19
United Church of Christ	0.1	2
African Methodist Episcopal	1.2	26
Baptist	52.1	1,083
Disciples of Christ	0.3	7
Methodist	10.4	218
CME (Methodist)	0.1	3
Apostolic	0.5	11
Church of Christ	1.2	25
Church of God	0.3	7
Church of God and Christ	1.2	23
Fundamentalist Baptist	1.4	30
Nazarene or Free Methodist	0.0	1
Pentecostal or Assembly of God	1.5	31
Salvation Army	0.0	1
Sanctified	0.6	11
Seventh Day Adventist	0.4	7
Southern Baptist	0.1	3
Other Baptist	0.0	1
Other Fundamentalist	0.0	1
Christian	0.7	15
Protestant (no denomination given)	0.8	17
Nondenominational Protestant Church	0.5	9
Community Church (no denomination given)	0.1	2
Other Protestant	0.0	1
Roman Catholic	6.3	132
Holiness	3.2	67
Jehovah's Witness	2.1	44
Latter Day Saints, Mormons	0.1	2
Spiritualist	0.2	5
Unity	0.1	3
Islam	0.7	15
Muslim, Moslem	0.2	5
Nation of Islam	0.0	1
Jewish	0.1	3
Buddhist	0.0	1
Bahai	0.0	1
None (no preference)	10.1	211
Atheist-agnostic	0.5	8
Other	0.2	4
Total	100.0	2,094

hood) and that of their parents were either Baptist or Methodist. One major difference between the respondents' religious affiliation (both current and childhood) and that of their parents is that respondents were slightly more likely to indicate a personal religious affiliation other than Baptist or Methodist, especially reports of current affiliation. Rates of nonaffiliation (no religious preference) were highest for reports of respondents' own current religious status, followed by fathers', respondents' childhood status, and mothers' religious status. Further, respondents were more likely to know their mother's religious preference than their father's.

Bivariate tests of significance and measures of association for the relationship between respondents' current religious affiliation and childhood and parental religious affiliations (data not shown) indicate strong relationships between the respondents' current religious affiliation and both childhood and parental religious affiliations. Respondents' mothers' religious affiliation had a stronger impact on respondents' current religious affiliation than did fathers' affiliation. Eight out of 10 respondents whose mothers were identified as Baptist reported that they were currently Baptist. Similarly, 6 out of 10 respondents whose mothers were Methodist reported that they were currently Methodist.

The observed relationship between respondent and parental religious affiliation is consistent with other work. Several researchers have reported at least 70% agreement on the religious affiliations of adult children and their parents (see Troll & Bengtson, 1979). Similarly, high levels of congruence between adult children and their parents have been found for both indicators of general religious orientation and specific religious attitudes and behavior (Troll & Bengtson, 1979). These findings support the view that, similar to other family values and customs, religious behavior, beliefs, and experiences are part of the culture and routinely transmitted from generation to generation (Argyle & Beit-Hallahmi, 1975). The finding that mothers' religious affiliation is more strongly related to respondents' current affiliation than is fathers' is also consistent with previous research findings. Several studies report higher levels of concordance on religious beliefs and practices for mothers and their offspring than for fathers (see Troll & Bengtson, 1979). Together, these findings support the view that religious socialization is customarily the domain of the mother.

Demographic Correlates of Religious Involvement

Research examining religious involvement emphasizes the importance of investigating diverse forms of religious expression, such as organizational (e.g., church attendance), nonorganizational (e.g., prayer) and attitudinal (e.g., subjective religiosity) measures of religiosity. A major criticism of prior research has been that indicators of organizational activity frequently were employed as the single indicators of religiosity. Consequently, individuals with health impairments or transportation difficulties or who were otherwise limited in their ability or willingness to attend services were, by definition, less religiously oriented than persons who demonstrated higher levels of organized religious participation. The present analysis examines a collection of organizational, nonorganizational, and attitudinal measures of religious involvement in order to provide a more adequate representation of the multidimensional nature of religiosity. This examination of the demographic correlates of religious involvement employs a full set of demographic variables as independent variables (i.e., gender, marital status, age, education, income, urbanicity, and region). Multiple regression analysis was used except when the dependent variable was dichotomous, in which case logistic regression was utilized. A more in-depth examination of several of these dependent variables is found in the work of Chatters and Taylor (1989a), Taylor (1986b, 1988b, 1988c), and Taylor and Chatters (1991).

The univariate distribution of the religiosity items is presented in Table 6.2. The data indicate that black Americans demonstrate a considerable degree of religious commitment. Fewer than 10% of all respondents reported that (except for weddings and funerals) they have not attended religious services as an adult (since 18 years of age). Of those respondents who have attended, roughly 70% reported that they attend religious services a few times a month or more frequently. Over 75% of these respondents felt that attending religious services was very important, and two out of three of them reported that they were official members of churches or other places of worship.

A general profile of participation in nonorganizational religious activities reveals that a full 78% of all respondents (including persons who have not attended church services as an adult) reported that they prayed nearly every day. Similarly, 27% indicated that they read religious books, 21% watched or listened to religious programs on

Table 6.2

Univariate Distribution of Religious Variables

Variable	Percent of Sample
Attend Church Services Since 18	
(excluding weddings and funerals)	
Yes	91.8
No	8.2
Total (N)	100.0 (2,102)
Church Attendance	
Nearly every day	4.5
At least once a week	35.5
A few times a month	30.6
A few times a year	19.4
Less than once a year	10.0
Total (N)	100.0 (1,922)
Importance of Attending Church	
Very important	77.2
Fairly important	17.0
Not too important	4.6
Not important at all	1.2
Total (N)	100.0 (1,723)
Church Membership	
Yes	67.6
No	32.4
Total (N)	100.0 (1,922)
Frequency of Reading Religious Materials	
Nearly every day	27.0
At least once a week	23.4
A few times a month	23.9
A few times a year	18.8
Less than once a year	6.9
Total (N)	100.0 (2,098)
Frequency of Watching and Listening to Religious Programs	
Nearly every day	21.0
At least once a week	46.8
A few times a month	14.4

Variable	Percent of Sample
Frequency of Watching and Listening to Religious Programs *(continued)*	
A few times a year	9.8
Less than once a year	8.0
Total (*N*)	100.0 (2,097)
Frequency of Prayer	
Nearly every day	78.0
At least once a week	8.3
A few times a month	6.4
A few times a year	4.2
Less than once a year	3.1
Total (*N*)	100.0 (2,094)
Frequency of Requesting Prayer	
Nearly every day	13.6
At least once a week	17.9
A few times a month	19.1
A few times a year	20.8
Less than once a year	28.6
Total (*N*)	100.0 (2,089)
Degree of Subjective Religiosity	
Very religious	34.1
Fairly religious	49.5
Not too religious	13.3
Not religious at all	3.1
Total (*N*)	100.0 (2,091)

television or radio, and 13.6% reported that they asked someone to pray for them on roughly a daily basis. In addition, 8 of 10 respondents considered themselves to be either very or fairly religious in their outlook.

Analyses of these measures of religious commitment revealed pervasive demographic differences. Gender differences in religious participation and involvement were the strongest and most consistent relationships observed. As compared to men, women were less likely to report that they have never attended religious services, attached greater significance to attending religious services, attended religious services more frequently, were more likely to be church members, participated in nonreligious activities more frequently, and depicted themselves as being religious to a greater degree. These findings are consistent with a body of work indicating that women exhibit a greater degree of religious commitment than men. Sasaki (1979) found that women prayed more frequently, were more likely to have strong religious beliefs, and were more likely to indicate that they were "born again" than were men. Blazer and Palmore's (1976) analyses revealed that women were more involved in religious activities and pursuits than men. Women, in general, and black women, in particular (Nelsen & Nelsen, 1975), attended church more frequently than their male counterparts. Similar to prior work on gender differences in religious behavior, these findings indicate that, irrespective of the religious commitment indicator (i.e., organizational, nonorganizational, attitudinal), women are more religious than men. (See Argyle & Beit–Hallahmi, 1975, for a review of this research.)

Age also has a pervasive influence on the various measures of religious commitment. Compared to younger persons, older black adults were more likely to have attended religious services since the age of 18, attended religious services more frequently, assigned greater significance to attending religious services, were more likely to be church members, participated in nonorganizational religious activities more frequently, and reported being more religious. Overall, these findings indicate that older black adults are more actively involved in religious pursuits than are younger persons.

Different theories and models of the relationship between age and religious involvement have been suggested in the literature (Argyle & Beit–Hallahmi, 1975). The stability model discounts the significance of age and suggests that there is little variation in religious involvement across the lifespan. Traditional theory proposes that declines in religious activity in early adulthood are followed by steady increases in the middle and late adulthood years. The family life-cycle model suggests that age differences in religious involvement are merely coincidental with the family events of parenthood and child rearing (during which religious participation is high). Finally, disengagement theory suggests that religious participation declines precipitously with advanced age.

The findings presented here of positive relationships between age and organizational, nonorganizational, and attitudinal religious measures are inconsistent with these models. In contrast to the suggestion that religious commitment has a curvilinear form or declines at specific ages, the overall pattern of results indicates a steady increase in religious involvement across age groups, with the highest levels occurring among the oldest respondents. A more extended discussion of the nature and form of age differences in religious involvement measures can be found in Chatters and Taylor (1989a).

Although income and education were significantly associated with indicators of public religious involvement, they failed to predict private behaviors and religious attitudes. Educational level was positively related to whether respondents ever attended church, church membership, and participation in auxiliary church activities; income was positively associated with whether respondents ever attended religious services and church membership. These findings are consistent with the view that persons of higher socioeconomic status (SES) generally are more involved in voluntary associations, and that religious participation is but one example of these organizations (Lenski, 1961). In contrast, the competing perspective (the deprivation model) that religious involvement is highest among lower SES persons because their participation in religious pursuits compensates for blocked or restricted access to other social institutions (Glock, Ringer, & Babbie, 1967) is not supported by these findings.

Theoretical approaches to examining marital status differences in religiosity emphasize the specific role that religion and religious institutions assume for persons who are not married. In essence, religious pursuits emerge as a surrogate for family roles and activities among persons who are not presently married (Glock et al., 1967). In contrast, the marital status differences noted here indicated that married persons distinguished themselves from other respondents in terms of *greater* religious involvement. Married persons attended church more frequently than all other groups; were more likely than never married, separated, and widowed persons to indicate that church attendance was important; were more likely to be church members than were widowed, divorced, and never married respondents; participated in nonorganizational religious activities more frequently than did never married persons; and reported higher levels of subjective religiosity than did never married and divorced respondents. Interpretation of these effects for marital status suggests that being married has socially integrative functions that are reflected in expressed religious attitudes and patterns of religious participation and involvement.

Investigations of urban-rural differences in religious involvement indicated that rural residents attended churches that held less frequent services. After controlling for frequency of services, rural respondents were more likely to attend services than were their urban counterparts. Further, rural respondents were more likely than urban respondents to be church members.

Regional differences indicated that persons residing in the South were distinctive from other regions in their level of religious involvement. Southern residents were less likely than persons in the Northeast and West to never attend religious services and were more likely to report a higher degree of subjective religiosity. Further, compared to respondents in all other regions, Southerners attended religious services and participated in auxiliary church activities on a more frequent basis and were more likely to be church members and to affirm that church attendance is important. These findings of regional differences among black Americans corroborate the general depiction of the South as the "Bible Belt." Research by Fichter and Maddox (1965) indicates that, compared with all other regions of the country, the South has more churches, they are more frequently attended, and greater numbers of people are affiliated with a church. The general tenor of Southern religion has been described as mostly Protestant, highly visible, very conservative, and heavily vested with emotional content. Consistent with other Southerners, black respondents in the South displayed a greater degree of subjective religiosity and more extensive religious involvement than their counterparts in other regions.

Socio-Historical Role of the Church

Theologians who have examined the position and historical traditions of black churches in this country argue that they have served a variety of roles and functions for black individuals and communities. Frequently debated is whether the functions and activities of black churches have been of benefit or detriment to black Americans as a group. Our interest in black respondents' views of the functions of black churches prompted an inquiry into perceptions of the role of this institution. A more in-depth discussion of this issue is presented in Taylor, Thornton, and Chatters (1987).

The NSBA questionnaire asked respondents the question, "In general, do you think the church has helped the condition of black people in America, hurt, or made no difference?" The overwhelming majority of respondents indicated that the church has helped the condition of blacks; 4.9% stated that the church has hurt the position of blacks; and 12.1% indicated that the church has made no difference (16 respondents indicated that the church has both helped and hurt). Multivariate analyses revealed important group differences in expressed attitude toward the black church. Women, older persons, and Southerners (as compared to persons in the Northeast) indicated that they felt that the church has helped as opposed to hurt the condition of black Americans. The fact that these groups of respondents endorse the view that the black church has been of benefit to blacks is consistent with the greater degree of religiosity and religious involvement observed among women, older persons, and Southerners.

All respondents, regardless of whether they viewed the church positively or negatively, were asked a follow-up question, "Why do you feel that way?" Responses for persons who felt that the church has helped indicated that the black church has (a) provided spiritual assistance, (b) had a sustaining and strengthening influence for communities and individuals, (c) provided personal support and aid, (d) promoted a set of guidelines for moral behavior, (e) functioned as a source of ideological unity, (f) provided an organizational infrastructure by serving as a community gathering place, and (g) actively encouraged social progress for black Americans. Respondents who felt that the church hurt the position of blacks reported that (a) churches and clergy are motivated by money; (b) organized religion does not reflect a true sense of personal religiosity and spirituality; and (c) Christianity, as a product of white culture, is inherently detrimental to the condition of blacks.

Church Support

Historical evidence indicates that black churches and religion were intricately involved in the day-to-day life and functioning of black communities, whether those communities were comprised of slaves or free blacks. Research on contemporary black American life suggests that black churches have retained several supportive functions and are extensively involved in the provision of assistance to their members. This section of the chapter examines the extent of participation and the role of church members in the informal social support networks of black Americans. Investigations of the role of church members in the support networks of elderly black adults can be found in Taylor and Chatters (1986a, 1986b).

In a recent analysis, Taylor and Chatters (1988) examined respondents' reports of receiving assistance from church members. Two-thirds of respondents (64.2%) indicated that church members provided some level of support. The religious variables of church membership, church attendance, subjective religiosity, and religious affiliation were related to the receipt of assistance. The salience of the religious involvement variables (i.e., membership and attendance) as support determinants is congruent with research on the reciprocal functions of informal support networks. In this regard, assistance is provided to respondents as a reward for their past record of participation in the activities of the church. Religious affiliation differences in church support indicated that Catholics were less likely to receive assistance from church members than were Baptists. The nature of Catholic worship, characterized by predominately white congregations, more formal church structure and hierarchy, and less communal religious practices, was viewed as an impediment to the transfer of assistance among church members.

Respondents' reports of the most important types of support that they received from church members (Table 6.3) were categorized as (a) advice and encouragement, (b) companionship, (c) help during illness, (d) prayer (religious, spiritual aid), (e) goods and services, (f) financial assistance, (g) transportation, and (h) total support. Advice and encouragement, the largest category of reported assistance, included responses such as: "If I have a problem, they help me solve it," "Help me when I'm down," and "Lift my spirits." Help during illness, the second most frequently mentioned category of aid, included assistance in the form of visiting, companionship, moral support, and instrumental services that were specifically provided to the respondent when he or she was ill, but which exclude specific nursing care.

Prayer as a form of support (i.e., help in a religious or spiritual manner) included responses such as: "They pray for me," "We worship together," "They help me live a Christian life." Respondents who mentioned assistance in the form of companionship emphasized themes of affiliation and friendship and the availability of someone to talk to when needed (i.e., a personal confidant). Of the several forms of instrumental aid, financial assistance was the most prevalent, followed by the provision of goods and services (e.g., meals and household services) and transportation. A small number of respondents reported that church members provided comprehen-

Table 6.3
Most Important Type of Help Received From Church Members (*N* = 875)

Type of Help Received	Percent of Sample
Advice and encouragement	24.0
Companionship	16.5
Goods and services	5.9
Financial assistance	6.5
Transportation	4.3
Help during illness	19.3
Help in a spiritual manner	17.0
Total support	6.5
Total	100.0

sive assistance (e.g., "They are there with money or anything I need," "They do anything I need").

The findings suggest that church members provided a variety of types of assistance to respondents. Although the majority of persons received socioemotional support, significant proportions reported instrumental aid (i.e., financial, material, and help with transportation) and total support (comprehensive assistance). Socioemotional support from church members may have an important impact on stresses arising from various personal crises and in the coping process to life events and transitions. Further, the availability of this support resource may be crucial in maintaining a positive self-evaluation and a sense of self-worth. The prominence of church support during times of illness is reflected in the variety of services that are mentioned. Church support of this sort may be critical in reducing the burden of care on family members, as well as countering the social isolation and loneliness that frequently accompany even short-term illnesses. Clearly, social support from church members is a significant, yet frequently overlooked, resource for black individuals and families.

Religion and Mental Health

The systematic investigation of the relationship between religion and mental health is a relatively new area of inquiry. In a recent analysis, Krause and Tran (1989) examined the influence of religious involvement and stress on self-esteem and feelings of personal control among older black adults. Increased levels of personal stress were related to a decline in self-esteem and a diminished sense of personal control. However, organizational religious involvement was positively associated with self-esteem, and nonorganizational/ subjective religiosity was positively associated with feelings of personal control. Consequently, the authors conclude that, although stress erodes feelings of self-esteem and personal control for older black adults, these negative effects are offset by different aspects of religious involvement.

Chatters and Taylor (1989b) examined the personal life problems of older black adults. The majority of respondents indicated that they had recently experienced at least one problem and identified problems in the areas of health and finances as the most significant. One in six respondents reported using prayer to cope with money problems, and 2.6% of respondents reported using prayer to cope with health problems. As a coping strategy, prayer is interesting because of the varied ways it can be used. Prayer can be an attempt to gain direct intervention in a problem, or alternatively, it may be used to alter one's perspective on the situation (e.g., an acceptance of God's will). Additionally, prayer may be important in handling the distress associated with a problem. These findings suggest that prayer, and more generally religion, are important coping resources for older black adults.

Analysis encompassing the entire age range of the NSBA data revealed that prayer was an option used by respondents to cope with a serious personal problem (Neighbors et al., 1982). Forty-four percent of respondents with such a problem stated that prayer was the coping strategy that was most beneficial. As the seriousness of problems increased, the likelihood that respondents used prayer as a coping response also increased. In addition, a large proportion of respondents reported that they sought specific assistance from ministers in coping with their serious personal problems.

Conclusion

This examination of religious attitudes, behaviors, and participation has underscored the breadth of religious commitment and involvement evident among black Americans. Overall, the findings suggest that black Americans are very religious as reflected in their reports of both public and private religious behaviors and self-descriptions as being religiously-oriented. This depiction of blacks is generally consistent with popular views of black religious life, as well as historical and contemporary scholarly evidence. As a departure from previous efforts, which frequently relied on qualitative methods, the present treatment addressed the question of black religious experience using data from a national probability sample of black adults and employing an analytic strategy to disclose possible subgroup variation in these behaviors. Further, this investigation explored a variety of religious items, encompassing private and public religious behaviors and religious attitudes, in an attempt to assess multiple facets of religiosity.

The present findings provided evidence that subgroups within the black population differ in their level of religious involvement. Similar to findings in the general population, women, older individuals, married persons, and residents of the South displayed a greater degree of religious commitment than did their counterparts; limited evidence for the effect of urbanicity on religious involvement was demonstrated. Theoretical explanations to account for social status variations in religiosity frequently lack sufficient development and elaboration (e.g., specification of relevant domains of behaviors and attitudes) and, consequently, are somewhat limited in their ability to adequately interpret these differences. The finding that greater religiosity was associated with gender and age is consistent with an interpretation that persons who occupy lower status positions (i.e., women and older adults) are more invested in religious concerns. However, marital status differences favoring married persons are inconsistent with both a social status interpretation and the family surrogate model of religious involvement. The data indicate that nonmarried persons are, on the whole, less likely than their married counterparts to be involved in religious pursuits. Finally, the absence of significant effects for socioeconomic indicators is at odds with a social status interpretation of religious involvement.

The centrality of religious concerns observed among black Americans relative to other population groups has been an area of enduring interest to religious and social science scholars. Emergent conceptualizations of the nature of black theology and religious beliefs and behavior recognize that, in a variety of ways and circumstances, black religion is adaptive for individuals and communities. Black religion and religious institutions traditionally have provided an emotional and psychological haven from a harsh and discriminatory social system. The characterization of black religious thought and practice as other-worldly and escapist, however, grossly misrepresents and distorts the history and traditions of black religion. The difficulty with this depiction is that it suggests that black religion, in providing an alternate frame of reference and experience for black Americans, effectively usurps individual and collective action directed toward changing the social system. Historical and current evidence attests to the fact that black religious thought and organized religion has consistently functioned as a foundation for social action and reform (McAdam, 1982; Morris, 1984). Deeply held religious beliefs were incorporated into the ideological core and principles of the struggle for civil and human rights and, further, provided the strategy and human resolution to participate in organized protest (i.e., civil disobedience, protest marches). Black religious institutions provided both the organizational base and the human resources necessary for the development of the Civil Rights Movement. The weight of evidence attests to the fact that, while black religious traditions are dedicated to the spiritual lives and concerns of individuals, black religious thought and experience remain deeply committed to the political and social betterment and advancement of black Americans, individually and collectively.

A recent review of the literature suggests that psychologists and social scientists in other disciplines have rediscovered religion as an area of legitimate scientific inquiry (Gorsuch, 1988). As interest in religion intensifies, researchers are beginning to address the role that religion and religious beliefs play in relation to other behaviors and attitudes, as well as examining the structural and organizational features of religious institutions. Specific areas of interest for black religious behaviors and experiences include (a) the relation of religious orientation to personal and group identity, (b) the effects of religion on perceptions of personal control and efficacy, (c) the relationship between religion and emotional well-being and mental health, (d) the role of black churches in the provision of social support, and (e) the position of black religious institutions within the broader black community.

Although black religious traditions and experiences have been represented and explored in historical and black theology literatures, considerably less is known about black religion in the context of empirical social science. Prior investigations of religion generally and the religious behaviors and attitudes of black Americans specifically were hampered by conceptual and methodological deficiencies such as restrictions in the scope of religious dimensions that were examined, limited sample representativeness, and failure to explore subgroup differences in religious expression among blacks. This chapter has attempted to bridge the gap between past scholarly traditions and current survey approaches to the study of black religious experiences, while addressing the conceptual and methodological limitations of past empirical work.

7

WORK LIFE

Phillip J. Bowman

The quality of work life among Americans of African ancestry has always been significantly influenced by structured racial inequality and inequities (Farley & Allen, 1987; Wilson, 1978). Shifting institutional barriers, both legal and informal, have restricted the occupational attainment of black Americans from one generation to the next. A substantial literature on white-black employment differences documents low status occupations, inadequate earnings, poor working conditions, and job instability as the major fault lines of black work life in America (Allen & Farley, 1985; Ferman, Kornbluh, & Miller, 1968; Vatter & Palm, 1972). These objective fault lines of black underemployment not only have eroded the quality of work life, but have also given way to persistent poverty. Moreover, chronic difficulties in work roles too frequently erupt in familial conflict, political disaffection, psychological distress, and problems in other domains of African American life.

Since the mid-1960s, increasing attention has been placed on the select group of upwardly mobile African Americans who have attained jobs that previously were reserved for white workers (America & Anderson, 1978; Freeman, 1973; Landry, 1988). However, despite this progress, the basic pattern of inequality in which black workers are grossly overrepresented in unskilled occupations has yet to change (Farley & Allen, 1987; Swinton, 1989; Wilson, 1987). The landmark report "Work in America" (1973) and other studies have consistently identified structural barriers as the major causal factors in the disproportionate number of blacks who either work unskilled jobs or are jobless: "This disproportion reflects the persistent, systematic discrimination and closed off opportunities that racial minority persons experience in work, education and other major institutions in society" (p. 52). Moreover, persistent black underemployment, and growing joblessness, are not mere parochial concerns relevant only to blacks. Black employment difficulties lie at the heart of a continuing American dilemma which is pivotal to some of the most serious economic and social problems facing the entire nation (Kinder, 1986; Myrdal, 1944; Wilson, 1987).

Racial inequalities in work organizations are essentially historical, stubbornly resist change, and have differential effects on the work life of black workers in low and high status jobs. Underemployment has characterized the work life of African Americans each year since their transition from slave to free labor in 1865. The clear progress made since the 1960s has leveled off and shows signs of reversing as we approach the 21st century. In the present chapter, findings from the National Survey of Black Americans (NSBA) are presented to better clarify the diversity of work life in the nation's largest racial-minority group. These unique national data provide a basis to go beyond past studies which have largely been limited to white-black comparisons on objective indicators. In contrast, this chapter emphasizes the growing diversity in African American work life with a social psychological consideration of both objective and subjective indicators.

Objective and Subjective Indicators

Concern over chronic underemployment and escalating joblessness in black America has resulted in a proliferation of reports. Particularly useful are special governmental reports based on the Decennial Census and Current Population Surveys (CPS).[1] These reports on large representative samples of the black population focus primarily on objective measures of occupational status, underemployment, unemployment, and earnings. To supplement these reports, other national studies have been conducted by university-based research programs such as the National Longitudinal Surveys (Sproat, Churchill, & Sheets, 1985), the Panel Study of Income Dynamics (Duncan & Morgan, 1980), and the Quality of Employment Survey (Quinn and Shepard, 1974). These longitudinal surveys provide data on more restricted national subsamples of African Americans than either the Census or the CPS. However, they also go beyond objective indicators and include some revealing self-reports of job perceptions, evaluations, and satisfactions. Building on these studies, the NSBA included a unique array of objective and subjective indicators which are particularly useful for understanding the quality of work life in black America.

Most existing studies on subjective aspects of African American work life have compared whites and blacks in rather restricted samples (i.e., Bloom & Barry, 1967; Miner & Brewer, 1983; Schmidt & Lappin, 1980; Watson & Barone, 1976). When racial differences have emerged, assumptions about black deficits rather than a consideration of black ethnicity and organizational barriers too often have guided interpretations (i.e., Bielby, 1987; Bowman, 1990; Feagin, 1987). An overreliance on categorical white-black comparisons has often resulted in a view of black workers as monolithic nonwhites instead of a diverse national population. However, studies do support the importance of distinguishing objective and subjective aspects of work life within diverse samples of black workers (Ash, 1972; Brenner & Tomkiewicz, 1982; Weaver, 1978). For example, black managers often react *more* negatively to their high status jobs than do white managers (Forgionne & Peters, 1982). In contrast, blacks in lower status jobs have been found to react *less* negatively than their white counterparts to objective job limitations (Bartel, 1981). We need to better understand subjective aspects of work life among high and low status black workers who differ on objective job characteristics.

In developing NSBA questions on work life, useful indices were adapted from past surveys and new measures were constructed to tap dimensions not considered in other studies. A sensitivity to the diversity of work experience within the black population combined with multidisciplinary economic, social, and psychological perspectives to yield a unique set of indicators. In addition to objective indicators, consideration was also given to the perceived causes of employment difficulties, job satisfaction, evaluations of work conditions, sources of stress in the workplace, appraisals of work role marginality, and perceptions of racial inequity. Such subjective indicators of attributions, affective reactions, expectations, and other work role perceptions provide unique insight into the quality of work life as African Americans actually experience it. Moreover, because these data are based on a rigorous national probability sample, these findings provide accurate descriptions of all black adult workers, a more externally valid basis to explore important relationships, and important baseline information for future studies to monitor changes in the work life of the black population.

Competing Perspectives: Inequality Versus Mobility

NSBA cross-sectional findings on work life need to be understood within the broader context of two competing theoretical perspectives. First, *dual labor market models* emphasize the persistence of historical inequalities that restrict the majority of black workers to low status jobs. In contrast, *human capital models* focus on individual sources of mobility among a select minority of black workers who have moved into high status jobs. These two divergent orientations result in very different pictures of work life in black America. Unfortunately, existing research and related policy recommendations too often emphasize one of these theoretical perspectives while undermining the significance of the other.

Inequality: A Dual Labor Market Perspective

The dual labor market paradigm was developed to explain problems of class with an emphasis on the structural sources of inequality and poverty (Harrison & Sum, 1980; Piore, 1977). Dual labor market models also have been adapted to explain job-related problems of black Americans and other groups facing racial inequalities in America (Bowman, 1980; McGahey & Jeffries, 1985). The dual labor market approach holds that black workers are systematically tracked into secondary jobs and lack access to primary sector jobs. A basic notion is that two largely separate labor markets exist, characterized by primary sector jobs "with a future" and secondary sector jobs that are "dead end." As discussed by Montaga (1977):

> The primary sector offers jobs with relatively high wages, good working conditions, chances of advancement, equity and due process in the administration of work rules, and above all, employment stability. In the secondary sector, jobs tend to be low-paying, with poorer working conditions, little chance of advancement, a highly personalized relationship between workers and supervisors which . . . is conductive to harsh and capricious work discipline; with considerable instability in jobs and a high turnover among the labor force. (p. 68)

Historical data from the Decennial Census (1890–1980) and the monthly CPS (1940–Present) provide a view of long-term trends which generally supports a dual labor market perspective. These official statistics clearly document the fact that in each generation from chattel slavery until the present, black workers have been disproportionately located in unskilled secondary jobs. Between 1890 and 1960, black workers made a massive employment transition from unskilled agricultural jobs to unskilled manufacturing and service jobs in response to the changing demands of an industrial labor market. At present, black males remain overrepresented in such unskilled industrial jobs despite the fact that postindustrial labor market changes will continue to displace such jobs at a rapid pace well into the 21st century (Bluestone & Harrison, 1982; Bowman, 1988; Rumberger, 1983). Therefore, despite improvements between the mid-1960s and the mid-1970s, black workers consistently have been underrepresented in primary sector jobs with a future, and overrepresented in unskilled, low-paying, and unstable secondary jobs.

Mobility: Competing Human Capital Models

As a direct result of the Civil Rights Movement, affirmative action policies enabled an unprecedented number of young, highly motivated, and highly educated blacks to gain mobility into primary sector jobs during the 1960s and 1970s (Allen & Farley, 1985; Farley & Allen, 1987; Wilson, 1978). The proportion of blacks in low status jobs was four times that of whites in 1948, but by 1970 the ratio showed blacks only twice as likely to be in less skilled jobs. However, the rate of progress slowed down considerably in the late 1970s. The 1980s brought further evidence of erosion, with black workers particularly vulnerable to postindustrial displacement, economic recession, and less aggressive affirmative action policies. Thus, the boundaries of mobility from secondary to primary sector jobs, made somewhat permeable for African Americans during the 1960s and 1970s, appear to be less penetrable as we approach the 21st century.

To explain mobility of black workers into primary sector jobs, popular human capital models tend to ignore persistent labor market inequality (Becker, 1975; Levine & Bane, 1978). In contrast to dual labor market models, human capital approaches suggest that motivation, ability, and investment in education are sufficient to promote mobility and to eradicate widespread black underemployment. Although some human capital models have considered past racial disadvantage, they fail to fully incorporate the pressing influence of current structural barriers that restrict black workers (Loury, 1981). By contrast, dual labor market models find it difficult to explain mobility among black workers who have moved into high status jobs through a combination of higher education and affirmative action. Unfortunately, both models have emphasized objective aspects of work life (i.e., job status, earnings) but have largely ignored the importance of subjective work experiences (i.e., job satisfaction, perceived inequities). Also, the overreliance on racial comparisons in both dual labor market and human capital research too often has masked the growing diversity of African American work life.

Inequality and Mobility: An Integrative Focus

Both dual labor market and human capital models provide unique insights into important aspects of black work life. However, human capital models are not sensitive to the broader labor market barriers, past and present, that restrict the quality of work life among black secondary sector workers. On the other hand, dual labor market models may understate the importance of educational investment in a postindustrial, post-civil rights, and multicultural American society. A more comprehensive research approach is needed to systematically investigate how both external labor market barriers and personal investment in education are linked to growing diversity in the quality of work life for black Americans.

Several propositions can be formulated from dual labor market and human capital models to guide a more integrative analysis of NSBA data:

1. Systematic barriers, past and present, continue to restrict the majority of black workers to low level secondary sector jobs.
2. A select group of black workers have gained mobility into the primary sector largely through affirmative action and higher education.
3. Disparities between secondary and primary workers have increased the diversity of objective and subjective aspects of work life quality within the black population.
4. Increasing unemployment and labor force dropout rates among African Americans largely reflect declines in the availability of unskilled secondary jobs in the industrial sector.

Objective differences in the working conditions of secondary and primary jobs have been documented in past dual labor market studies. However, pivotal antecedents of differential occupational attainment of black secondary and primary workers are less clear, but may well involve mechanisms from both dual labor market and human capital models. Moreover, we know even less about differences between black secondary and primary workers in subjective aspects of their work life. It is plausible to expect that objective advantages in the jobs held by black primary sector workers should have positive effects on the subjective quality of their lives, both inside and outside work organizations. However, this plausible expectation requires empirical testing along with several other issues raised by the growing diversity between black secondary and primary workers.

National Findings

The analysis of NSBA data presented in the following sections addresses several crucial questions: How do gender, age, intergenerational background, and social networks differentiate black workers in secondary and primary sector jobs? In line with objective job improvements, is job satisfaction higher among blacks in primary than in secondary occupations? Are perceptions of job stress, underemployment, and job instability greater for black workers in secondary sector jobs? Does perceived racial discrimination decline in significance among blacks who move into primary sector jobs? Although descriptive in nature, national findings that address these issues provide a basis to synthesize dual labor market and human capital approaches. By comparing black workers in the secondary and primary sectors, we are able to go beyond the common tendency in white-black comparative studies to view blacks in monolithic and global terms.

Secondary and Primary Jobs: Diversity Among Black Workers

Findings in this section address three specific issues. How are black workers distributed in various dual labor market sectors, substrata, and occupational roles? Are black men more likely than black women to hold upper stratum primary sector jobs in line with general patterns of gender inequality in America? Did the Civil Rights Movement enable only younger black men and women to attain primary jobs, while middle-aged and older blacks remain more restricted to secondary jobs?

A Dual Labor Market Typology

A common basis for analyzing occupational attainment among blacks and other groups in America is the detailed code developed by the Bureau of the Census (Blau & Duncan, 1967; Farley & Allen, 1987; Porter, 1974). Most research using the several hundred occupational categories in this code either groups jobs into broad classes (i.e., blue collar vs. white collar) or assigns socioeconomic status values to specific jobs based on prestige ratings, education, and/or income. The approach taken in this chapter retains census occupational codes but regroups them into secondary and primary job sector categories according to theoretical criteria emerging from dual labor market paradigms.

The two broad dual labor market sectors, two primary sector substrata, and specific occupational roles in this classification scheme are shown in Figure 7.1. The three major job categories are viewed as differing on conventional criteria of prestige, pay, and skill level as well as advancement opportunities, work conditions, and stability. The *secondary sector* includes lower level unskilled labor, operative, and service jobs. To aid a more meaningful analysis, the *primary sector* has been further subdivided into a lower and upper stratum. Craft, clerical, and sales jobs make up the *lower stratum* of the primary sector. The *upper stratum* has been broken down into managerial/administrative and various professional/ technical jobs. As basic elements of social stratification, Montaga (1977) and others have shown how these dual labor market job categories locate black workers in the social structure of American society; location in each major sector has far-reaching consequences in other areas of their lives. This dual labor market classification scheme represents a useful organization not only for white-black comparisons, but also for examining the diversity of work life within black America.

Gender, Inequality, and Mobility

Figure 7.1 presents the distribution of black men and women in each dual labor market sector, substratum, and occupational role. Exactly identical proportions of each gender group in the NSBA sample were located in secondary sector, lower stratum primary sector, and upper stratum primary sector jobs. Among both black men and women, the majority (52%) were in secondary sector jobs; 29% were in lower primary sector roles, and only 19% had upper stratum primary sector careers. In contrast to the general pattern of gender inequality in the American labor force, black men were no more likely to be found in primary sector jobs than black women. Instead, both gender groups were heavily concentrated in secondary jobs.

132

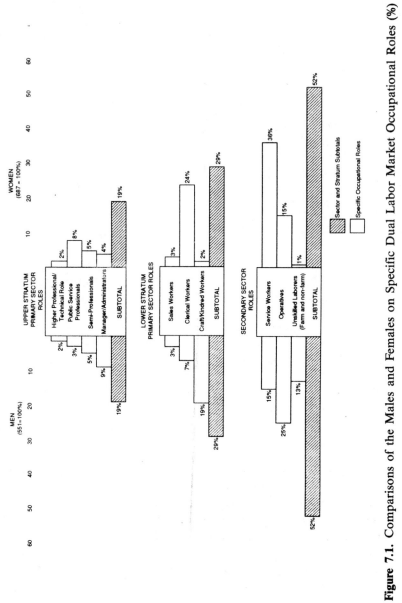

Figure 7.1. Comparisons of the Males and Females on Specific Dual Labor Market Occupational Roles (%)

Despite the gender similarity across the broader sectors, there were major differences between black men and women within each sector. Within the secondary sector, black women were more than twice as likely to be service workers (36% vs. 15%) and black men were disproportionately concentrated in jobs as operatives (25% vs. 15%) and unskilled laborers (13% vs. 1%). The relatively large portion of secondary workers in unskilled service occupations may reflect the rapid postindustrial growth in service jobs and the parallel decline in demand for unskilled laborers and operatives. Because of their overrepresentation in vulnerable operative and unskilled labor jobs, black males may increasingly be forced to compete with other groups for either lower level service or primary sector jobs. The growing labor force dropout trends among black men may well reflect their current difficulties in such competition (Bowman, 1988; Farley & Allen, 1987).

When we turn to primary sector jobs, a similar pattern of gender typing appears. Black women were more likely than black men to be clericals (24% vs. 7%) and public service professionals (8% vs. 3%), whereas black men were disproportionately craft/kindred workers (19% vs. 2%) and managers/administrators (9% vs. 4%). Very small but identical proportions of black men and women were found in sales, semi-professional, and higher professional roles (3, 5, and 2%, respectively). To better clarify the picture among black workers in the primary sector, a more detailed breakdown of men and women in upper stratum jobs is presented in Table 7.1. CPS data from 1980 are also presented on blacks (as a percentage of all employed men and women) in comparable job categories to highlight the extent of their underrepresentation.

Regardless of gender, blacks in the NSBA sample were extremely rare in the higher professional roles of physician/pharmacist (0.4%), lawyer (1.7%), engineer (2.2%), college professor (3%), or accountant (3.4%). As expected, blacks who had reached the professional ranks were primarily females concentrated in specific public service and semi-professional jobs. In upper stratum jobs, black women were disproportionately grade school teachers (30.2% vs. 7.8%) and nurses/health technicians (18.7% vs. 5.9%). In contrast, black men were more likely to work as "other" managers or administrators (27.1% vs. 6.2%). Thus, we see that almost a third of upper stratum black women were grade school teachers and over a fourth of black men in this highest stratum were managers coded as "other." These predominantly male managers did not fit the conventional managerial categories in the

Table 7.1
Distribution of Black Males and Females in Upper Stratum Primary Jobs

	1979–80 National Survey of Black Americans Data [a] (% of national sample)			1980 Current Population Survey Data [b] (Blacks as % of all workers)	
	Total Sample (N = 232)	Men (N = 103)	Women (N = 129)	Men	Women
High Level Professional/ Technical Jobs					
Physicians	.4	1.0	0.0	2	5
Engineers	2.2	2.9	1.5	2	0
Lawyers	1.7	1.9	1.5	3	7
College professors	3.0	3.9	2.3	3	5
Accountants	3.4	1.9	4.7	4	7
Traditional Public Service Professional Jobs					
Social workers	6.5	3.9	8.5	16	17
Career/Vocational counselors	2.2	2.9	1.5	15	18
Personnel/Labor relations	1.3	0.0	2.3	8	11
Grade school teachers	20.3	7.8	30.2	6	10
Religious workers	1.7	3.9	0.0	6	0
Other Professional/Technical Jobs					
Nurses/Health technicians	13.0	5.9	18.7	21	17
Computer specialists	3.4	5.8	1.5	4	9
Engineering technicians	5.2	5.8	4.7	6	7
Writers/Artists/Entertainers	4.7	6.8	3.1	4	4
Managers and Administrator Jobs					
General office/ Financial managers	7.3	10.7	4.7	3	5
Restaurant/Bar/Sales managers	6.0	3.9	7.8	6	8
School administrators	2.2	3.9	0.8	6	12
Other managers	15.5	27.1	6.2	—	—
Total	100.0	100.0	100.0		

a. Includes respondents employed in upper stratum primary jobs only.   b. United States Department of Commerce. (1980). *Current Population Survey: Annual Demographic File, 1980.* (Machine-readable data file.) Washington, DC: U.S. Department of Commerce, Bureau of the Census (Producer). Ann Arbor, MI: Inter-University Consortium for Political and Social Research (Distributor).

census code. However, a comparison of the CPS and NSBA data suggests that some of these black men who report managerial duties may be social workers, vocational counselors, or nurses. Moreover, some black women coded as grade school teachers in the NSBA sample may have been coded in official CPS statistics as vocational counselors, social workers (i.e., in schools), and school administrators.

CPS data show interesting patterns of black underrepresentation among both males and females in high level occupations. Blacks represent about 12% of the American population, but black men and women made up far less than this proportion in high level professional and technical jobs. Underrepresentation is clearest among black men who made up only 2% of physicians and engineers, 3% of the college professors and lawyers, and 4% of the accountants. However, black men and women made up over 15% of all social workers, career counselors, and nurses/health technicians.

Age Cohorts, Gender, and Mobility

Comparing different age groups provides a basis to consider how younger black workers (18–34) who largely entered the labor force since the Civil Rights Movement of the 1960s differed from older cohorts (35–54 and 55–plus) who largely made the transition from school to work prior to 1965. Based on findings in Table 7.2, it appears that the post-civil rights cohort of young black women were more likely than young black men to have improved their position relative to their older counterparts. The 35.9% of black females 18 to 34 years old in secondary jobs was clearly less than the percentages of middle-aged (55.3%) or older black women (87.6%) in these low level jobs. However, younger black males (18–34 years old) were as likely as older black men (age 35 and older) to be in lower level secondary jobs. Therefore, mobility from secondary to primary sector jobs among blacks since the mid-1960s may be largely characterized by young black females moving into lower stratum clerical jobs instead of domestic service roles where older black women are still largely concentrated.

Tracking and Mobility Mechanisms

Given the growing diversity among black workers, it is important to identify factors associated with the differential occupational attainment of those who hold secondary and primary sector jobs. Descriptive findings below explore the role of intergenerational mechanisms, racial segregation, sociodemographic factors, and job networks.

Table 7.2
Relationship of Age and Gender to Dual Labor Market Attainment (in percent)

Dual Labor Market Attainment	Young adults (18 to 34 years)		Middle-aged (35 to 54 years)		Older adults (55 + years)	
	Male (N = 263)	Female (N = 295)	Male (N = 201)	Female (N = 284)	Male (N = 83)	Female (N = 105)
Upper Stratum Primary Jobs						
Schoolteacher	1.5	4.4	1.5	7.0	1.2	1.9
Professional & technical workers	8.8	13.6	9.0	9.8	7.2	0.9
Managers/Administrators	6.1	3.1	10.4	4.6	12.1	2.9
Lower Stratum Primary Jobs						
Sales worker	3.8	3.7	1.5	2.8	2.4	1.0
Craft/Kindred worker	21.3	2.7	20.4	1.8	10.8	0.0
Clerical worker	8.8	36.6	6.0	18.7	2.4	5.7
Secondary Jobs						
Service worker	12.5	18.3	11.9	40.5	27.7	72.4
Operative	26.2	15.6	27.9	14.1	14.5	15.2
Unskilled laborer (farm & non-farm)	11.0	2.0	11.4	0.7	21.7	0.0
Total	100.0	100.0	100.0	100.0	100.0	100.0

NOTE: Includes employed and laid-off workers in dual labor market primary and secondary jobs only.

Intergenerational Mechanisms

Evidence on intergenerational and other structural employment barriers has consistently demonstrated the powerful impact of family socioeconomic background on occupational attainment (Bowman, 1988; Duncan, 1967, 1968; McGahey & Jeffries, 1985; Wilson, 1987). Table 7.3 presents findings relevant to the intergenerational transmission of historical inequalities through the occupational and educational status of parents. These data clearly show that black workers were most likely to hold secondary sector jobs if their parents were secondary rather than primary workers and had less than a high school education. Conversely, black workers were more likely to have attained high-level primary sector jobs if their parents either held such jobs or were college graduates. Such intergenerational findings reflect the historical roots of the current job inequalities faced

Table 7.3

Relationship of Intergenerational Factors to Dual Labor Market Attainment

Intergenerational Factors	Dual Labor Market Attainment			
	Secondary Job (%)	Lower Primary Job (%)	Upper Primary Job (%)	Percent (N)
Father's Occupation				
Secondary sector	55.3	27.7	17.0	100 (743)
Lower stratum primary sector	43.4	32.4	24.2	100 (173)
Upper stratum primary sector	38.0	21.5	40.5	100 (79)
Mother's Occupation				
Secondary sector	52.4	31.2	16.4	100 (666)
Lower stratum primary sector	35.6	40.7	23.7	100 (59)
Upper stratum primary sector	29.7	31.1	39.2	100 (74)
Father's Education				
Less than high school	52.1	27.2	20.7	100 (507)
High school graduate	36.8	38.2	25.0	100 (136)
Some college	15.2	33.3	51.5	100 (33)
College graduate	25.7	28.6	45.7	100 (35)
Mother's Education				
Less than high school	53.6	27.9	18.5	100 (567)
High school graduate	39.1	36.7	24.2	100 (248)
Some college	27.7	36.1	36.2	100 (47)
College graduate	14.6	26.8	58.6	100 (41)

NOTE: Includes employed and laid-off workers in dual labor market primary and secondary jobs only.

by black secondary workers whose fathers and mothers were often restricted by legal, educational, and employment barriers.

Racial Segregation

Recent literature on the black underclass suggests that racial isolation in economically depressed urban areas increases employment difficulties among unmarried parents (Bowman, 1988; Glasgow, 1980; Wilson, 1978, 1987). This literature suggests that racial segregation in central cities combines with other demographic risk factors to increase employment disadvantages among black Americans. To explore this issue, Table 7.4 presents data that compare specific underclass "risk groups" on dual labor market occupational attainment.

Findings on racial composition reveal that the proportions of blacks in one's high school and current neighborhood were associ-

Table 7.4

Relationship of Selected Sociodemographic Risk Factors to Dual Labor Market Attainment

	Dual Labor Market Attainment			
Risk Factors	Secondary Job (%)	Lower Primary Job (%)	Upper Primary Job (%)	Percent (N)
Racial Segregation				
Racial Composition of High School				
All black	51.8	26.6	21.6	100 (500)
Mostly black	46.9	35.4	17.7	100 (147)
Half black	48.4	39.1	12.5	100 (161)
Mostly white	35.2	40.3	24.5	100 (196)
All white except respondent	21.1	23.6	55.3	100 (38)
Racial Composition of Current Neighborhood				
All black	61.8	23.2	15.0	100 (487)
Mostly black	50.2	30.1	19.7	100 (432)
Half black	40.8	34.9	24.3	100 (169)
Mostly white	41.3	41.3	17.4	100 (92)
All white except respondent	27.2	27.3	45.5	100 (33)
Demographic Factors				
Degree of Urban Development				
Central city	45.7	32.7	21.6	100 (610)
Suburb/Small city	52.2	30.0	17.8	100 (393)
Non-metropolitan	69.4	17.9	12.7	100 (235)
Region				
West	41.7	33.3	25.0	100 (84)
North Central	49.1	30.4	20.5	100 (273)
Northeast	51.2	31.7	17.1	100 (240)
South	55.4	26.8	17.8	100 (641)
Marital Status				
Married	51.6	28.9	19.5	100 (579)
Unmarried (never married, divorced, separated, widowed)	53.0	29.2	17.8	100 (655)
Dependent Children				
No	55.4	24.2	20.4	100 (538)
Yes	50.0	32.8	17.2	100 (692)

NOTE: Includes employed and laid-off workers in dual labor market primary and secondary jobs only.

ated with occupational attainment. Surprisingly, however, neither racial segregation (all-black environments) nor racial balance (half black/half white environments) showed any clear employment disadvantages or advantages. What is most striking was the clear link between being the only black in one's high school or neighborhood and attainment of high status jobs. For example, a full 55.3% of respondents who had been "solo blacks" in all-white high schools had attained upper primary jobs compared to only 12.5% of blacks from racially balanced schools. Similarly, 45.5% of solo blacks living in all-white neighborhoods held upper primary jobs compared to only 24.3% of blacks in racially balanced neighborhoods. However, although very few blacks were solos in either all-white high schools ($n = 38$) or all-white neighborhoods ($n = 33$), the majority had attended all-black high schools ($n = 500$) and lived in all-black neighborhoods ($n = 487$). In contrast to solo blacks, the majority of workers from all-black or substantially black environments were somehow tracked into low status secondary jobs.

Demographic Risk Factors

In terms of other demographic risk factors, studies on the underclass have emphasized the truly disadvantaged circumstances of blacks who are unmarried and have children in central cities, especially within declining north central industrial states (Wilson, 1987). Contrary to the expected pattern, Table 7.4 shows that the black workers most likely to be in secondary jobs lived in rural areas rather than inner cities, and in southern rather than north central states. Therefore, despite the special psychosocial risks facing the black underclass in midwestern cities, we should not lose sight of the persistent employment disadvantages facing the large number of African Americans who still live in the rural South. Unexpectedly, unmarried workers were equally likely to hold low status jobs (53%) as married workers (51.6%). Parental status also made little difference as workers with (50%) and without (55.4%) children were about equally likely to hold secondary jobs.

Job Networks

Beyond the broad social networks represented by the sociodemographic factors discussed above, more specific job networks may also help differentiate the occupational attainment of black workers (D'Amico, 1984; Raelin, 1983; Wielgosz & Carpenter, 1983). Table 7.5 presents findings on linkages between the first and present job and

Table 7.5

Relationship of Job Network Characteristics to Dual Labor Market Attainment

Job Network Characteristics	Dual Labor Market Attainment			
	Secondary Job (%)	Lower Primary Job (%)	Upper Primary Job (%)	Percent (N)
Entry Into the Labor Force				
"What was your first regular permanent job?"				
Secondary job	71.9	20.7	7.4	100 (676)
Lower stratum primary job	27.5	53.3	19.2	100 (302)
Upper stratum primary job	10.0	12.9	77.1	100 (140)
Recent Job Network				
"How did you first hear about a job at the place you're now working?"				
Relative	63.1	27.0	9.9	100 (203)
Friend/Acquaintance	59.1	24.4	16.5	100 (514)
Employment/Social agency	51.9	29.5	18.6	100 (129)
School/Training program	28.0	32.0	40.0	100 (25)
Printed want ads	38.4	42.0	19.6	100 (112)
Direct information	34.9	38.7	26.4	100 (106)
Other sources	33.3	28.6	38.1	100 (84)

NOTE: Includes employed and laid-off workers in dual labor market primary and secondary jobs only.

the sources of information that led to the current job. Respondents were asked to describe their first "regular, permanent job." There is a clear relationship between the type of first job and the current job, despite some upward and downward mobility. For example, 71.9% of the respondents whose first regular, permanent job was a secondary job still held such a job; similarly, 77% of those whose first job was an upper primary job still held such high level jobs. Therefore, upon labor force entry, the majority of black workers appear to get tracked into a specific job network which yields similar jobs throughout their careers.

To further explore specific job networks, respondents were also asked: "How did you first hear about a job at the place you're now working?" followed by a series of probes. As shown in Table 7.5, most respondents had first heard about their jobs through friends or acquaintances, followed by relatives, employment agencies, want ads, and direct contacts. Generally, workers who relied on relatives, friends, or employment/social agencies were more likely to attain secondary jobs. In contrast, those who heard about their jobs from schools, direct employer contact, or want ads more often attained primary sector jobs. Further probing showed that the majority of the friends or relatives who told our respondents about the job at their current work setting not only worked there, but also did specific things to help them get their job. In order of frequency, black workers noted that these informal helpers either used their influence, made formal recommendations, gave them direct aid or encouragement, or sometimes actually hired them. Those who helped secondary workers were more likely to use their personal influence, whereas helpers for those who attained primary jobs were more likely to either give formal recommendations or actually do the hiring.

Quality of Work Life

Compared to black secondary workers, the reduction in objective difficulties facing black primary workers should enhance job satisfaction, lower job stress, increase job security, and decrease the significance of racial discrimination. Are black upper primary workers generally more satisfied with their jobs than lower primary or secondary workers? Are all facets of work life more stressful for secondary than primary workers? Are work role marginality and racial inequity perceived as problems only among secondary workers? To explore these issues, findings in this section compare black workers in secondary and primary sector jobs on several subjective indicators of work life quality.

Job Satisfaction

Job satisfaction has usually referred either to the global psychological disposition people have toward their jobs or to a set of attitudes toward specific facets of work life (Hackman & Oldham, 1976; Locke, 1983; Quinn & Shepard, 1974). To measure "global" job satisfaction, employed respondents were first asked: "All in all, how satisfied are you with your job?" Contrary to expectation, Table 7.6 shows that about equal portions of secondary (42.9%) and upper stratum primary (42%) workers reported that they were "very satisfied" with their jobs. Lower primary workers were less likely to report that they were "very satisfied" (34%). Therefore, despite objective job limita-

Table 7.6

Comparisons of Dual Labor Market Job Categories by Indicators of Job Satisfaction

Indicators of Job Satisfaction	Dual Labor Market Job Categories [a] (% of Total)		
	Secondary Job (N = 622)	Lower Primary Job (N = 344)	Upper Primary Job (N = 226)
Global Job Satisfaction			
"All in all, how satisfied are you with your job?"			
Very satisfied	42.9	34.0	42.0
Somewhat satisfied	40.4	46.2	43.0
Somewhat dissatisfied	10.6	15.4	10.6
Very dissatisfied	6.1	4.4	4.4
Total	100.0	100.0	100.0
"How satisfied would you be if a son/daughter of yours had your job as a regular, permanent job?"			
Very satisfied	21.0	22.1	43.3
Somewhat satisfied	27.8	43.7	39.3
Somewhat dissatisfied	22.3	18.0	8.9
Very dissatisfied	28.9	16.2	8.5
Total	100.0	100.0	100.0
Work Role Values			
"Which one of these things is most important to you—the thing you want most in a job?"			
Allow use of skills and abilities	16.5	27.5	39.4
No hassles	15.4	10.5	7.7
Friendly co-workers	15.4	11.4	5.0
Autonomy	15.4	5.4	5.9
Promotion opportunities	12.3	20.8	9.0
Interesting work	10.0	15.1	26.7
Good supervisor	9.0	6.6	3.6
Good physical environment	6.0	2.7	2.7
Total	100.0	100.0	100.0

Indicators of Job Satisfaction	Dual Labor Market Job Categories [a] (% of Total)		
	Secondary Job (N = 622)	Lower Primary Job (N = 344)	Upper Primary Job (N = 226)
	Job Stress[b]		
"What would you say bothered you most about your job?"			
Poor pay and benefits	11.3	15.2	10.3
Physical environment (dirty, physical strain)	10.7	6.5	6.7
Co-workers (unfriendly, unhelpful)	9.2	10.3	13.4
Lack opportunities (promotions, challenge)	6.4	9.1	8.9
Undesirable work schedule	5.4	5.9	7.6
Supervisor (unfriendly, unhelpful)	4.3	5.3	6.7
Customers or people I serve	4.1	4.6	11.6
Other factors	14.4	17.6	19.2
Nothing bothers me	34.2	25.5	15.6
Total	100.0	100.0	100.0

a. Includes employed and laid-off workers in dual labor market primary and secondary jobs only. b. Includes first mentioned responses only.

tions, black secondary workers were as satisfied as upper level primary workers on this conventional measure of global job satisfaction. However, the expected "secondary job-dissatisfaction" pattern is much clearer on a second, less conventional measure of job satisfaction.

Employed respondents were also asked: "How would you feel if a son/daughter of yours had your job as a regular permanent job?" On this item, 43.3% of upper level primary workers responded "very satisfied" (almost the identical proportion as on the more conventional indicator). In contrast to the pattern on the first indicator, only 22.1% of lower level primary workers and 21% of the secondary workers were "very satisfied" on this alternative measure. The negative impact of objective job limitations is reflected dramatically in the increase in proportion of upper primary (17.4%), lower primary (34.2%), and secondary workers (51.2%) who expressed dissatisfaction ("very dissatisfied" plus "somewhat dissatisfied") with the thought of their child having their job. These contrasting findings on two alternative indicators of global job satisfaction raise some interesting measurement and conceptual issues.

Work Values and Job Stress

To explore possible sources of global job satisfaction, respondents also were asked about the specific job facets (other than pay) they most valued and whether their jobs provided what they most valued (Table 7.6). Secondary workers expressed concern about a wider range of job characteristics, but primary workers especially valued three specific aspects of work life: use of skills and abilities, interesting work, and promotion opportunities. Of all the specific job facets, "a job that lets you use your abilities and skills" was most highly valued, regardless of job level. However, the salience of this facet increased systematically at each job level, from 16.5% among secondary workers, to 27.5% among lower primary workers, to a full 39.4% among upper primary workers. A similar pattern emerged on "interesting work," another job content factor. Only 10% of secondary workers perceived interesting work as what they wanted most out of a job, compared to 15.1% of lower primary workers and 26.7% of upper primary workers.

Although skill utilization and interesting work were clearly the predominant concerns for upper primary workers, several other facets of work life were as important for lower level primary and secondary workers. For example, lower level primary workers were more often concerned about "promotion opportunities" (20.8%) than either upper primary (9%) or secondary (12.3%) workers. Consistent with dual labor market predictions, secondary workers were at least twice as likely as upper level primary workers to be concerned about "no hassles," "friendly co-workers," "autonomy," "good supervisors," and "a good physical work environment." As expected, secondary workers were least likely to report that their jobs actually provided what they most valued. Accordingly, lower and upper level primary workers more often received what they desired most from their jobs.

Since the mid-1970s, increasing attention has been placed on job stress not only as a source of job dissatisfaction but also as a major psychosocial risk factor in mental and physical illness (Israel, House, Schurman, Heaney, & Mero, 1989; Kahn, 1981; McLean, 1979). As shown in Table 7.6, secondary and primary workers also were asked about job stress to further explore sources of dissatisfaction. Each respondent was asked: "What would you say bothers you the most about your job?" In line with dual labor market predictions, 15.6% of upper primary workers reported low stress ("nothing bothered them") compared to 25.5% of lower primary workers and 34.2% of secondary workers. Secondary workers were more likely than primary workers to perceive the physical work environment, boring work, and a range of other factors as stressful. However, in order of frequency, a few workers at all levels were most bothered by perceived difficulties with pay, co-workers, supervisors, customers, or blocked opportunities.

Perceived Work Role Marginality

According to dual labor market models, chronic work role marginality may be a greater source of stress for workers in the secondary than primary sector. In addition to transient hassles or life events, secondary workers may be especially threatened by marginality in work roles that is enduring, persistent, and recurring. To explore this issue, secondary and primary workers were compared on subjective indicators of job instability, skill underutilization, downward mobility, and restricted promotion opportunities.

As shown in Table 7.7, some aspects of work role marginality were perceived as problems by black workers regardless of job level, whereas others were more problematic for secondary than primary workers. Regardless of job level, only about one-half of all respondents felt secure about the future of their current job, and four-fifths believed that they had "skills and abilities" for a better job. Specifically, only 44.3% of secondary workers, 43.8% of lower primary workers, and 49.6% of upper primary workers reported high job security ("not likely at all" that they would lose their job "during the next couple of years"). A full 75.2% of secondary workers, 83.7% of lower primary workers, and 82.3% of upper primary workers responded "yes" when asked: "Do you feel that you have the skills and abilities for a job better than the one you now have?" However, as expected, lower level workers more often reported downward career mobility from a better job as well as limited opportunity for a promotion on their current job. When asked, "Did you ever have a job better than the one you now have?" 41.8% of secondary workers, 38.1% of lower primary workers, and 27.8% of upper primary workers responded "yes." Similarly, a full 61.5% of secondary workers perceived their chances for promotion as "not very good" compared to only 40.9% of lower primary and 41.5% of upper primary workers.

Racial Experiences in Work Organizations

For African Americans, stress in the workplace may often involve personal experiences of racial isolation, episodes of discrimination,

Table 7.7

Comparisons of Dual Labor Market Job Categories by Indicators of Perceived
Work Role Marginality

	Dual Labor Market Job Categories (% of Total)		
Indicators of Perceived Role Marginality	Secondary Job (N = 622)	Lower Primary Job (N = 344)	Upper Primary Job (N = 226)
"How likely is it that you will lose the job you have during the next couple of years?"			
Not likely at all	44.3	43.8	49.6
Not too likely	35.8	35.9	36.2
Fairly/Very likely	19.9	20.3	14.2
Total	100.0	100.0	100.0
"Do you feel you have skills and abilities for a job better than the one you now have?"			
No	24.8	16.3	17.7
Yes	75.2	83.7	82.3
Total	100.0	100.0	100.0
"Did you ever have a job better than the one you now have?"			
No	58.2	61.9	72.2
Yes	41.8	38.1	27.8
Total	100.0	100.0	100.0
"At the place you now work, what are your chances for getting promoted?"			
Not very good	61.5	40.9	41.5
Good	18.6	28.0	27.8
Very good	19.9	31.1	30.7
Total	100.0	100.0	100.0

NOTE: Includes employed and laid-off workers in dual labor market primary and secondary jobs only.

or broader perceptions of racial inequity in the organization of work
(Bielby, 1987; Feagin, 1987; Pettigrew & Martin, 1987). Racial inequities not only may occur as stressful events or hassles, but also may be
perceived as discriminatory institutional patterns or biased organi-

zational practices. To explore the racial experiences of black Americans in work organizations, Table 7.8 presents findings on racial composition of work groups, race of supervisor, perceived racial discrimination, and appraisals of racial segmentation.

About two-thirds of the secondary workers and three-fourths of primary workers in the NSBA sample held jobs that required them to work in groups. In reference to racial composition of work groups, secondary workers were more often members of predominantly black work groups, whereas primary workers were more often members of predominantly white work groups. About half (52.3%) of the secondary workers were in all or mostly black work groups, compared to 36.2% of lower and 30.9% of upper primary workers. By contrast, upper primary workers were more likely (31.7%) than secondary workers (18.9%) to have a mostly white work group, and over three times more likely (22.3% vs. 6.4%) to be a solo black in an all-white work group. Regardless of job level, the clear majority of all black workers had white supervisors, while about one-fourth had a black supervisor.

As shown in Table 7.8, perceived racial discrimination appears to be a significant issue for black primary as well as secondary workers. Twenty-three percent of secondary workers, 30.7% of lower primary workers, and 27.2% of upper primary workers reported that blacks were "treated unfairly or badly" within their workplace. Moreover, secondary workers were less likely (5.1%) than either lower primary (10.0%) or upper primary workers (9.0%) to believe that they had personally been "turned down for a job because they were black." In contrast to interpersonal racial inequities, secondary workers appeared more vulnerable than primary workers to broader racial segmentation in the work organization. Compared to upper primary workers, secondary workers were only slightly more likely to report that "blacks tend to get certain kinds of jobs" where they worked (46.9% vs. 37.1%); however, they were three times more likely to perceive their own job as "one that black people tend to get more than whites" (41.5% vs. 14.2%). The majority of both secondary and primary workers agreed that in their workplace the jobs that blacks got were worse than jobs that whites tended to get. Therefore, mobility of black workers into the primary jobs may (a) fail to reduce interpersonal racial inequities, (b) increase sensitivity to racial discrimination in promotion, but (c) decrease perceived vulnerability to institutionalized racial segmentation.

Respondents who reported that blacks were treated badly or unfairly were probed, "In what ways?" Comparing the responses of sec-

Table 7.8

Comparisons of Dual Labor Market Job Categories by Racial Experience
in the Work Organization

Indicators of Racial Experience	Dual Labor Market Job Categories (% of Total)		
	Secondary Job (N = 647)	Lower Primary Job (N = 359)	Upper Primary Job (N = 232)
Interracial Exposure			
Racial Composition of Work Group			
All/Mostly black	52.3	36.2	30.9
About half black	22.4	20.6	15.1
Mostly white	18.9	27.9	31.7
All white except respondent	6.4	15.3	22.3
Total	100.0	100.0	100.0
Race of Supervisor			
White	60.2	66.7	58.9
Black	24.8	25.1	27.2
Other (Hispanic, multiracial)	5.8	5.3	5.0
No supervisor	9.2	2.9	8.9
Total	100.0	100.0	100.0
Perceived Racial Discrimination			
"At your work place, are black people treated unfairly or badly?"			
No	76.7	69.3	72.8
Yes	23.3	30.7	27.2
Total	100.0	100.0	100.0
"At the place where you work now, have you ever been turned down for a job you wanted because you are black?"			
No	94.9	90.0	91.0
Yes	5.1	10.0	9.0
Total	100.0	100.0	100.0

Indicators of Racial Experience	Dual Labor Market Job Categories (% of Total)		
	Secondary Job (N = 647)	Lower Primary Job (N = 359)	Upper Primary Job (N = 232)
	Perceived Racial Segmentation		
"In the place where you work, do black people get certain kinds of jobs?"			
No	53.1	55.6	62.9
Yes	46.9	44.4	37.1
Total	100.0	100.0	100.0
"Is your job one that black people tend to get more than whites?"			
No	58.5	78.1	85.8
Yes	41.5	21.9	14.2
Total	100.0	100.0	100.0

NOTE: Includes employed and laid-off workers in dual labor market primary and secondary jobs only.

ondary and primary workers provides new insight into the diversity of racial experience among blacks within work organizations. The most typical response focused on restrictions to advancement and included comments such as "whites are favored for promotion," "few blacks get to be supervisor," and "blacks are in dead-end jobs and don't get trained." Such complaints were made by 37% of upper primary personnel, 34% of lower primary employees, and 29% of secondary workers who felt that blacks were treated badly in their work setting. These results further bear out the pattern noted earlier suggesting a special sensitivity to advancement barriers among blacks in primary jobs. Other racial inequities noted disproportionately by primary workers included the underutilization of black personnel and bad treatment of blacks by co-workers. The factors contributing to such perceived inequities are likely multiple and complex, but both growth needs and racial composition of work groups probably

150 LIFE IN BLACK AMERICA

play some role. As shown earlier, blacks in upper primary jobs were more concerned about growth needs, such as skill utilization, and were most often members of predominantly white work groups.

Lower primary personnel, such as clericals and craft/kindred workers, were more likely than higher or lower level workers to report that blacks received harsher discipline and less privileges. Specific complaints included "rules are waived for others, but always enforced for blacks," and "blacks can't take vacations when they want." The finding that secondary workers were more likely than other personnel to complain that blacks tend to get the "dirtiest," "hardest," or "lowest" jobs further reflects their particular sensitivity to racial segmentation within work organizations. Racial inequities noted equally by black workers in the three dual labor market job categories included "unequal pay," "job security," and "worse treatment by supervisors."

Summary and Implications

Going beyond traditionally white-black comparisons, this chapter systematically investigated differences between black workers in low level secondary and higher status primary jobs. An integrative focus on both dual labor market and human capital models helped to clarify the complex patterns of inequality and mobility that increasingly characterize African American work life. The focus on both objective and subjective indicators also provided further insight into the diversity of work life in black America. Findings not only presented accurate national estimates, but also explored crucial relationships that raise some interesting issues for more definitive study.

Gender Issues

Consistent with dual labor market models, black males were primarily in secondary jobs as operatives or laborers, whereas females tended to be unskilled service workers. Of those who had scaled the occupational ladder into the primary sector, few had attained higher level primary jobs as doctors, lawyers, accountants, professors, or engineers. However, despite their underrepresentation in these higher level professional/technical jobs, black men and women were well represented as teachers, other public service professionals, and nontraditional managers or administrators. Moreover, findings suggest that much of the mobility of black workers from the secondary to the primary sector since the 1960s Civil Rights Movement involved young-er black women moving into clerical jobs. Despite the widely publi-cized mobility of blacks into primary sector jobs, the occupational center of gravity among both males and females remains dispropor-tionately rooted in less skilled, low-paying jobs with poor working con-ditions, little advancement opportunity, and increasing risks for joblessness. Nonetheless, the increased portion of blacks in various primary sector jobs has had the clear effect of creating greater diversity in the work life of African Americans as we approach the 21st century.

The tendency for young black women to be less restricted than young black men to secondary jobs and more often in professional jobs raises some controversial questions. For example, after con-trasting gender patterns between white and black workers, an early study by Bock (1969) concluded that black women had an "unnatu-ral superiority" over black men in professional employment. He sug-gested that because black parents perceive less societal resistance to mobility for their daughters, they may give them preference in edu-cation and proactively orient them toward mobility. In contrast, other researchers emphasize the double jeopardy of black females who are more often than black males channeled into low-paying, gen-der segregated jobs and restricted by family responsibilities (Farley & Allen, 1987; King, 1988). To be sure, such race by gender complexi-ties represent fertile ground for future inquiry.

Tracking and Mobility Issues

In line with human capital models, higher education clearly has been a necessary condition for increasing the representation of blacks in primary sector jobs. However, data on structural barriers is con-sistent with studies that suggest that increased schooling may not be sufficient because it may have only marginal payoffs for blacks rela-tive to whites. For example, Erbe (1975) found that blacks with equal education to whites do not always attain equal jobs:

> Blacks with professional degrees are less likely to be managers than whites with only a high school diploma; blacks with college degrees are less likely to be sales workers than whites who have not completed high school. And black males with high school diplomas are less likely to be in skilled crafts occupations than whites with an eighth grade educa-tion or less. (p. 156)

Despite the importance of education, such findings question simplistic human capital approaches that limit analysis of black occupational inequality to educational underinvestment due to ability or motivational deficits.

To be sure, structural barriers facing past generations of African Americans were reflected in the relation of parents' education and occupation to occupational attainment of the respondents. Such findings are consistent with status attainment studies which show that secondary and primary jobs are largely transmitted across the generations (Blau & Duncan, 1967; Montaga, 1977; Porter, 1974). Many blacks in secondary jobs are largely products of parents and grandparents who were systematically denied both quality education and quality jobs. These secondary workers started off with historically structured disadvantages not usually faced by white youth or the few privileged young blacks whose families somehow overcame such barriers during earlier generations. Unfortunately, many African Americans in secondary jobs continue to be burdened by such intergenerational barriers, despite the fact that civil rights policies of the 1960s and 1970s enabled unprecedented numbers to overcome them.

More definitive studies should also further clarify the role of racial segregation, sociodemographic risk factors, and job networks in the occupational attainment of black secondary and primary workers. Multivariate analyses that consider complex interaction effects may provide greater support for the "underclass hypothesis" that racial isolation within economically depressed urban areas places unmarried black parents at special risk (Bowman, 1988; Wilson, 1987). Nevertheless, in light of past research, descriptive findings in the present study suggest that several other issues should also be considered (St. John, 1975; Raelin, 1980; Wielgosz & Carpenter, 1983). Why wasn't occupational attainment higher among blacks from racially balanced environments (half white/half black) than among those from segregated environments (all-black)? Why did the few solo blacks from all-white environments experience such clear employment advantages? Should there be more concern for African Americans with chronic employment difficulties in the urban north than in the rural south? Do first jobs have pivotal consequences for the long-term career problems of black secondary workers? Does an over-reliance on informal networks and employment agencies rather than schools, direct employer contacts, and job advertisements restrict the job options of secondary workers?

Quality of Work Life Issues

The national data support the notion that job satisfaction level not only depends on objective conditions of work, but also on the specific measures used and diverse orientations that workers bring to the workplace. Differential findings on conventional and less conventional measures of global job satisfaction raise crucial conceptual and measurement issues. Future inquiry should explore why black secondary workers expressed unexpectedly high global satisfaction on the conventional measure, but extreme dissatisfaction with the idea of their daughters or sons holding their low level job (Quinn, 1972). On the conventional measure, did black secondary workers favorably compare their low status job situation with growing numbers of jobless blacks rather than with blacks or whites in primary jobs? Are secondary workers better able to accommodate themselves to low level jobs when they believe that their children will attain better jobs? The less conventional measure, which asked respondents to evaluate their jobs in terms of their goals for their children, may represent a more valid indicator, insofar as it proved to be more responsive to objective characteristics of secondary and primary sector jobs.

A particularly important direction for future research is to investigate the manner in which work orientations, job stress, work role marginality, and racial inequity affect job satisfaction among black workers (Bartel, 1981; Bowman, 1990a; Forgionne & Peters, 1982). Although black secondary and primary workers differed on work orientations and job stress, work role marginality and racial inequity were perceived to be serious problems regardless of job level. Consistent with the general literature on work motivation, black secondary workers were concerned with a wider range of extrinsic work conditions, whereas those in primary jobs were especially orientated toward intrinsic job content—interesting work that utilized their skills and abilities (Hackman & Oldham, 1976; Locke, 1983). Job stress appears particularly problematic for black secondary workers, but perceived skill underutilization and work role marginality may erode job satisfaction regardless of job level (Bowman, 1990b; McGrath, 1983). Although primary workers often escape institutionalized racial segmentation, predominantly white work groups and ambitious mobility orientations may increase their vulnerability to race-related interpersonal conflicts and their sensitivity to promotion difficulties (Bass, 1984; Hoffman, 1985; Katz, 1970; Pettigrew & Martin, 1987).

Policy Implications

Findings in this chapter suggest that effective policy to improve the work life of African Americans must focus both on external organizational barriers and individual investment activities. The integrative focus in this chapter disagrees with the common tendency among both researchers and policymakers to narrowly focus on either external mechanisms that restrict opportunities or internal mechanisms that promote mobility. Despite intergenerational barriers, these findings suggest that educational policies that promote post-secondary training and retraining are of paramount importance for vulnerable black secondary workers. However, findings on pervasive skill underutilization also support the importance of policy initiatives in other arenas to improve the returns from education among black primary and secondary workers. Strong affirmative action policies show promise in facilitating the mobility of highly trained black workers. However, the unique work life difficulties of black males and females, black underclass entrapment in urban and rural areas, widespread perceptions of work role marginality, and perceived racial inequities within work organizations may call for policies beyond traditional affirmative action. In future efforts to formulate effective policies, ongoing studies that further analyze the rich set of objective and subjective indicators highlighted in this chapter may help to broaden the scope of relevant policy discourse.

Notes

1. For example, the Bureau of Labor Statistics within the U.S. Department of Labor has published a quarterly report, *Employment in Perspective: Minority Workers*, since February 1980. These statistical summaries are based on data from the Current Population Survey, a sample survey of 56,000 U.S. households conducted monthly by the Bureau of the Census. The U.S. Bureau of the Census also issues comprehensive reports such as *The Socio and Economic Status of the Black Population in the United States: An Historical View, 1790–1978*. Such reports update and extend data from earlier reports. This series of publications provides detailed information on the labor force, employment, and occupational status, comparing blacks and other nonwhites with white workers.

The National Longitudinal Surveys are directed by Herbert S. Parnes at Ohio State University's Center for Human Resource Research. These surveys include a wide range of indicators and are particularly useful in research on human capital issues, unemployment, as well as labor supply and demand. The Panel Study of Income

Dynamics is directed by James N. Morgan and Greg Duncan at the University of Michigan's Institute for Social Research. Data from this unique time series study are particularly useful for investigating what causes family income to rise and fall below poverty level. The guiding orientation is that attitudinal variables affect and are affected by economic status. A major focus is on how economic behavior intervenes between attitudes and economic status as well as how other forces affect all three. Although both data sets include indicators of social psychological dimensions of labor force behavior, the quality of jobs and experience within work settings has been relatively neglected. The focus has also been on indicators geared toward black-white comparisons rather than measures particularly useful in investigating the heterogeneity of work experience within the black population.

JOBLESSNESS

Phillip J. Bowman

The growing numbers of African Americans who are jobless face difficulties even more severe than the low pay, marginality, and inequity that burden those who hold menial jobs. An argument that even a menial job is usually better than no job at all is persuasive. Joblessness has become a concern for Americans of all races, but increasingly looms as a major threat to economic security and psychosocial well-being among African Americans. Official statistics show that overall unemployment surpassed the 10 million mark in 1982, a larger number than at any other time since the Great Depression of the 1930s (Swinton, 1983). Black-white differences on traditional indicators clearly document the relative severity of joblessness among the nation's largest racial-minority group.

Black workers are more frequently displaced from jobs during economic recession, are jobless for longer periods, become more discouraged in job search, drop out of the labor force more often, and experience greater economic hardship as a result of joblessness (Bowman, 1984; Brimmer, 1988; Swinton, 1983). These fault lines of chronic joblessness too often erupt in other areas of African American life with deleterious effects on mental health, family stability, organizational participation, and community functioning (Bowman, 1980, 1988, 1989; Duster, 1988; Farley & Allen, 1987). In this chapter on joblessness in black America, critical issues and perspectives are first highlighted followed by a discussion of national findings based on a unique set of objective and subjective indicators.

Critical Issues: Official Versus Hidden Unemployment

According to government statistics, the official jobless rate among black workers has been at least twice that of whites throughout the post-World War II period. Swinton (1983) observed that this two-to-one ratio applies "for blacks of all ages, both sexes, all educational levels, in all regions of the country, [in] cities and in the suburbs" (p. 66). Although this official rate differential is indeed striking, it still underestimates the severity of black joblessness because it does not include all black Americans who want or need a job. Rather, official statistics are based on the more restrictive "active job search" definition used to tabulate monthly jobless data from the government's Current Population Surveys (CPS) (U.S. Department of Labor, 1980):

> Unemployed persons are those who (a) were not working during the survey week and made specific efforts to find a job in the preceding 4 weeks; (b) were on layoff and waiting to be recalled; or (c) were waiting to report to a new job within 30 days. (p. 3)

Official unemployment statistics based on this operational definition have a serious limitation; they do not include the hidden unemployed who want and need a job but who do not "actively look" for employment. Yet, the only reason why many African Americans join the ranks of the hidden unemployed is because they become so discouraged in job search that they give up hope of finding work and stop active job search (Bowman, 1984; Bowman, Jackson, Hatchett, & Gurin, 1982; Ondeck, 1978; Wool, 1978).

In 1967 the government began to document one group of the "hidden unemployed" who wanted a job but did not actively look for work because they believed that there was no job for them. However, these jobless "discouraged workers" are not considered part of the official labor force and have never been included in official unemployment counts. National data on the jobless who are "discouraged workers" strongly suggest that the level of hidden unemployment is even more severe in black communities than official unemployment (Bowman et al., 1982; Hill, 1981). While blacks represent about 12% of the total American population, and over 20% of the officially unemployed, they have been found to constitute as much as 40% of the discouraged workers who have dropped out of the labor force due to frustration in job search. Even this alarming disproportion may be a conservative estimate because it is widely known that large numbers of blacks (particularly discouraged males) are undercounted in government surveys based on household samples.

The National Urban League (NUL) periodically reports findings from their "Hidden Unemployment Index" to show how official rates grossly underestimate the severity of joblessness in black America. For example, Hill (1981) noted that

> while official figures indicate that about 13 percent of all black workers were unemployed during 1980, the NUL Hidden Unemployed Index, which takes account of discouraged workers, puts that actual total black jobless rate at 25 percent in 1980. Thus, a minimum of one out of every four black workers are jobless today—which is equal to the unemployed rate for the nation at the peak of the Great Depression in the 1930s. It is clearly no exaggeration to assert that while the rest of the nation is in a recession, the black community is in the throes of a severe economic depression. (p. 7)

By the second quarter of 1982, the Hidden Unemployment Index showed that nonwhite joblessness had jumped to 30.2% with prospects of greater escalation.

Compared with official unemployment, very little is known about hidden unemployment or its consequences within black communities. Future research on black joblessness should go beyond official definitions to better clarify the experiences of the hidden unemployed. This phenomenon of hidden joblessness is central to increasing public policy debates about an emerging underclass in urban America, especially in predominantly black inner city neighborhoods with high structural unemployment (Auletta, 1982; George, 1988; Glasgow, 1980; Wilson, 1987). Moreover, research on discouragement among the hidden unemployed and others faced with chronic difficulty in major life roles has important theoretical implications for understanding the social psychology of role strain and adaptation (Bowman, 1989, 1990a, 1990b; Jackson, 1986).

The NSBA questionnaire included measures to estimate the official jobless rate as well as other dimensions of joblessness relevant to hidden unemployment. Particular attention was placed on measures to tap both objective job search difficulty and subjective reactions to labor market barriers. A social psychological focus on objective aspects of the last job, and conditions of joblessness as well as more subjective perceptions, expectations, and evaluations provides a basis to examine more fully how black Americans actually experience joblessness—official and hidden—as we approach the 21st century.

Perspectives on Black Joblessness

As with menial jobs, there are two general theoretical perspectives on the problem of chronic black joblessness (McGahey & Jeffries, 1985; Wilson, 1978). First, the human capital model explains black joblessness in terms of deficits that reduce individual productivity—motivation, education, or skills (Becker, 1975; Harrison, 1972; Levine & Bane, 1975). In contrast, restricted opportunity models of black joblessness emphasize racial discrimination or other systematic barriers in the labor market (Bluestone & Harrison, 1982; Harrison & Sum, 1980; Ogbu, 1986). In the preceding chapter, we discussed the basic principles of dual labor market theory and proposed that "increasing unemployment and labor force dropout rates among African Americans largely reflect declines in the availability of unskilled secondary sector jobs." In line with this proposition, it is insightful to consider findings on official and hidden joblessness within the context of dual labor market dynamics (Harrison & Sum, 1980; Piore, 1977). The persistent dilemma of race in America makes both racial discrimination and postindustrial displacement major labor market concerns of the black jobless (George, 1988; Kinder, 1986). However, the increasing labor market skill demands of a postindustrial economy also make education and other human capital investments important considerations (Mills, 1983; Rumberger, 1983).

Existing longitudinal data suggest that the *historical restriction of African Americans to unskilled secondary sector jobs has interacted with other factors across time to increase the severity of their joblessness* (Brimmer, 1985; Parnes, 1982; Sproat, Churchill, & Sheets, 1985; Swinton, 1989). Although menial secondary sector jobs have been a problem for black people since their transition from slave to free labor in 1865, the problem of severe black joblessness is a more recent phenomenon. In fact, from 1890 to 1930, the proportion of blacks who worked was at least 10 percentage points higher than that of whites. During that 40-year period, the number of black Americans gainfully employed expanded with the rapid growth in unskilled industrial jobs. Since the 1930s, however, black and white labor force participation rates have converged, with both groups reaching 57% by 1970. Thus, since the era of the Great Depression, increasing numbers of whites and decreasing numbers of blacks have been gainfully employed.

The widely reported movement of more white women into the labor force is a major factor in the statistical convergence of labor force participation rates between blacks and whites. Another major factor, which is less frequently studied, is the precipitous and continuous decline in the number of black men gainfully employed. Despite this reverse trend, it does not follow that the entry of white women has directly forced black men out of the labor force. White women have entered the labor force primarily as clericals, service workers, and professionals. In contrast, black men have been displaced primarily from jobs as unskilled and semi-skilled industrial workers. Although the social implications are not well understood, the decreasing number of black men with jobs is well documented (Farley & Allen, 1987; Swinton, 1989). National CPS data show a marked decrease between 1948 and 1980 in the proportion of black men with gainful employment. This decline occurred among black men at each age and educational level, but is particularly dramatic among teenagers, older men, and those with less education.

Black women have sometimes been found to have even higher rates of official unemployment than black men. However, black males are alone in their increasing tendency to drop out of the labor force for reasons other than homemaking, schooling, or retirement. With fewer black men gainfully employed, more jobless black women are assuming the role of sole family provider, which may further spur active job search, increase labor force participation, and official unemployment counts (Allen & Farley, 1985; Glick, 1988). However, as noted earlier, unknown numbers of black males who drop out of the labor force are not enumerated in CPS surveys. Although some black males may not be attached in a stable manner to households surveyed, many others are disproportionately in prisons, the military, and other institutions not included in most national surveys (Duster, 1988; Gary, 1981). Thus, national surveys of households are likely to underrepresent hidden unemployment among black males, many of whom are residentially dislocated or institutionalized.

Periodic recessionary downturns in the American economy tend to have a more severe impact on official and hidden unemployment of black people, largely because the secondary jobs they disproportionately hold are hit hardest (Anderson, 1982; Brimmer, 1976, 1984, 1985). For example, the Great Depression in the 1930s had devastating effects on the labor force participation rates of the largely unskilled black population, whose job losses were even greater than those of whites. Every economic downturn since the Depression has made blacks, largely because of their concentration in marginal secondary jobs, lag even further behind whites. The eminent economist Andrew Brimmer (1973) observed that the resulting "lag can be seen in several measures—including a lower growth in the black labor force, the smaller share of new jobs obtained by blacks, and the continued climb in black unemployment" (p. 42). Thus, black workers lose jobs at a faster rate during economic recession and regain employment at a slower rate when economic recovery occurs.

In the last quarter of the 20th century, several economic recessions have helped to systematically erode the employment gains made by African Americans between the mid-1960s and mid-1970s (Allen & Farley, 1985; Brimmer, 1985; Farley & Allen, 1987). The early 1980s recession, which was the deepest economic downturn since the Great Depression, had an especially devastating impact on black joblessness. The adverse impact of the early 1980s downturn has been exacerbated by rapid technological change, ineffective education and training policies, and growing segregation of jobless African Americans into depressed inner city neighborhoods (Barth, 1982; Bowman, 1988; Duster, 1988; George, 1988; Wilson, 1987). Automation and deindustrialization are permanently displacing the specific secondary sector jobs which black workers continue to depend on disproportionately for their economic livelihood (Bluestone & Harrison, 1982; Mills, 1983; Swinton, 1989). Even the most optimistic forecast must acknowledge the particular difficulty faced by the growing numbers of unskilled African Americans who must adapt to rapid deindustrialization and a depressed inner city economy. Although jobless blacks who are unskilled and have secondary sector job histories appear most vulnerable, those who are better prepared and seek primary sector jobs may also be challenged with stiff competition as well as lingering racial and cultural insensitivity.

National Findings

As suggested above, a meaningful examination of African American joblessness must go beyond the conventional focus on official unemployment among those who actively seek jobs. Therefore, national findings in this section also focus on the hidden unemployed, or those who want and need a job but do not actively look for one.

National data are presented to explore the nature, contributing factors, and consequences of both official and hidden unemployment among black workers. As proposed in dual labor market paradigms, findings in the chapter on work suggested that African Americans may be systematically channelled into unskilled secondary jobs. If vulnerable secondary jobs contribute to black joblessness, then tracking mechanisms associated with such unstable jobs should also be linked to hidden and official unemployment.

To begin to unravel the unique circumstances of joblessness in black America, the data presented below build on dual labor market considerations to explore a range of potential antecedents and consequences. The focus goes beyond the typical demographic analysis of labor force participation. Descriptive analyses explore the relation of intergenerational background, employment history, and job search experience to joblessness in black America. The economic and social psychological consequences of joblessness are also explored. The rather straightforward comparative analysis can help identify specific variables that differentiate the hidden unemployed from the not-interested-in-working, the officially unemployed, and the employed. Although such findings do not permit conclusive causal inferences, they can raise important questions for more definitive research and public policy consideration. What specific intergenerational factors differentiate the unemployed from the employed? Is a dual labor market job history linked to hidden or official unemployment? Do the hidden and officially unemployed differ on reasons for leaving their last job, or in the duration of their joblessness? Is a history of unstable secondary jobs linked to job search behaviors or to a tendency to become discouraged in job search? What are the economic consequences of hidden and official joblessness? Do the hidden and officially unemployed perceive the major causes of their joblessness in a similar manner?

Labor Market Status

Table 8.1 presents data on the labor market status of the NSBA sample as a basis to distinguish hidden unemployment from other forms of joblessness. Fifty-seven percent of the sample (1,199 respondents) was working for pay, with 43% (906 respondents) not employed. As noted earlier, these jobless respondents would be classified as officially unemployed only if they had specifically looked for a job within 4 weeks immediately before the interview or were laid

Table 8.1

Comparison of Three Unemployment Status Distributions

Labor Market Status	Total Sample (N = 2107) (%)	Labor Force [a] (N = 1397) (%)	Jobless (N = 906) (%)
Employed for pay	56.9	85.8	
Officially unemployed	9.4	14.2	21.9
Hidden unemployed[b]	15.5		36.0
Not interested in job	18.2		42.1
Total	100.0	100.0	100.0

a. Labor force is officially defined as those persons either employed or officially unemployed. b. Hidden unemployed are those persons who want a job but have not actively looked for a job within the four weeks prior to the interview.

off but expecting to return to their prior job. Only 22% of the jobless (198 respondents) met this criteria, with 117 actively seeking work and 81 laid off. These 198 officially unemployed respondents make up 14.2% of the active labor force, which is the official unemployment rate in this national sample of African Americans. Government statistics define the labor force as only those persons either employed or officially unemployed.

In addition to the officially unemployed, the data reveal that an even larger portion of the jobless (36%) can be classified as the hidden unemployed. Of the 326 hidden unemployed, 41 were looking for a job but not actively enough to be counted among the officially unemployed, 203 reported that they would definitely take a job if offered one, and 82 others indicated that they were interested in working but would not be able to start a job at the time they were interviewed. Thus, our data support the notion that there is a larger number of African Americans among the hidden unemployed than among those who are officially counted as unemployed. Although not typically considered part of the active labor force, the orientations of the hidden unemployed toward work may be very different from those not interested in working. Moreover, the line between the hidden and officially unemployed may be quite permeable.

Many among the hidden unemployed may actively seek work when more jobs become available. Such transitions from hidden to official unemployment might explain the curious increases in the official jobless rate which sometimes occur despite economic growth and more available jobs. In contrast, when economic downturns decrease available jobs, some of the officially unemployed may become discouraged and stop looking for work. In our national sample, we found that one in six of the hidden unemployed had stopped looking for work because they lost hope of finding a job. Therefore, extreme discouragement, or a belief that job search is hopeless, may be one factor that distinguishes the hidden unemployed from those not interested in working because of preferences for retirement, homemaker, or student roles. In addition, the one fourth of the officially unemployed who reported extreme discouragement may be at high risk to discontinue active job search and join the ranks of the hidden unemployed. Guided by findings in this chapter and related studies, future research needs to clarify the cognitive and behavioral dynamics that separate the official and hidden unemployed (Bowman, 1984; Bowman et al., 1982; Ondeck, 1978).

Demographic Factors

As shown in Table 8.2, findings on demographic factors were not striking but do show some interesting differences and similarities. Hidden unemployment occurred among all sex, age, and marital-parental status subgroups, but some differences did emerge. Females were more represented among the hidden unemployed, males among the employed, but there were no clear gender differences in official unemployment. Moreover, older workers (55 years or older) were more likely to be among the hidden unemployed and least often officially unemployed. As expected, prime working aged workers (35–54 years) were most likely to be employed, and equally as likely as younger respondents to be actively seeking work.

Marital-parental status did not clearly differentiate the hidden unemployed, although unmarried parents were the most likely to be officially unemployed and least likely to be employed. It is also interesting that the small number of adults who were married without children were the most likely to be employed. Neither urbanicity, region, nor racial composition of one's current neighborhood differentiated the hidden unemployed from either the officially unemployed or employed. This is somewhat surprising, given ongoing underclass debates which often focus on chronically jobless African Americans in the North Central industrial states, inner cities, and racially segregated neighborhoods (Bowman, 1988; Glasgow, 1980; Wilson, 1987). However, despite the lack of a direct association, fu-

Table 8.2
Comparisons of Selected Demographic Subgroups on Employment-Unemployment Status

	Employment-Unemployment Status[a] *(% of sample)*			
Selected Demographic Subgroups	*Employed for Pay (N = 1199)*	*Officially Unemployed (N = 198)*	*Hidden Unemployed (N = 326)*	*Total*
Sex				
Male	78.3	10.4	11.3	100
Female	64.0	12.1	23.9	100
Age				
18 to 34 years	65.4	16.9	17.7	100
35 to 54 years	78.4	7.9	13.7	100
55 years or older	63.2	3.7	33.1	100
Marital-Parental Status				
Married with children	77.7	7.2	15.1	100
Unmarried with children	60.9	14.5	24.6	100
Married, no children	84.1	7.3	8.6	100
Unmarried, no children	67.5	15.0	17.5	100

NOTE: Region of country, urban-rural residence, and racial composition of neighborhood were not associated with employment-unemployment status.
a. Excludes those who were not working and not interested in working.

ture inquiry may do well to explore how these demographic variables emphasized in underclass debates are linked to other risk factors (i.e., stress, drugs, crime) that may exacerbate either joblessness or its harmful human consequences.

Intergenerational Background

Table 8.3 presents findings on selected intergenerational variables that may differentiate hidden unemployment and other employment outcomes. Respondents' employment status was significantly linked to their fathers' occupation, but not to their mothers' occupation, fathers' education, or mothers' education. Respondents whose fathers had secondary sector jobs were about twice as likely to appear among the hidden unemployed (20.3%) than those whose fathers had upper primary jobs (11.4%). These findings are somewhat surprising in that education and occupation of mothers, rather than fathers, have of-

Table 8.3

Comparisons of Intergenerational Subgroups on Employment-Unemployment Status

Intergenerational Background	Employment-Unemployment Status (% of sample)			
	Employed for Pay	Officially Unemployed	Hidden Unemployed	Total (N)
Father's Occupation				
Secondary sector	69.1	10.6	20.3	100 (1038)
Lower stratum primary sector	70.5	11.8	17.7	100 (237)
Upper stratum primary sector	81.3	7.3	11.4	100 (96)
Mother's Occupation				
Secondary sector	69.0	12.1	18.9	100 (935)
Lower stratum primary sector	76.6	9.1	14.3	100 (77)
Upper stratum primary sector	67.3	14.0	18.7	100 (107)
Father's Education				
Less than high school	72.6	9.4	18.0	100 (679)
High school graduate	67.3	15.8	16.9	100 (196)
Some college	64.8	19.7	15.5	100 (71)
College graduate	78.3	4.3	17.4	100 (23)
Mother's Education				
Less than high school	71.8	11.3	16.9	100 (768)
High school graduate	69.1	14.0	16.9	100 (343)
Some college	69.5	13.7	16.8	100 (95)
College graduate	87.0	0.0	13.0	100 (23)

NOTE: Excludes those not working and not interested in working.

ten been considered pivotal to status attainment outcomes among African American youth, who are increasingly raised by unmarried mothers (Epps, 1969; Farley & Allen, 1987). Therefore, fathers' occupational difficulty emerged as a particularly critical risk factor in hidden joblessness. Studies suggest that the impact of fathers' occupation on youths' future employment prospects may be mediated by one's own educational training and background (Guttman, 1983; Levine & Bane, 1975; Wilson, 1978).

Secondary Job History

A father's secondary sector occupation and a low level of educational attainment may further combine with a history of secondary jobs to increase the likelihood of official and hidden unemployment. To provide insight into the job history-unemployment link, Figure 8.1 shows differences between the employed and unemployed on specific dual labor market occupational roles. Data on the employed are based on their present jobs, whereas corresponding data on the unemployed indicate the labor market location of their last job. When asked if they had ever worked for pay, 73% (385) of the officially and hidden unemployed reported that they had held a job before. If chronic joblessness is linked to unstable secondary jobs, we would expect the unemployed to be disproportionately channelled from secondary rather than primary sector jobs. As expected, only 52% of employed respondents were located in unstable secondary sector jobs, but a full 72% of the unemployed had been channelled from such unstable jobs. Only 4% of the unemployed were channelled from upper level jobs compared to 19% of the employed who still held such stable primary sector jobs. Therefore, compared to the distribution of employed black workers, a larger portion of the unemployed were channelled from unstable secondary jobs than primary sector jobs.

As shown in Figure 8.1, the special vulnerability of unstable secondary jobs is also reflected in the proportions of employed and unemployed in specific occupational roles. Within the secondary sector, this employment-unemployment ratio shows that unskilled service workers made up 26% of the employed blacks but 41% of the unemployed. Employed-unemployed differences are less striking for unskilled laborers and semi-skilled operatives, despite the fact that these secondary jobs are much more vulnerable than unskilled service jobs. However, workers from the more vulnerable jobs more often ended up among the hidden unemployed (interested in working but not actively seeking a job because of discouragement or some other reason). The employed-unemployed ratio increases as we move up the occupational ladder from manager/administrators (3:1), to semi-professionals (5:1), to public service professionals (6:1), to higher professional/technical roles (2:0). Therefore, high-level primary sector jobs increased chances for employment, whereas vulnerable secondary jobs systematically increased risks for both official and hidden unemployment.

Findings also suggest a perceived racial dimension to dual labor market problems among the black jobless in America. Jobless respondents were asked: "In the place where you worked on your last job, did black people tend to get certain kinds of jobs?" Despite the

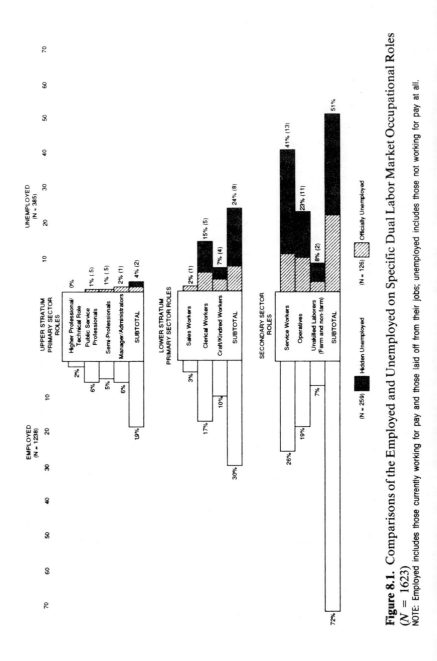

Figure 8.1. Comparisons of the Employed and Unemployed on Specific Dual Labor Market Occupational Roles (N = 1623)

NOTE: Employed includes those currently working for pay and those laid off from their jobs; unemployed includes those not working for pay at all.

168

fact that many worked in all-black settings, 44% of the hidden unemployed and 48% of the officially unemployed responded "yes." Moreover, almost one half of those who reported the presence of racially segmented jobs in their last work organization also noted that their last job was one "that black people tended to get more than whites." About one in five of both the hidden and officially unemployed also believed that they had been turned down for a promotion in their past jobs because they were black. However, despite such perceptions of racial bias, racial discrimination was seldom given as the major reason for leaving their last job. Instead, in order of frequency, external labor market factors (i.e., layoffs, plant closure, fired), voluntary departures (i.e., quit, decided to try something else), health-related factors (i.e., illness, disability), family circumstances (i.e., child care, residential relocation), and education (i.e., school re-entry, training) were reported as the major reasons. None of the officially unemployed and only 12% of the hidden unemployed mentioned retirement. In contrast, a full 50% of the jobless not interested in working gave retirement as the major motivation for leaving their last job.

Job Search Experience

The preceding results suggest that unstable secondary jobs, racially capricious employment practices, and labor market displacement may all contribute to black joblessness. These labor market barriers may increase the job search difficulties of both the officially and hidden unemployed. For example, 33% of active job seekers and 18% of the hidden unemployed responded "yes" to the question: "Have you ever not been hired on a job because you are black?" Moreover, 35% of the officially unemployed and 23% of the hidden unemployed also responded "yes" to a related question: "Are there any other ways you have been treated unfairly or badly because you are black while working or looking for work?" These data suggest that the job search experience of black Americans may often be aggravated by perceived racial discrimination. In addition to direct interpersonal racial discrimination, the more institutionalized tracking of black workers into secondary sector jobs may also have adverse effects on their job search experience.

The data in Table 8.4 explore possible associations between dual labor market employment history and job search experience. Dual labor market models would predict that jobless blacks with an employment history in the secondary rather than primary sector would

Table 8.4

Comparisons of Secondary and Primary Sector Job Seekers on
Selected Indicators of Job Search Experience

Job Search Experience Indicators	Dual Labor Market Job History [a] (% of sample)	
	Secondary Sector Job Seekers (N = 120)	Primary Sector Job Seekers (N = 50)
What kind of job are you looking for?		
Secondary sector job	71.6	35.0
Lower stratum primary sector job	25.7	45.0
Upper stratum primary sector job	2.7	20.0
How long have you been looking for work?		
1 to 17 weeks	43.9	61.9
18 weeks or more	56.1	38.1
How many places have you been to in the last 4 weeks to look?		
None	24.8	20.8
1 to 4 places	35.8	31.3
5 or more places	39.4	47.9
What things have you been doing to find a job?[b]		
Nothing	6.0	2.0
Generally looking	6.9	14.6
Contact family/Friends	7.7	2.1
Employment agencies	22.2	14.6
Want ads	23.9	25.0
Direct employer contacts	33.3	41.7
How hard has it been for you to find what you want?		
Not hard to fairly hard	26.1	24.5
Extremely hard to almost impossible	73.9	75.5
A lot of people would like to work but have lost hope that they can find a decent job. Do you feel this way?		
No	70.0	78.0
Yes	30.0	22.0

a. Includes unemployed respondents who have looked for work only.   b. Includes first mention responses only.

experience special job search difficulties. Job seekers from secondary and primary jobs indeed differed on the type of jobs they sought,
the duration of their job search, and the number of places they had

looked. However, differences were much less clear on specific job search strategies used, perceived difficulty of job search, and the tendency to lose hope of finding a job. Not surprising, job seekers who had held a prior job tended to seek jobs in the same sector as their last job. For example, 71.6% of the job seekers from the secondary sector were searching for similar jobs; only 2.7% sought jobs in the upper primary sector. The largest portion of those from primary jobs were seeking work in the lower primary sector (45%), while 20% reported seeking upper primary sector jobs. Surprisingly, however, over one third of the job seekers with a primary job history were searching downward for a job in the secondary sector. These findings suggest that there may be as much or more sinking as mobility reflected in the job search orientations of African Americans.

As expected, when compared to job seekers from primary sector jobs, secondary job seekers had been looking for a longer period of time and were less active in their job search. For example, 56.1% of the secondary job seekers had been looking for over 17 weeks, whereas only 38.1% of the primary job seekers had been searching that long. Only 39.4% of these secondary job seekers were looking very actively (5 or more times in 4 weeks) compared to 47.9% of the primary job seekers. Specific job search strategies of secondary and primary job seekers were similar with both using, in order of frequency, direct employer contacts, want ads, employment agencies, and informal contacts (i.e., family and friends). A full three fourths of both groups of job seekers perceived their job search to be extremely difficult to almost impossible, with about one fourth admitting that they had become so discouraged that they had lost hope of finding a job. To be sure, findings suggest that frustrating barriers often make job search a discouraging experience for African Americans.

Consequences: Economic and Psychosocial

Whatever the contributing factors, numerous studies suggest that chronic joblessness and job search discouragement are likely to have far-reaching consequences (Bowman, 1984; Brimmer, 1988; Fryer, 1986; Jahoda, 1982; Kelvin & Jarrett, 1985). In this final section, data are presented to explore both the economic and psychosocial correlates of joblessness.

Table 8.5 compares the employed and unemployed on both objective and subjective indicators of economic well-being. Again, these data separate the officially and hidden unemployed to explore the

Table 8.5

Comparisons of the Employed and Unemployed on Indicators of Economic Well-Being

Economic Well-Being	Employment-Unemployment Status [a] (% of sample)		
	Employed for Pay (N = 1199)	Officially Unemployed (N = 198)	Hidden Unemployed (N = 326)
Objective Indicators			
Personal Income			
< $5,000	25.4	58.8	73.6
$5,000 to $10,000	32.0	25.8	16.9
> $10,000	42.6	15.4	9.5
Family Income			
< $5,000	10.1	36.5	46.8
$5,000 to $10,000	24.0	32.0	28.4
> $10,000	65.9	31.5	24.8
Number Supporting Household			
One	44.3	57.6	65.4
Two or more	55.7	42.4	34.6
Subjective Indicators			
Worry About Family Subsistence			
None to a little	75.9	53.6	59.7
A lot to a great deal	24.1	46.4	40.3
Major Source of Jobless-Related Stress[b]			
Financial		72.0	51.4
Boredom/Lack of activity		14.4	16.2
Other		1.6	4.7
Nothing		12.0	27.7

a. Excludes those not working and not interested in working.   b. Includes first mention responses only.

economic consequences of both types of joblessness. Overall, the findings on objective indicators clearly demonstrate that the jobless—both official and hidden—experience much greater economic hardship than the employed. On personal income, only 25.4% of the employed received under $5,000 compared to 58.8% of the officially unemployed and a striking 73.6% of the hidden unemployed. This tendency for the hidden unemployed to experience even greater economic disadvantage than the officially unemployed or employed also occurred on family income, although less dramatically. Only 10.1% of the employed reported a family income under $5,000 compared to

36.5% of the officially unemployed and 46.8% of the hidden unemployed. As expected, the low family income of the hidden unemployed correlated with the smaller number of people who contributed income to their households. Only 34.6% of the hidden unemployed had two or more family providers compared to 55.7% of the employed.

Unexpectedly, the tendency for the hidden unemployed to experience greater economic hardship than the officially unemployed is not expressed in the subjective indicators of economic well-being. To assess anxiety about family subsistence, each respondent was asked: "How much do you worry that your total family income will not be enough to meet your family's expenses and bills?" In response, almost one half of both the officially unemployed (46.4%) and hidden unemployed (40.3%) worried "a lot" to "a great deal." In contrast, less than one fourth of the employed expressed such high levels of anxiety about family subsistence. The tendency for the hidden unemployed, despite more objective economic disadvantage, to express less subjective distress than the officially unemployed is even more clear on a measure of jobless-related stress. All jobless respondents were asked: "What is the *one* thing that bothers you most about not working full-time?" A full 72% of the officially unemployed emphasized financial problems, compared to 51.4% of the hidden unemployed. By comparison, only 16% of those not interested in working emphasized financial problems, with the majority reporting that nothing bothered them about not working full-time.

The tendency for the officially unemployed to react subjectively to economic difficulty with more intensity may be linked to their younger age or more frequent frustration in job search. Moreover, less intense subjective reactions among the hidden jobless may also be linked to other objective factors, such as sources of financial support, or to a range of psychological factors. With respect to sources of financial support, the hidden unemployed were indeed less likely than the officially unemployed to depend on temporary unemployment insurance. However, both the officially and hidden unemployed were equally likely to depend on family members or welfare assistance.

This chapter concludes with a comparison of the employed, officially unemployed, and hidden unemployed on two general measures of psychological well-being—global life satisfaction and sense of personal efficacy (Table 8.6). There are no striking differences, but as expected, the unemployed groups are consistently more likely than

Table 8.6

Comparisons of the Employed and Unemployed on Indicators of Psychological Well-Being

Psychological Well-Being Indicators	Employment-Unemployment Status [a] (% of sample)		
	Employed for Pay (N = 1199)	Officially Unemployed (N = 198)	Hidden Unemployed (N = 326)
Global Life Satisfaction In general, how satisfied are you with your life as a whole these days?			
Dissatisfied	20	37	31
Satisfied	80	63	69
Global Personal Efficacy Some people feel they *can run their lives* pretty much the way they want to; others feel the *problems of life are sometimes too big* for them.			
Problems of life too big	30	39	45
Can run own life	70	61	55

a. Excludes those not working and not interested in working.

the employed to express dissatisfaction with life and a low sense of efficacy in coping with life problems. For example, 37% of the officially unemployed were either somewhat or very dissatisfied "with life as a whole" compared to only 20% of the employed. Similarly, 45% of the hidden unemployed felt that "the problems of life are just sometimes too big for them" compared to only 30% of the employed. Therefore, the employed generally were more satisfied with their lives and more likely to feel that they could run their lives pretty much the way they wanted to. However, the rather small differences that emerged suggest that future inquiry should build on research that has begun to identify a range of naturally occurring protective mechanisms. Ongoing studies suggest that adaptive cultural resources among jobless African Americans may help reverse discouragement, reduce self-blame, and mitigate the deleterious psychological consequences of joblessness (Bowman, 1989; Feather & Davenport, 1981; Hill, 1971; Weiner, 1985).

Summary and Implications

As we begin the transition to the 21st century, chronic joblessness among Americans of African ancestry has become a critical issue with far-reaching consequences (Auletta, 1982; Bowman, 1988; Wilson, 1987). The rapid displacement of unskilled industrial jobs and continued racial antagonism has spurred the emergence of an unprecedented black jobless underclass which is increasingly entrapped in segregated inner city neighborhoods. National studies based on governmental data have been limited largely to gross black-white comparisons or related demographic analysis of official unemployment and labor force participation rates (Brimmer, 1988; Farley & Allen, 1987; Parnes, 1982; Sproat et al., 1985; Swinton, 1988). More qualitative studies, which have been based on small unrepresentative samples, have characterized particular subpopulations of the black jobless to highlight distinct patterns of pathology (Auletta, 1980), oppression (Glasgow, 1980), or coping (Ladner, 1973; Liebow, 1965).

Going beyond past studies, the national findings presented in this chapter have relevance for future research and public policy discourse related to black joblessness. We still know far too little about the nature, antecedents, and consequences of chronic joblessness among African Americans despite its growing severity and widespread implications. Figure 8.2 presents a conceptual model that links present findings to past and future research directions (Bowman, 1984, 1989; Bowman et al., 1982; Hill, 1971; Sproat et al., 1985). This model seeks to highlight critical issues to guide both more definitive research and more responsive public policy discourse on black joblessness.

Generally, the findings suggest that black joblessness should be viewed as a bi-dimensional social psychological concept that is influenced by a broad set of variables and has a wide range of human consequences. Conceptually, a meaningful consideration of African American joblessness must make the critical distinction between *official* and *hidden* unemployment. Despite their lack of active job search, the hidden unemployed were more similar to the officially unemployed than to those truly not in the labor force (not interested in working because of preferences for retirement, homemaker, student, or other roles). Data revealed that the only reason many among the hidden unemployed did not seek work as actively as the officially unemployed was because they had become so discouraged in their job

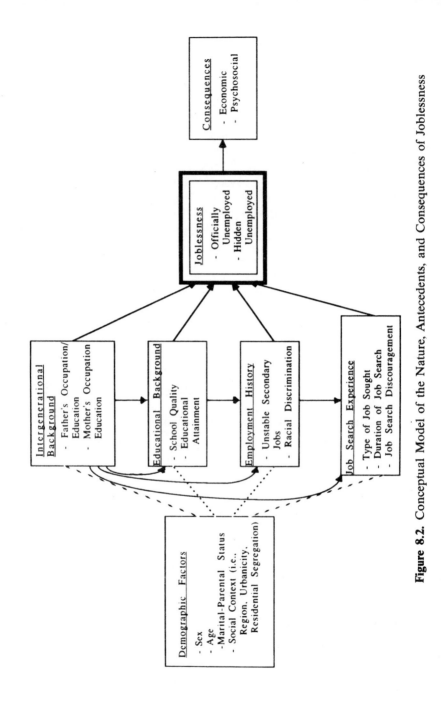

Figure 8.2. Conceptual Model of the Nature, Antecedents, and Consequences of Joblessness

search that they had completely lost hope of finding a job. Similarly, many among the officially unemployed had also begun to believe that job search was hopeless, which may well place them at high risk for reduced job search, labor force attrition, and a transition to hidden unemployment. Therefore, future research on black joblessness must go beyond official unemployment and also consider the apparently larger number of black Americans who want and need a job but for various reasons discontinue active job search.

With respect to antecedents, national studies must move beyond demographic profiles to clarify the joint effects of intergenerational factors, educational background, employment history, and job search experience. The present study suggests that occupation of father, displacement from unstable secondary jobs, and job search discouragement all may be important precursors of black joblessness—both official and hidden. We need to examine further how gender, age, marital-parental status, and urban underclass entrapment combine with these important precursors of joblessness. Moreover, educational attainment and sociocultural variables may mitigate the relationship between chronic joblessness and its potentially devastating human consequences. Future studies should also seek to clarify effects of both official and hidden unemployment on a wide range of economic and psychosocial consequences. For example, we need to better understand why the severe economic hardships associated with hidden unemployment were less often accompanied by psychosocial distress.

The national findings in this chapter, as well as more definitive studies based on the foregoing conceptual model, can inform public policy discourse on black joblessness. Given the caveats that must always be placed on the policy-use of comparative analysis of cross-sectional data, the practical relevance of present findings is less in the determination of program decisions and more in raising questions for policy discourse. Findings suggest that policy discussions on the issue of hidden unemployment among African Americans be broadened with a serious consideration of both race-specific and more general initiatives to confront broader postindustrial issues. It also appears that current policies that focus narrowly on black unmarried mothers should be broadened to consider ways to break the intergenerational link found between black fathers' secondary job difficulties and joblessness in subsequent generations.

Education and training policies seem especially urgent in efforts to break this link because of both their potential impact and their tendency to minimize ideological conflict in policy debates. Results suggest that public school policies need to shift the emphasis from "racially balanced schools" to policies that foster "effective schools" that graduate black students and prepare them to seek the advanced training necessary for employment in postindustrial America. Also, in addition to marketable skills, employment training targeted toward the chronically jobless in black communities should also prepare trainees to cope with unstable jobs, racial discrimination, and labor market changes. Deficit training strategies, which emphasize deep-seated pathologies, too often have concentrated on acculturation rather than on the academic, technical, and coping skills necessary to succeed in a rapidly changing and sometimes racially insensitive labor market. Findings also support the need to go beyond Affirmative Action to ensure that qualified black workers can compete fairly for primary sector jobs. In the short term, innovative community-based human service interventions should be encouraged to reduce the potentially devastating economic and psychological consequences of growing black joblessness—both official and hidden. In addition, some form of long-term industrial policy is needed to address the differential impact that postindustrial displacement of unskilled jobs is having on underprepared black workers who increasingly drop out of the labor force because of job search discouragement.

RETIREMENT

Rose C. Gibson

This chapter presents a global picture of the retirement experiences of black Americans. It begins with a basic framework of retirement as a dynamic phenomenon and proceeds through descriptive analyses of the National Survey of Black Americans (NSBA) data within this general model. The aim is to align findings from the NSBA with central features of the retirement constuct as an event, a role, and a precipitator of other life events. The purpose is to stimulate studies that will advance research on the retirement of black Americans in a concerted manner. Retirement broadly discussed, especially in a chapter of this size, perforce carries the price of a lack of thoroughness. This limitation warrants future in-depth examinations of particular questions raised by the present analyses.

Retirement is conceptualized here as a tripartite phenomenon composed of (a) the process of retirement that eventuates in the decision to retire, (b) retirement as a social role, and (c) retirement as a trigger of other life events (Atchley, 1976; Carp, 1972; George & Maddox, 1977; Streib & Schneider, 1971). The threats to validity in drawing conclusions about a dynamic retirement process from the cross-sectional NSBA data are far from trivial. Nonetheless, as we shall see, the retirement construct as dimensional and as an ongoing interplay of forces is a useful framework within which to approach analyses of the black retirement experience.

The chapter begins with a demographic profile of the black American retiree. Next, retirement as an event, a role, and as having consequences for the older black individual is discussed. The chapter closes with recommendations for new research on the retirement of black Americans.

Over 50 years of retirement research caution against analyzing retirement as a simplistic, discrete, and static phenomenon. Rather, it seems more productive to conceptualize retirement as continuing, giving momentum to, and being shaped by the interplay of both structural and individual factors. Within this model, considerable research attention has been devoted to the decision process as a component of the retirement construct. The decision to retire has been found to be influenced by poor health (Barfield & Morgan, 1969; Irelan & Bell, 1972; Kingson, 1980; Morgan, 1980a; Quinn, 1979; Reno, 1976; Streib & Schneider, 1971); socioeconomic status (Palmore, George, & Fillenbaum, 1982); financial readiness (the availability of a private pension in addition to Social Security) (Boskin, 1977; Bould, 1980; Morgan, 1981; Murray, 1979; Quinn, 1977); the interaction of poor health and financial readiness (Morgan, 1980b; Palmore et al., 1982); job dissatisfaction (Morgan, 1981; Parnes & Nestel, 1981; Quinn, 1977); extended periods of unemployment (Bould, 1980; Epstein, 1966); and work and retirement values and attitudes (Atchley, 1982a; Fillenbaum, 1971; Goudy, Powers, & Keith, 1975; Kimmel, Price, & Walker, 1978).

Despite the abundance of this research, social scientists have devoted relatively little attention to the retirement decision process among blacks. The findings of a few race comparisons do suggest, however, that blacks compared with whites are more likely to retire at earlier ages, retire because of poor health, have been forced to retire, have been unemployed in the 12-month period prior to retirement, and have reported job dissatisfaction and job search discouragement prior to retirement (Abbott, 1977; Bould, 1980; Gibson, 1982a, 1982b, 1982c, 1983; Morgan, 1980a, 1981; Palmore, Fillenbaum, & George, 1984; Palmore et al., 1982; Parnes & Nestel, 1981).

Taken as a whole, these two bodies of research suggest race differences in the retirement process, especially in the relative weights of factors that determine the retirement event. While poor health and disadvantaged labor market experiences appear more influential for blacks than whites, financial readiness seems to exert more influence for whites than blacks.

Poor health, unfavorable labor force experiences, and financial unreadiness (likely to be characteristic of the life courses of disadvantaged blacks in the present elderly cohorts) may be difficult to idenfity as discrete benchmarks of the transition into retirement for this group. On the other hand, more advantaged blacks, who experienced favorable health, labor force, and economic conditions over the life course, may see the retirement event more clearly as a transitional point (Jackson & Gibson, 1985). These contrasting lifetime work experiences of blacks, then, allude to subgroup differences in the black population in regard to the retirement decision process and its culmination in the retirement event.

Quite in contrast, the older black population seems less heterogeneous on the validity of financial unreadiness as a predictor of the retirement event because very few in the present elderly birth cohorts could look forward to postretirement private pensions, assets, investments, or annuities (Abbott, 1977). Thus, although health and work factors may be differentially valid as predictors of the retirement decision in subgroups of the black population, financial readiness may be an invalid construct in the retirement decisions of blacks regardless of subgroup membership.

The second dimension of the retirement construct, retirement as an achieved social role, has been analyzed within identity (Mutran & Reitzes, 1981), competing role (Gibson, 1987a, 1987b, 1988), and sick role theories (Chirikos & Nestel, 1983; Ellison, 1968). Competing role theory, extrapolated to retirement, suggests that individuals assume the retirement role when forced out of the work role, when the work role is no longer appropriate, or when the retirement role offers greater benefits than the work role.

The secondary gains of the disabled-worker role, as these benefits discourage adoption of alternate roles, have been the focus of both theoretical (Lamb & Rogawski, 1978; Ludwig, 1981; Prince, 1978) and empirical analyses (Chirikos & Nestel, 1983). The connecting theme of these analyses is that the greater economic and psychological benefits of the disabled-worker role encourage disadvantaged socioeconomic and racial groups to assume this role in preference to the less advantageous retirement role.

Gibson (1987a), moving this one step further, examined empirically the association between the disabled-worker and the retirement roles among blacks. Adoption of the disabled-worker role was found to be the major deterrent to adopting a retired role. Other factors found to discourage blacks' adoption of a retired role were an indistinct line between lifetime and old age work patterns, a recognition that occasional work is necessary well into old age, and an absence of income from private retirement pensions.

Focusing more specifically on the interplay of the disabled-worker role, its special rewards, and the retirement role, Gibson (1991c) identified a role adoption process among older blacks that began with perceptions of a discontinuous, disadvantaged work life and economic and psychological need. Perceptions of lifetime disadvantaged work decreased the propensity to adopt the retirement role; whereas both economic and psychological need decreased the inclination to assume a retirement role by first increasing the propensity to adopt the disabled-worker role. These findings also intimated that those blacks who experience disadvantaged work lives and pressing psychological and economic needs have more difficulty than advantaged blacks in assuming a retired role. The older black population also may be heterogeneous in the retirement identification process.

These studies on the secondary gain aspects of the disabled-worker role provide clear theoretical and some empirical grounds for analyzing retirement for blacks as a social role in competition with more attractive alternate roles. Thus, competing role theory shows considerable promise as a framework within which to analyze the retirement roles of blacks.

A third frequently examined dimension of retirement is the post-retirement milieu. Researchers have examined such diverse factors as morale (happiness, life satisfaction, and adjustment and satisfaction in specific life domains), physical and mental health status, and leisure and productive activities (Atchley, 1982b; Barfield & Morgan, 1969; Beck, 1982; Kimmel et al., 1978; Mutran & Reitzes, 1981; Palmore et al., 1984.)

Although this body of retirement research has increased steadily over the past two decades, work that focuses specifically on blacks (Lambing 1972a, 1972b) has not kept pace. Reducing the findings of a small number of race comparative studies to their essence, however, indicates that compared with whites, blacks postretirement are more disadvantaged physically, socially, and economically (Abbott, 1977; Beck, 1982; Bould, 1980; Campbell, 1981; Dowd & Bengston, 1978; Gibson, 1986a, 1986b, 1986c; Jackson, Bacon, & Peterson, 1977, 1978; Jackson & Wood, 1976; Morgan, 1980a, 1981; Orchowsky, 1979; Palmore et al., 1984; Parnes & Nestel, 1981; Stanford, 1983). These findings were generally interpreted to mean that race disparities in social, economic, and physical resources cause race disparities in morale. A few studies have suggested, however, that the racial distance in morale was not commensurate with the racial distance in resources (Beck, 1982; Campbell, 1981; Jackson, Chatters, & Neighbors,

1982; Parnes & Nestel, 1981). The speculations were that such factors as religion, supportive networks, and close ties with family moderate the effects of adversity on the well-being of older blacks (Ortega, Crutchfield, & Rushing, 1983; Watson, 1983).

Another explanation of the apparent race, resources, and morale interaction could be that the present cohort of elderly blacks is relatively better off socially and financially after retirement than before. Peace of mind brought about by the more dependable, if not more adequate, Social Security and Supplemental Security income has replaced the vagaries and vicissitudes of disadvantaged work and sporadic pay. Race not only seems to change the relationship between adversity and morale in retirement, but the relationship between work in old age and morale, as well. Although the morale of white retirees is frequently found to be lower than that of older white workers (e.g., Parnes & Nestel, 1981), the reverse seems to be true of black retirees. Black retirees have higher morale than older black workers (Jackson & Gibson, 1985). This difference in well-being between older black workers and retirees appears associated with adverse conditions in the labor force for older blacks who must work despite poor health.

In summary, retirement as a three-dimensional phenomenon—an event, a role, and a trigger of events—is a reasonable framework in which to begin to analyze the retirement of black Americans. Factors leading to the retirement event and their respective influences on the decision to retire, however, may be different for blacks and whites and for subgroups of the black population. Competing role theory seems a plausible framework in which to analyze social role aspects of black retirement, particularly the competing propensities to adopt the retirement and disabled-worker roles. Race disparities in health and socioeconomic status may not be commensurate with race disparities in morale. Certain factors may be buffering the effects of these adversities on the psychological well-being of blacks in retirement. We turn now to an analysis of some of these issues in the NSBA data within a general model of retirement as event, social role, and trigger of subsequent life events.

A Profile of the Black American Retiree

The NSBA sample of black elderly (aged 55 and over) was divided into three comparison groups to explicate ways in which different past and current work experiences of subgroups of the black population might differentially impact their experiences of retirement as an event, as a role, and as having certain consequences for the individual. Group 1, the workers (n = 142), were currently working 20 or more hours per week. Group 2, the retired (n = 252), were not working at all or working less than 20 hours per week and when asked the reason for not working or not working more, responded "retired." Group 3, the nonretired (n = 150), also were not working or working less than 20 hours per week, but when asked why they were not working (or not working more) gave reasons other than retirement. The distinction between the retired and the nonretired was their self-defined retirement. In 1979, as Table 9.1 indicates, about 26% of the 544 black elderly in the sample were working, 46% were retired, and 28% were nonretired. Thus, only half the sample was retired in the traditional sense.

A typical black retiree is poor (family income less than $6,000 per year), poorly educated (0–8 years of school), a former laborer or domestic worker, widowed, age 67 or older, and an urban and Southern dweller. This profile of the black retiree is consistent with most past research. The large proportion (79%) of traditionally retired blacks in the oldest age category is perhaps due in part to the rapidly increasing longevity of blacks aged 80 and over.

The picture of the nonretired is more dire than that of the retired. Comparing the nonretired, retired, and workers, the nonretired were the most likely to have family incomes in the lowest category, the working black elderly were the least likely, and the traditionally retired were in between these two groups. This ranking of the groups on income also held for education and occupation. The nonretired were the most likely to be poorly educated and to have worked in low-level occupations. Thus, the nonretired were in the lowest socioeconomic group; the working black elderly, as might be expected, were in the highest group; and the retired were in between.

The working elderly were slightly more likely than the retired and nonretired to be married, divorced, or separated and less likely to be widowed. This is perhaps a function of the differing age structures in the three groups. The working elderly tended to be younger, the traditionally retired older, but the nonretired were both young and old. It is interesting to note that about a third of the nonretired elderly were 67 years of age or older and still did not call themselves retired despite their nonworking status. Chronological age did not seem to be a criterion for self-defined retirement. The nonretired group also contained the largest proportion of women and individuals who lived in rural areas and in the South.

Summarizing to this point, this portrait of the black traditionally retired individual is consistent with past race comparative research that found the black retired to be poor, poorly educated, and widowed. The contrasting characteristics of the three groups, however, highlight the diversity of the older black population and identify the nonretired as an even more socioeconomically deprived subgroup of the black American elderly than are the retired. The disadvantaged nonretired have not been previously identified in race-comparative research.

The Retirement Event Among Black Americans

This section of the chapter focuses on the 252 traditionally retired individuals. They were not working full-time, were receiving some type of retirement pay, and viewed themselves as retired. In contrast to the nonretired, retirement seems more of an identifiable transition point from work to retirement for this group.

Table 9.2 indicates that the largest proportion of traditionally retired blacks had left the labor force early (before age 65). It is interesting, however, that nearly 15% of the group had retired at age 70 or older. These very old workers may be the group to which Jackson (1980) referred when she stated that blacks "die from" rather than retire from the work force. Prolonged labor force attachment, however, seems more characteristic of the few than the many.

The traditionally retired subsample was rather evenly divided on planned and voluntary aspects of the retirement event. About half had planned to retire, retired unexpectedly, retired willingly, and retired unwillingly. Among those who retired unexpectedly, poor health was the most frequently cited reason for retirement, followed by job-related and family responsibility reasons. Financial readiness was the least mentioned reason. This clear rank-ordering of poor health, job-related issues, and financial readiness supports the premise that financial readiness as an explanatory factor in the retirement decisions of blacks is an inappropriate construct.

This description of the retirement event among blacks parallels what is already known, that is, blacks tend to retire at early ages (Atchley, 1976; Gibson, 1982a, 1982b, 1982c; Morgan, 1980a) for reasons associated with job and poor health. Financial readiness, however, may be a more valid construct for whites than for blacks.

Table 9.1

Percentages Comparing the Characteristics of Working, Retired, and Nonretired Blacks Aged 55 and Older

Characteristics	Working	Retired	Nonretired
Total Family Income, 1978			
< $6,000 per year	25.2	65.4	72.9
$6,000 to $19,999	52.8	29.9	23.0
> $20,000	22.0	4.7	4.1
Total Respondents	123	208	122
Number of Grades of School Completed			
0 to 8 years	33.3	61.7	69.1
9 to 11 years	27.7	14.5	18.1
12 years	26.2	12.9	9.4
Some college, college graduate	12.8	10.9	3.4
Total Respondents	141	248	149
Occupation			
Professional, managerial	11.9	6.8	0.7
Clerical, sales, craftspersons	11.2	12.8	7.5
Operatives	18.2	17.6	10.2
Laborers, private household	26.5	34.3	35.0
Service	31.5	21.6	22.6
Not ascertained	0.7	1.0	2.0
Never worked	0.0	5.9	22.0
Total Respondents	142	252	150
Marital Status			
Married	42.3	37.3	37.3
Divorced, separated	24.7	12.7	16.0
Widowed	31.0	46.0	42.7
Never married	2.0	4.0	4.0
Total Respondents	142	252	150
Age in Years			
55 to 61 years	59.9	3.6	48.0
62 to 64 years	15.5	6.3	12.7
65 to 66 years	9.2	11.1	6.0
67 years or older	15.4	79.0	33.3
Total Respondents	142	252	150

Characteristics	Working	Retired	Nonretired
Sex			
Male	48.6	42.5	18.0
Female	51.4	57.5	82.0
Total Respondents	142	252	150
Urban/Rural			
Large urban	47.9	46.0	34.7
Small urban	28.2	29.0	25.3
Rural	23.9	25.0	40.0
Total Respondents	142	252	150
Region			
Northeast	21.8	15.5	14.0
North Central	21.8	18.7	15.3
South	47.9	62.7	66.0
West	8.5	3.1	4.7
Total Respondents	142	252	150

NOTE: Working means working 20 or more hours per week for pay. Retired means working less than 20 hours per week and giving the reason for not working as retired. Not retired means, although working less than 20 hours per week, the reason for not working or not working more was given as something other than retired.

Retirement as a Social Role Among Black Americans

A comparison of the lifetime and current work patterns of the traditionally retired and the nonretired is instructive. The different work experiences of these two groups suggest that the retirement event, being more ambiguous for the nonretired, results in this group's failure to view themselves as retired, thus rejecting the retiree role. Table 9.3 reveals that the retired were less likely than the nonretired to be currently working and, if working, were more likely to be working fewer hours. The retired also were more likely to have worked during their lifetime, to have had a full-time job, and to have worked full-time since they were age 18. Thus, the retired experienced more advantaged and continuous types of lifetime work patterns that terminated more abruptly, while the nonretired experienced more dis-

Table 9.2
The Retirement Event Responses of Traditionally Retired Blacks in 1979–80 ($N = 252$)

Characteristics	Percent of Sample
Age at Retirement	
< 55 years	13.8
55 to 64 years	44.8
65 years	11.3
66 to 69 years	15.5
70 years or older	14.6
Characteristics of the Retirement Event [a]	
Planned to retire	48.5
Retired unexpectedly	51.5
Retired willingly	56.4
Retired unwillingly	43.6
Reasons for Retirement [b]	
Job related	18.5
Age	7.5
Health	47.9
Other (e.g., personal, new interests)	4.2
Family responsibilities	12.3
Financial readiness	2.1
Mandatory	7.5

a. Categories are not mutually exclusive.   b. Multiple mentions are possible. Asked only of those who retired unexpectedly and are currently working less than 20 hours per week.

advantaged and discontinuous lifetime work patterns that apparently are still current.

These findings compare favorably with Gibson's (1987a, 1987b) multivariate findings which identified an indistinct line between lifetime and old age work patterns and occasional current work as factors related to a rejection of the retirement role. The findings also are in line with Gibson's (1991c) more recent work which suggests that adopting the retirement role is a process incorporating perceptions of a discontinuous work life, economic need, and the antagonistic propensity to adopt the disabled-worker role.

Lifetime and current work experiences, then, are differentiating factors in the older black population and provide some insight into why the meaning of the retirement role might be different for sub-

Table 9.3

A Comparison of Lifetime Work Patterns of Retired and Nonretired Blacks
Aged 55 and Older in 1979–1980

Work Patterns	Retired (N = 252) %	Nonretired (N = 150) %
Number of Hours Per Week Presently Working		
0 hours	94.0	86.0
0 to 10 hours	3.6	7.3
11 to 19 hours	2.4	6.7
Total Respondents	252	150
Previous Work Experience		
Never worked for pay	0.8	11.7
Worked for pay	99.2	88.3
Total Respondents	237	128
Full-time Work Experience		
Never had full-time job	5.1	15.4
Had full-time job sometime in life	94.9	84.6
Total Respondents	234	116
Job Permanency		
Never had regular, permanent job	3.1	0.0
Had regular, permanent job sometime in life	96.9	100.0
Total Respondents	192	82
Type of Job in Life		
Worked mainly in different jobs in life	39.1	41.2
Worked mainly in same job/occupation	60.9	58.8
Total Respondents	220	97
Part-time Work Experience		
Worked part-time some years since age 18	54.8	72.2
Worked full-time all years since age 18	45.2	27.8
Total Respondents	221	97

NOTE: Retired means working less than 20 hours per week and giving the reason for not working as retired. Not retired means although working less than 20 hours per week, the reason for not working or not working more was given as something other than retired. Varying totals for respondents in the categories are due to the fact that some respondents with differing work characteristics were asked different questions.

groups of the older black population. Thus, in accord with the Chirikos and Nestel (1983) and the Gibson studies, meanings of the retirement role for blacks may be most effectively studied within a
competing role theory framework by examining the relative benefits
of the disabled-worker and retirement roles.

Consequences of Retirement for Black Americans

The post-retirement milieu of traditionally retired blacks is described by comparing their data with those of the workers and the
nonretired. In general, the findings are not at odds with the idea that
the psychological resources of retired blacks are counterbalancing
some of the negative effects of poverty and poor health.

Economic Conditions

Table 9.4 suggests that most older blacks regardless of retirement
status are highly dependent on Social Security and Supplemental
Security Income (SSI). They virtually have no savings, investments,
or other assets. The retired were more likely than the nonretired to
receive some type of retirement pay, whereas the nonretired were
more likely to receive income from their own or spouse's work and
from public funds (e.g., welfare and Aid to Dependent Families with
Children). Contrary to conventional wisdom, few blacks in either retirement status group received financial assistance from family
or friends.

Although both the retired and nonretired were more likely to report income from single than from dual sources, the retired were
more likely to receive support from dual sources. The nonretired
were more likely to have packages composed of income from their
own or spouse's work and another source, while the retired were more
likely to have a combination of two types of retirement income. The
contrasting subject feelings of financial well-being between the retired and nonretired also reflect the more dire economic circumstances of the nonretired. They were more likely than the retired to
feel worse off financially than three years ago and twice as likely to
worry a great deal about bills (Table 9.5).

These findings, then, underscore the fact that the nonretired are
the most economically deprived group of the black elderly. And since
they are still contributing to their income through their own work

Table 9.4

A Comparison of Sources of Income of Retired and Nonretired Blacks
Aged 55 Years and Older in 1979

1978 Income	Retired (N = 252) %	Nonretired (N = 150) %
Single Source		
Welfare, ADC, AFDC, or food stamps	1.2	7.3
Social Security or SSI	30.2	23.3
Work of self or spouse (for pay or goods)	2.3	14.7
Retirement pay, pensions, or annuities	11.9	7.3
Savings, investments, or rental properties	0.8	0.0
Children, parents, other relatives, friends	1.6	2.7
Other governmental (Workmen's Compensation, disability pay, unemployment pay, or other governmental pay)	0.8	2.7
Not ascertained	6.0	7.9
Total Respondents	143	96
Dual Sources		
Work of self or spouse combined with another source (welfare, SSI, Social Security, retirement pay, family, or other governmental sources)	10.7	17.3
Welfare combined with another source (SSI, Social Security, or retirement pay)	4.8	2.7
Retirement pay, pensions, annuities, combined with another source (SSI, Social Security, or a second type of retirement pay)	18.7	2.7
Savings, investments, or rental property combined with another source (retirement pay, SSI, Social Security or other governmental pay)	2.8	2.0
Other governmental pay combined with another source	2.3	7.3
Family or friends combined with another source	3.6	4.0
Social Security combined with SSI	0.4	0.0
Total Respondents	109	54

NOTE: Within dual sources of income, the work category could include any of the other sources as a source second to work. All other categories exclude work as a second source. Categories do not sum to 100% because they are not mutually exclusive.

and disability pay, they may see the line between work and retirement less clearly. This ambiguity may in turn discourage adoption of a retired role.

Table 9.5
A Comparison of the Physical Health and Morale of Working, Retired, and
Nonretired Blacks Aged 55 and Older in 1979–1980

	Working %	Retired %	Nonretired %
Number of Health Problems			
None	16.9	12.7	2.7
One or more	83.1	87.3	97.3
Total Respondents	142	252	150
Extent to Which Health Problems Limit Work or Daily Activities			
No limiting health problems or have			
health problems that do not limit	57.0	31.0	18.0
Only a little	33.1	36.5	22.7
A great deal	9.9	32.5	59.3
Total Respondents	142	252	150
Satisfaction with Health Status			
Satisfied (very or somewhat)	85.2	87.7	70.7
Dissatisfied (very or somewhat)	14.8	12.3	29.3
Total Respondents	141	252	150
Better Off Financially Now Than 3 Years Ago			
Better	56.2	38.0	37.6
Same	32.8	47.6	39.6
Worse	11.0	14.4	22.8
Total Respondents	137	250	149
Worry About Bills			
Great deal	16.9	14.5	28.6
Little	25.7	23.8	25.9
None	57.4	61.7	45.5
Total Respondents	136	248	147
Life Satisfaction			
Very satisfied	44.7	54.4	46.0
Somewhat satisfied	43.3	33.6	36.0
Somewhat dissatisfied/very dissatisfied	12.0	12.0	18.0
Total Respondents	141	250	150

	Working %	Retired %	Nonretired %
Happiness			
Very happy	36.6	59.9	42.7
Pretty happy	54.2	32.9	46.7
Not too happy	9.2	7.2	10.6
Total Respondents	142	249	150
Personal Efficacy			
Low efficacy	39.6	33.3	43.2
Medium efficacy	19.4	22.0	27.7
High efficacy	41.0	44.7	29.1
Total Respondents	139	246	148
Got What You Hoped For Out of Life			
Mostly	69.5	79.4	68.7
Less	30.5	20.6	31.3
Total Respondents	141	247	147

NOTE: Failure of number of respondents in each category to equal column totals due to missing data. Working means working 20 or more hours per week for pay. Retired means working less than 20 hours per week and giving the reason for not working as retired. Not retired means, although working less than 20 hours per week, the reason for not working or not working more was given as something other than retired.

Physical Health

Although large proportions of all three groups had one or more health problems, the nonretired had the poorest physical health. They were the most likely to have health problems, be limited a great deal by these problems, and be dissatisfied with their health.

Morale

A majority of the traditionally retired seemed in fairly high spirits. Most were satisfied with life, were happy, had feelings of high efficacy, and felt they had received mostly what they had hoped for out of life. There were subgroup differences, however, that supported the speculation that leaving the labor force when black and elderly promotes psychological well-being. Morale, in fact, appeared to vary inversely as the number of hours spent in the labor force. The retired were the most likely not to be working, and exhibited the best psychological adjustment; the full-time workers exhibited the least; and the nonretired, who were part-time and sporadic workers, lie in between on this continuum of well-being. The retired were the most likely to be very satisfied with life, be very happy, report feelings of high personal efficacy, and have gotten what they had hoped for out of life. These higher feelings of personal efficacy among the retired than the working black elderly also are consistent with Gibson's findings (1982a) from longitudinal analyses of the Panel Study of Income Dynamics. In that study, feelings of control increased as older black female heads of household retired from the labor force.

Leisure Activities and Productive Behaviors of Retired Blacks

Focusing exclusively on the traditionally retired, the most common responses to a question asking how they spent their time in order of frequency were: housekeeping, leisure activities such as sports and hobbies, gardening, "nothing," sitting, and resting (Table 9.6). Only 9% of the responses were church or church-related. This was surprising given the purported centrality of religion and religious activities in the lives of older blacks. The finding is consistent, however, with Gibson's (1982c) longitudinal cohort analyses of the Americans View Their Mental Health data. In those analyses declines in religion and religiosity were observed within older black cohorts over a 19-year period.

A small percentage of the responses to the time-use question (about 7%) were reading, listening to the radio, watching television, visiting, and talking. Even smaller percentages of the responses were in the more productive behavior categories of caring for others, clubs, organizations, and volunteer work. And very few named travel. When asked what they liked best about retirement, one third of the retirees said "freedom," while a much smaller percentage said they missed their previous jobs. Nearly half of the retirees said they liked retirement, and about 43% said they had no problems with retirement. These figures (not shown in a table) do suggest that life out of the labor force is fairly good for older blacks.

In summary, the black retired are heavily dependent on public funds and in poor health and economic circumstances. Despite this lack of physical and economic resources, however, retired blacks seemed to maintain fairly high levels of morale (Gibson & Jackson, 1987;

Table 9.6
Leisure Activities and Productive Behaviors of Traditionally Retired Blacks
in 1979–1980 (*N* = 252)

Activities	*N*[a]	*Percent*[b]
Housekeeping	80	20.0
Gardening	52	13.0
Helping others	12	3.0
Church related	36	9.0
Clubs/Organizations	16	4.0
Sports, hobbies, other leisure (includes walk/exercise)	63	15.8
Travel	11	2.7
Reading, radio, television	26	6.5
Visiting, talking	28	7.0
Volunteer work	10	2.8
Paid work	5	1.0
Nothing, sitting, resting	51	12.7
Other	10	2.5
Total	400	100.0

NOTE: Multiple mentions were possible. The 252 respondents generated a total of 400 responses.
a. Number of responses in the category.   b. Percent of the total responses.

Jackson et al., 1977). There is a possibility, then, that certain factors moderate the negative effects of poor health and poverty on morale.

Discussion

This chapter presented a global picture of the retirement of black Americans, beginning with a basic framework of retirement as a dynamic phenomenon and proceeding with descriptive analyses of the NSBA data within this general model. The aim was to associate elements of the NSBA data with central features of the retirement construct as an event, a role, and a precipitator of other life events. The purpose was to initiate research seemingly lacking in the extant literature, but nonetheless critical to accumulating a systematic body of knowledge on black retirement. The cost of this broad discussion of black retirement was a lack of thoroughness. Therefore, several in-depth analyses warranted by the findings are discussed below.

In general, the findings in this chapter on the retirement experiences of black Americans were consistent with past race-comparative retirement research. Contrasting characteristics in three analysis groups, however, highlighted the diversity of the older black population on issues of work and retirement. A most deprived subgroup of the black American elderly was identified. This extremely disadvantaged group, the nonretired, was not only the most socioeconomically and psychologically deprived of the black elderly, but also had characteristics that departed most dramatically from traditional models of retirement as an event and social role. Ironically, this group by definition would be screened out of national retirement research, planning, and policy. The group merits future research focus.

Findings on the retirement event among blacks generally supported findings extant in the literature; that is, blacks tend to retire at early ages for reasons associated with job problems and poor health (Atchley, 1982b; Gibson, 1986a; Morgan, 1980a). The findings were contrary, however, to the idea that financial readiness is a valid construct for predicting the retirement process and decision. The influence of financial readiness on the decision to retire is apparently different for the races.

Differences also seem to exist within the black population on factors associated with the retirement process and the retirement event. Lifetime and current work experiences differentiated the sample and suggested different meanings of the retirement event for these subgroups of the black population. New research should investigate these differences in the retirement process and event between blacks and whites and among various subgroups of the black population. Such analyses should attempt to carefully monitor, describe, and explain the precursors of retirement over time and in juxtaposition to specific trends such as labor force, disability, and availablity of disability pay.

Competing role theory, because it allows for the secondary gains of the disabled-worker role as an alternate to the retirement role, seems a useful framework in which to study the different meanings of the retirement role for various subgroups of blacks. There is a need to identify the intricacies and timing of the relationship among work, disability, and retirement roles. What, for example, are some effects on black work and retirement roles of social trends and events? These secular trends would include the increasing availability of disability pay, increases in the physical disability of older blacks, their declining labor force participation, and aftermaths of the Civil Rights Movement.

Retired blacks in the NSBA had fairly high levels of morale despite low levels of physical and economic resources. Ways in which factors such as religion and social support moderate this adversity-morale relationship are important questions for new research. An analogous relationship is that race seems to change the relationship between work in old age and morale. Our findings supported past work which found older black workers to be the least well off in psychological well-being, the retired to be the best off, and the nonretired to lie in between these polarities on the well-being continuum. This set of findings seriously calls into question the utility of older worker programs for the present generation of black elderly.

A much neglected topic in retirement research, and one not dealt with in this chapter, is the extent to which blacks and whites differ on the role of gender in the definitions, process, event, and outcomes of retirement. Gender seems a less important factor in the retirement of blacks than whites (Gibson, 1987a, 1987b), because the work lives of black men and women have been much more similar than those of their white counterparts. A question that needs to be asked is whether the long history of black women in the labor force makes their retirement experiences distinct from those of their white counterparts who have been more recent participants.

Methodological Issues for New Research on Black Retirement

Because retirement is more productively thought of as dynamic, longitudinal in contrast to cross-sectional data would produce more valid descriptions of, inferences about, and explanations of the retirement process among blacks. The task for new research is to compare the races and subgroups of the black population on the timing and sequencing of events that lead to the retirement decision and postretirement conditions. The analysis of longitudinal data, however, requires several important considerations. First, there might be a confound of the effects of age, period, and cohort on the retirement process, event, and consequences. One approach to this problem is to alternately hold each of these types of effects constant while allowing the remaining two to vary—for example, repeating the measures at several points in time, following the aging of a birth cohort through time, and comparing several birth cohorts through cohort-sequential designs.

A second difficulty inherent in the analysis of longitudinal data on black retirement will be establishing the causal sequencing of such events and outcomes as job dissatisfaction, disability, and the various elements of the retirement process. The task here is to identify spurious relationships in the causal chain and alternate possible causes of the effect under investigation. Replications of these causal explanations of the retirement process should be attempted across data of different methods, times, places, and conditions. Findings from such multiple applications could lend greater confidence in hypothesized causal patterns. For those who would collect primary longitudinal data on black retirement, the close articulation of the longitudinal design of the study with the eventual analysis of the data is a crucial consideration (Gibson, 1989).

The dearth of research on the retirement process among blacks and race differences in this process is not justified because several high quality longitudinal and retrospective datasets exist for secondary analysis. Seldom have investigators capitalized on the longitudinal nature of datasets such as the Longitudinal Studies of Labor Market Experiences, The Panel Study of Income Dynamics, and the National Retirement History Longitudinal Survey (1969–1979), to name a few.

Retirement research cast in molds such as those recommended in this chapter could result in policy that more effectively enhances the lives of all groups of the retired in black America.

$$\boxed{10}$$

PHYSICAL HEALTH

Linda M. Chatters

In recent years the state of health among black Americans and other racial and ethnic minority groups has been of increasing interest. Research on health status and health service utilization has attempted to address a number of important questions concerning this population group's health. Despite advances in medical and scientific knowledge and accumulating information concerning the dissemination of health resources, improvements in the health status of minority groups generally, and blacks in particular, continue to lag behind that of whites. Information for one indicator, overall life expectancy, demonstrates that for whites, life expectancy is 74 years compared to 69 years for nonwhites and 68 years for blacks (U.S. Bureau of the Census, 1983). Analysis of the black-white differential in life expectancy (Keith & Smith, 1988) indicates that cardiovascular diseases, homicide, cancers, and infant death are the major contributors to the race differential among males. For females, cardiovascular diseases, cancers, homicide, and infant death contribute significantly to the racial disparity. Comparison of the male-female life expectancy differential within the black population indicates that cardiovascular diseases, nonmedical deaths (excluding suicides, homicides, and motor-vehicle accidents), cancers, and homicide are major contributors to the sex disparity in life expectancy.

Until recently, specific and directed attention to the health status of black and other minority populations (and their identified subgroups) was sporadic at best. (Harwood's 1984 edited volume on black health status and Jackson's 1988 edited volume on the status of older black adults are exceptions.) Previous efforts to describe the health of black Americans have been based on data in which limited numbers of black respondents were available in study samples and, as a consequence, the ability to examine subgroup variation in health among the black population was limited. Further, work in the area was frequently disjointed and fragmentary, lacking a clear and consistent focus on relevant health problems and indicators.

The public health and scientific communities, as well as the various agencies in the federal government concerned with issues of health, recognized these deficiencies in the knowledge base on black and minority health. The U.S. Department of Health and Human Services (DHHS) and the National Institute on Aging specifically addressed these problems in their efforts to review available information on the health of blacks and other minority groups. In 1985 the charge of the Secretary's Task Force on Black and Minority Health was to remedy this situation by compiling a comprehensive and integrated picture of the health status of black and minority America. Focusing on six broad categories of disease and injury (i.e., cancer; cardiovascular and cerebrovascular diseases; chemical dependency; diabetes; homicide, suicide, and unintentional injuries; and infant mortality and low birth weight), the Task Force sought to develop recommendations directed toward the expansion of the information base on minority health, as well to address health delivery and financing issues and human resource needs.

In 1986, the National Institute on Aging (NIA) commissioned a panel of experts in the areas of physical and psychosocial functioning to address issues of health status as they pertain to the aging black population. Their efforts, contained in the edited volume, *The Black American Elderly: Research on Physical and Psychosocial Health* (Jackson, 1988), are comparable to the work of the DHHS Task Force with regard to those diseases and illnesses that are prevalent among older persons. However, the NIA group addressed an expanded set of concerns as reflected in their emphasis on psychosocial functioning and mental health and their explicit focus on issues which are of particular significance to older persons and to the aging process (e.g., nutritional status, age differences in metabolic function, and medical drug interactions). *The Report of the Secretary's Task Force on Black and Minority Health* (DHHS, 1985) and *The Black American Elderly: Research on Physical and Psychosocial Health* (Jackson, 1988) are up-to-date and comprehensive treatments on the subject of black health and are valuable resources for students of minority health.

The research efforts represented by the National Survey of Black Americans (NSBA) dataset predate the activities of the DHHS Task Force on Black and Minority Health and the National Institute on Aging, and in addition, embody a somewhat different focus of concerns. Specifically, the NSBA sought to develop and test a collection of self-report measures of health status and service utilization in the context of a general survey of a representative sample of the adult black population. Further, the NSBA health measures investigated the individual's perceptions of health problems and concerns, attitudes toward the quality and adequacy of health care, and the relationship between specific aspects of personal health and other experences and behaviors. As such, the information obtained from the NSBA can be utilized as a complement to reports that are based on health and vital statistics data and provides a sense of the personal meaning of health to individuals. A particular strength of the NSBA data, as compared to several previous investigations of black health status, is the ability to examine group differences in self-reported health measures as defined by age, gender, socioeconomic standing, and other status dimensions.

The objectives of this chapter are to: (a) present information contained in the NSBA that is relevant to the health status of American blacks and (b) provide data on subgroup differences in health within the NSBA sample as defined by age, gender, and socioeconomic status. The chapter begins with a brief section profiling the health status of blacks in general, as defined by age, gender, and socioeconomic status. Next, the chapter provides a description of the health measures included within the NSBA dataset. Basic profiles of health are presented for the sample as a whole, and among identified age, sex, and socioeconomic subgroups.

A Health Profile of Black America

Current data on the health of black Americans indicates that significant disparities exist in their status relative to white Americans.[1] Black-white differences in life expectancy and years of life remaining at specified ages demonstrate significant and persistent disparities in the health of black Americans relative to the white population. Morbidity profiles and mortality statistics for major categories of disease and injury corroborate and elaborate the picture of poor health among blacks. The information summarized here on morbidity and mortality status focuses on the major groups of diseases and conditions that are most significant in their effects (i.e., leading causes of death and disability) on the health of blacks. Further, the diseases and conditions that are discussed in this chapter were represented in the NSBA survey. (Other significant influences on the health of blacks, which are not addressed in this chapter, include infant mortality and homicide.)

Major Causes of Morbidity and Mortality

The following section provides a summary profile of disease categories that represent significant causes of morbidity and mortality in the black population. Data on the collection of illnesses comprising cardiovascular and cerebrovascular diseases indicate that blacks are disproportionately represented (i.e., using various incidence and prevalence statistics) among persons having coronary heart disease, myocardial infarction, stroke, and end-stage renal disease, as well as associated risk factors for these diseases (i.e., hypertension, elevated cholesterol, cigarette smoking, and diabetes mellitus). Further, blacks have poorer outcomes from these conditions in the form of higher mortality rates from coronary heart disease, stroke, and sudden death from acute myocardial infarction.

In relation to cancers of various sites, blacks have the highest overall age-adjusted rates for cancer incidence and mortality of any group within the U.S. population (DHHS, 1985). Blacks demonstrate a lower survival rate for 22 out of the 25 cancer sites that are monitored by the SEER Program of the National Cancer Institute; the overall 5-year survival rate is 12% lower for blacks compared to whites. Blacks demonstrate higher incidence and mortality rates overall (for selected primary cancer sites), as well as for specific cancer sites (e.g., cervix, esophagus, prostate, stomach). Black women demonstrate higher incidence and mortality rates and poorer survival rates for cancers of the corpus uterus and breast relative to white women. Cancers, as a group of diseases, are particularly prominent among black men and indicate an overall profile of higher incidence and mortality.

Diabetes mellitus represents a group of disorders (i.e., non-insulin dependent diabetes mellitus, insulin dependent diabetes mellitus, and gestational diabetes) that have a disproportionate impact on the health of black Americans and other minorities. Non-insulin dependent diabetes mellitus (NIDDM) affects the majority of black Americans with diabetes. It has been suggested that significant numbers of the black population have undiagnosed or latent diabetes. The effects of diabetes mellitus on morbidity and mortality are wide ranging and frequently underestimated due to its implication in other serious conditions. Diabetes mellitus is associated with the development of stroke, heart disease, kidney disease, vascular disease and amputation, blindness, and a range of adverse pregnancy outcomes. Age and sex are recognized risk factors for several forms of diabetes, and in particular, black women are susceptible to the development of NIDDM and have higher diabetes mortality rates. Risk factors for the complications associated with diabetes include: limited access to health care; specific disparities in diabetes education, management, and care; and lifestyle differences (e.g., cigarette smoking, hypertension, and obesity) which are frequently associated with lower socioeconomic status.

Subgroup Differences in the Health of Black Americans

As evidenced by these broad health profiles for major diseases, the status dimensions of age, gender, and socioeconomic status (SES) occupy a critical position in defining the nature, distribution, and the course of the disease and illness experiences of black Americans. Social status position reflects crucial differences in the distribution of and access to material, social, and personal resources, which can be used to promote health. Status position, as defined by these dimensions, is related to the social roles (e.g., worker, spouse, and parent) that individuals occupy and which may have an impact on health phenomena. Specifically, factors that are associated with social roles (i.e., role behaviors, values) may be important for efforts to maintain health or relate to differential exposures to specific health risks (e.g., occupational hazards). Finally, social status position may shape general life conditions and circumstances, which represent specific risk factors for poor health status.

The decision to examine age, sex, and SES differences in the self-reported health of NSBA respondents was based on several considerations. A significant amount of work has investigated the unique contributions of each factor to health, and there are substantial literatures that describe the effects of age, sex, and SES on the health of population groups who vary on the basis of geography, culture, and historical period. Important conceptual and methodological issues and concerns related to research on age, sex, and SES differences in health have been discussed in a thorough and extended manner in critical reviews of the literature (McKinlay, 1972; Verbrugge, 1985). Further, these status dimensions have demonstrated their past utility in differentiating the health experiences of the black population. Age, sex, and socioeconomic status are of major importance in understanding the specific characteristics (i.e., prevalence, incidence, and risk factors) of those diseases and conditions that are most significant (i.e., leading causes of death and disability) to the health of black Americans.

NSBA Measures of Health Status and Service Utilization

This section of the chapter begins with a description of the measures of health status and service utilization that were employed in the NSBA (1979–80), followed by a presentation of descriptive and bivariate results. Then, multivariate findings are provided, and a summary of age, gender, and socioeconomic differences concludes the chapter.

NSBA respondents were asked a series of questions regarding their current health status and medicine use, the use of traditional and nontraditional health care resources, informal support resources for assistance when ill, subjective judgments of their health, and attitudes about the care that they receive from health and medical providers.[1] A general question asks respondents if they have had a health problem within the past month or so and the degree to which that problem was emotionally upsetting to them. The number of reported health problems and level of health disability were derived from a series of questions which asked respondents whether they had been told by a doctor that they had a particular health problem from among a list of 11 conditions. The number of health problems is a simple summation of reported and volunteered health conditions (a maximum of three additional mentions were coded). For the health disability measure, respondents who indicated having had at least one health problem were asked a subsequent question as to how much each identified problem kept them from working or carrying out their daily tasks.[2] Finally, respondents were asked to rate their overall satisfaction with their health status.

Respondents provided information on current medicine use (prescription and over-the-counter drugs). A follow-up question asked whether respondents ever missed taking their medication and the circumstances involved in failure to take medication. Several questions provided information concerning the use of health care resources. Respondents were asked if they had ever received medical help from a list of care providers (i.e., private doctor, public health clinic, independent nurse practitioner, visiting nurse, hospital emergency room, and hospital outpatient clinic) and their assessment of the level of assistance they received from each. Respondents also indicated whether they had ever utilized nontraditional practitioners and healers (i.e., faith healer, acupuncturist, astrologer, herbalist, and reader of tea leaves or palms).

Respondents provided information on their use of informal resources (e.g., family, friends, neighbors, and co-workers) for assistance when they were sick or disabled. A question addressing medical and health insurance coverage asks whether respondents are currently enrolled in such a plan. Finally, respondents assessed the level of difficulty they experienced in obtaining needed medical services and care and whether they thought that they needed medical care or treatment that they were not presently receiving.

Descriptive and Bivariate Findings

Descriptive findings and results for the full sample and identified subgroups are organized under the general categories of health status and medicine use, formal and informal health resource use, and health care coverage and adequacy. For the sake of brevity, bivariate analyses for gender, age, and socioeconomic groups focus primarily on instances of significant differences between status categories. Each of the independent factors was divided into discrete and mutually exclusive categories. The sample was divided into three broad age groups: 18 to 34 years, 35 to 54 years, and 55 years and older. Education was categorized as 0 to 11 years of education, high school graduate, some level of college training, and college graduate. Family income was divided into four groups corresponding to respondents with incomes below $5,000, $5,000 to $9,999, $10,000 to $19,999, and $20,000 and over.

Overall Health Characteristics

Health Status and Medicine Use

Overall, 35% of the sample indicate that they do not have any of the listed health conditions and volunteer no health problems.

Twenty-seven percent indicate they have one problem, 17% identify two health problems, and 10% have three problems. The remaining 11% of the sample indicate having four or more health problems, with a maximum number of nine conditions mentioned (mean = 1.44). The average level of disability from health problems is 1.7. The most prevalent health problems among this sample are high blood pressure (31.6%), arthritis (24%), and an unspecified nervous condition (21.9%). Considerably fewer respondents report having a kidney problem (9.6%), a blood circulation problem (8.6%), ulcers (8.7%), diabetes (7.1%), stroke (2.2%), cancer (2%), a liver problem (2%), and sickle cell anemia (1.5%). Twenty-seven percent of the sample (n = 574) indicate they had a problem with their health within the month prior to the interview. Of these individuals, 41% indicate it caused them "a great deal" of upset, 13% report "a lot," 35% state "only a little," and 11% say "not at all."

With regard to medicine (prescription and over-the-counter) use, 43% (n = 891) of the sample indicate they have taken a medication recently. Of this group, 47% indicate they sometimes fail to take their medicine at its scheduled time. Respondents cite adverse side-effects from the drug (55.3%) as the main reason why they fail to take their medicine, along with fear of dependency on the medicine (14.8%), the medicine being unavailable to them (13.6%), a lack of money to purchase the medicine (7.2%), a dislike of taking the medicine itself (1.4%), and other miscellaneous reasons (8.1%). Overall, respondents are largely "very satisfied" with their health (52%); 32% are "somewhat satisfied"; 12% are "somewhat dissatisfied"; and 4% are "very dissatisfied."

Formal and Informal Health Resource Use

Twenty percent (n = 422) of the sample respondents indicate they have never gone to a private doctor in an independent office setting. Among respondents who have seen a private doctor (n = 1,678), overall physician effectiveness ratings are high. Sixty percent indicate they received "a great deal" of help, while equal percentages (19%) of respondents report they received "a lot" and "only a little" help. Less than 2% report receiving no help at all. With reference to informal assistance during illness episodes, only 2% of the sample indicate they had no one from whom they could request help. Equal percentages (15%) of respondents report they have one or two individuals who would help them, while the majority of respondents (68%) indicate they have three or more persons who could help during an illness (an average of 2.5 helpers). Finally, only 9% of the sample (*n* = 192) report using nontraditional sources of assistance, such as a faith healer (51%), an astrologer (31%), a reader (38%), a root healer (28%), or an acupuncturist (11%).

Health Care Coverage and Adequacy

The majority of the sample (79%) is covered by health insurance, while the remaining 21% are uninsured. Perceptions of difficulty in receiving medical care indicate that 10% of the sample respondents report that it is either "very" or "fairly" hard to get medical services, while 26% indicate that it is "not too hard" and 64% state that it is "not hard at all." When asked whether they need more care than they currently receive, 12% of the sample indicate that they have unmet health care needs, while the majority of respondents (88%) judge their current level of care to be sufficient.

Gender Differences

Comparisons of health problems for women and men indicate that 42% of men report they do not have any of the doctor-diagnosed health problems listed, whereas only 30% of women have no health problems. The average number of health problems is 1.1 for men and 1.6 for women. Comparisons of average levels of disability from reported health problems indicate that women (1.73) report higher levels of disability from their health problems than do men (1.67). Similarly, women are significantly more likely to report they have particular health conditions or problems, specifically arthritis, cancer, high blood pressure, diabetes, a kidney problem, a nervous condition, and a blood circulation problem. Women are significantly more likely than men to indicate that they had a health problem within the past month and to report greater distress from that problem. Profiles of medicine (over-the-counter and prescription) use reveal women are more likely than men to take medicine. Of those respondents who do take medicine, women are less likely than men to adhere with taking their medicines. There are, however, no differences between men and women in the stated reasons why they miss taking their medicines. With regard to overall assessments of their health, women are more likely than men to indicate dissatisfaction with their health status.

Women are more likely than men to indicate they have sought medical help from a private doctor (office-based) and to report a higher level of physician effectiveness. Women are also more likely than men to have used a visiting nurse, public health clinic, emergency room, outpatient clinic, or nontraditional health resources. When asked about who would assist them in the event of illness, women and men report comparable numbers of helpers (averages of 2.51 and 2.47, respectively); women, though, are slightly more likely to indicate multiple helpers. Equal proportions of women and men are covered by health insurance. However, women are more likely than men to indicate they need more medical services than they currently receive and to report greater difficulty in receiving health care.

Age Differences

With regard to the number of identified health problems, younger respondents on average have fewer conditions than do older persons (18–34 years old, 0.81 problems; 35–54, 1.45; 55–101, 2.35). Fully half of the youngest age group report no health problems, compared to 31% of the middle-aged group and 11% of the older group; 40% of the oldest group have three or more conditions. Comparisons of average levels of disability reveal significant increases in limitations with age. The youngest group had an average disability score of 1.54, the middle-aged group had an average of 1.67, and the older group had an average of 1.88.

Age differences in the prevalence of particular conditions are noted, with increasing age being associated with reports of arthritis, high blood pressure, diabetes, kidney problems, liver problems, a blood circulation problem, stroke, and an unspecified nervous condition. Age comparisons for ulcers indicate that the middle-aged group has the highest prevalence, followed by the older group, and then the younger age group. The oldest group is four and a half times more likely (55%) than are young respondents (12%) and three times more likely than middle-aged respondents (36%) to report they have high blood pressure. For diabetes, older respondents (17%) are 17 times more likely than young respondents (1%) and nearly three times more likely than middle-aged respondents (6%) to report having the disease. Similar age gradients, from young to old, are noted for blood circulation problems (2.8%, 7.9%, 18.2%) and stroke (0.2%, 0.5%, 7.1%).

Age is positively and significantly related to whether the respondent has had a problem with health in the month prior to the interview. However, young and middle-aged groups are more likely than older respondents to indicate that health problems upset them "a great deal" or "a lot." Medicine use is highest among the oldest group of respondents and older persons are more likely than young and middle-aged persons to adhere to taking their medicine. Middle-aged respondents have the lowest adherence. There are no significant age differences in the reasons why medicine is not taken. Overall, the likelihood of being "very satisfied" with health decreases across the three age groups, whereas reports of being "somewhat satisfied" increase with age.

Age is positively and significantly related to having seen a private doctor, as are perceptions of physician effectiveness. Older respondents, however, are significantly less likely to have used a public health clinic, a nurse practitioner, or emergency room facilities. Middle-aged respondents are significantly more likely than younger and older respondents to have used an outpatient clinic. Among persons using emergency rooms, age was positively associated with perceived effectiveness. Older respondents have fewer individuals to whom they can turn for help when ill, on average, 2.3 persons, compared to 2.5 for middle-aged and 2.6 for young persons. Fully three quarters of the young group indicate that there are three or more persons whom they could call upon for help when ill, whereas 70% of the middle-aged and 55% of the old group indicate a similar level of informal resources. Age is significantly and positively related to the likelihood of having health insurance coverage. There are no age differences in the perception of needing additional medical services and care. Although all three age groups clearly endorse the view that obtaining required medical services is not difficult for them, middle-aged respondents are nearly unanimous in that perception, with 92.4% indicating that it is "not too hard" or "not hard at all."

Income and Educational Attainment Differences

Income level is negatively related to the number of identified health conditions. Among persons with family incomes of less than $5,000 a year, 23% report that they are without health problems (average of 2.1 health conditions). An average of 1.4 health conditions are found for persons with family incomes of $5,000 to $9,999; 32% of this group are without health problems. For persons with incomes of $10,000 to $19,999, 41% have no identified problems, with an average of 1.1 health conditions; and for the family income category of $20,000 and above, 44% are without health problems, with an average of 1.0 health conditions. Comparing groups with the lowest (less than $5,000) and highest (greater than $20,000) incomes, persons in the highest income category are almost twice as likely to report that they have no identified health problems. Average disability levels indicate a similar significant decrease in disability accompanying increases in income.

Lower levels of family income are associated with an increased likelihood of having particular health conditions. Comparing the lowest to the highest income categories, persons with the lowest incomes are twice as likely to have ulcers, a kidney problem, and high blood pressure; 2.5 times as likely to have arthritis and a nervous condition; three times as likely to have diabetes; four times as likely to have a blood circulation problem; and 6.5 times as likely to suffer stroke. Although lower family income is associated with having had a health problem in the month prior to the interview, income groups are comparable in the amount of distress this problem caused. Lower income groups are more likely to indicate that they take medications, although there are no income differences in adherence. Overall, higher incomes are associated with the likelihood of being "very satisfied" with one's health, while lower incomes are related to greater dissatisfaction with health.

Persons with higher family incomes are more likely to report having seen a private doctor, although there are no income differences in perceived effectiveness of physicians. Lower family incomes are associated with having used a public health clinic and visiting nurse; and persons with lower incomes are more likely to rate public health clinics as being effective in addressing their problem. Lower levels of family income are associated with fewer informal helpers; among persons reporting incomes less than $5,000, close to 5% indicate that they have no informal helpers and 54% indicate that they have three or more persons who could help in the event of illness (mean = 2.28). In comparison, only 1% of respondents with incomes ranging from $5,000 to $9,999 are without informal resources and 69% have three or more support persons (mean = 2.53). Comparable figures for income ranges of $10,000 to $19,999 indicate that less than 1% have no informal help resources and 72% have three persons to help during illness (mean = 2.56); for incomes in excess of $20,000, 1% have no informal helpers and 78% indicate the presence of three helpers (mean = 2.6).

Income is significantly and positively related to whether respondents have health insurance coverage. Persons with higher incomes are more likely to report that the medical services they currently receive are adequate for their needs, whereas those with lower incomes endorse the opposite view. Similarly, persons with higher incomes are less likely to indicate difficulty in obtaining needed medical care. Among respondents with family incomes greater than $20,000, 3.2% report that it is "very" or "fairly" hard and 79.4% state that it is "not hard at all." In contrast, among persons with incomes of less than $5,000, 15.8% state that it is "very" or "fairly" hard, and 54.5% indicate that obtaining needed services is "not hard at all."

Educational differences in health status, to some extent, mirror those found for income. However, persons with lower levels of education, especially the category represented by respondents who have no formal education to 11 years of schooling, are particularly distinctive from groups with higher levels of educational attainment. Among persons with 0 to 11 years of education, 24% have no health problems (averaging 1.87 problems), as compared to high school graduates, of whom 42% are without health problems (averaging 1.16 problems); persons with some college, of whom 45% have no health problems (with an average of 1.06 problems); and college graduates, of whom 44% are without problems (averaging 0.91 problems). Average levels of disability from health problems significantly decrease with increasing levels of education.

With few exceptions (i.e., a liver problem, cancer, sickle cell anemia), educational level is negatively associated with the presence of particular health problems. Several conditions, however, clearly demonstrate substantial differences between persons with the lowest level of education (0–11) and those possessing more years of education. Respondents with 0 to 11 years of education were two to three times more likely than persons with more schooling to have arthritis, twice as likely to have high blood pressure and diabetes, and between one-and-a-half and three times as likely to have a nervous condition. Similar to findings for income level, the likelihood of taking medicines is highest among the least educated. (There are no education differences in adherence rates.) In contrast to findings for income, educational level is unrelated to both whether one had a health problem in the month prior to the interview and overall ratings of satisfaction with health.

Educational level is positively related to the likelihood of having gone to a private doctor. Physician effectiveness ratings are highest for respondents with the highest and the lowest levels of educational attainment (69.8% of college graduates and 62.3% of persons with 0 to 11 years report receiving "a great deal" of help), whereas persons with some college training are least favorable in their assessments of physicians (25.2% report "only a little" help or "none at all"). College graduates are the least likely to have used a public health clinic. Although there are no significant education differences in the use of emergency rooms, persons with 0 to 11 years of education rated them as being more effective. Increases in educational level are associated with increases in the proportion of respondents who report the availability of three or more informal helpers. Sixty-one percent of persons with 0 to 11 years versus 78.3% of college graduates report having three or more helpers.

Parallel to findings for family income, educational level is significantly and positively related to the likelihood of having health insurance coverage. Persons with fewer years of education are more likely to state that they need additional medical services, with persons with 0 to 11 years of education (14.7%) endorsing that view at close to twice the rate of college graduates (7.7%). College graduates are the group most likely to feel that obtaining needed medical care is not difficult (78.6% state "not hard at all") and least likely to report difficulty in actually obtaining care (2.7% state "very hard" or "fairly hard"). In contrast, persons with the lowest level of education are the least likely to report that obtaining care is not difficult (56.5% state "not hard at all") and the most likely to state that it is "very" or "fairly" hard to obtain the care they need (14.6%).

Multivariate Analyses

To examine the independent effects of age, gender, income, and education, regression analyses of selected health indicators were conducted using an expanded set of demographic factors (i.e., region, urbanicity, and marital status, in addition to the four primary variables) as predictors (see Table 10.1). Although several significant relationships which are consistent with previous work are noted, for the most part the amounts of explained variance are low. The regression for number of health problems indicates that being older, female, possessing lower levels of income and education, and residing in the North Central region (as opposed to the South) are associated with having more health problems (R^2 = 23%). In a similar manner, age, income, and education are significant predictors of the average level of disability from health conditions (R^2 = 12%). Older respon-

Table 10.1
Selected Health Indicators Regressed on Demographic Factors

Predictors	Number of Problems	Average Disability	Health Satisfaction	Informal Resources	Difficulty Getting Care
Age	.028 (.002)[c]	.003 (.001)[a]	−.00 (.001)	−.004 (.001)[b]	−.008 (.001)[c]
Gender					
Men	−.461 (.068)[c]	−.06 (.04)	.13 (.041)[c]	−.12 (.04)[b]	−.06 (.03)
Income	−.045 (.008)[c]	−.02 (.005)[c]	.017 (.005)[b]	.02 (.005)[c]	−.03 (.005)[c]
Education	−.05 (.011)[c]	−.03 (.006)[c]	.007 (.007)	.011 (.007)	−.03 (.006)[c]
Marital Status					
Widowed	−.039 (.11)	−.04 (.06)	−.01 (.07)	−.17 (.06)[a]	.17 (.06)[b]
Separated	.11 (.11)	−.05 (.06)	−.04 (.07)	−.02 (.06)	−.07 (.06)
Divorced	.10 (.10)	−.08 (.06)	−.08 (.06)	.00 (.06)	−.09 (.06)
Never married	−.08 (.09)	−.10 (.06)	.07 (.05)	−.09 (.05)	−.15 (.05)[b]
Urbanicity					
Rural	−.03 (.08)	−.02 (.05)	.06 (.05)	.04 (.05)	.07 (.04)
Region					
Northeast	−.006 (.09)	.02 (.05)	−.12 (.05)[a]	−.19 (.05)[c]	.02 (.05)
North Central	.17 (.08)[a]	.03 (.05)	−.00 (.05)	−.22 (.05)[c]	−.06 (.04)
West	.17 (.13)	.03 (.08)	.01 (.08)	−.19 (.08)[a]	−.10 (.07)
Adjusted R^2	.23	.12	.026	.057	.078

NOTE: Several predictors are represented by dummy variables; Gender, 0 = women, 1 = men; Marital status, married is the excluded category; Urbanicity, urban is the excluded category; Region, South is the excluded category.
a. $p < .05$;   b. $p < .01$;   c. $p < .001$.

dents, women, and those with lower incomes (and residents of the North Central and Northeast regions) are significantly more likely to have had a health problem in the month prior to the interview (Table 10.2). Degree of emotional distress (analysis not shown) associated with the problem is higher among women and residents of the Northeast ($R^2 = 2.3\%$). Satisfaction with health (Table 10.1) was predicted by gender, income, and region; women, persons with lower incomes, and residents of the Northeast had lower satisfaction ($R^2 = 2.6\%$).

Table 10.2

Logistic Regressions for Health Indicators

Predictors	Recent Health Problem	Unmet Health Care Needs
Age	.013 (.00)[b]	−.01 (.00)[b]
Gender		
Men	−.80 (.12)[c]	−.15 (.16)
Income	−.03 (.01)[a]	−.07 (.02)[c]
Education	−.02 (.02)	−.06 (.02)[a]
Marital Status		
Widowed	−.18 (.18)	.41 (.25)
Separated	.23 (.18)	.26 (.25)
Divorced	−.04 (.18)	−.18 (.27)
Never married	−.15 (.17)	.18 (.21)
Urbanicity		
Rural	−.04 (.15)	.14 (.19)
Region		
Northeast	.38 (.15)[a]	.09 (.21)
North Central	.33 (.14)[a]	.21 (.19)
West	.45 (.23)	.43 (.31)
Chi-square	114.43	52.67
df	12	12

NOTE: For health indicators, 0 = no, 1 = yes. Several predictors are represented by dummy variables: Gender, 0 = women, 1 = men; Marital status, married is the excluded category; Urbanicity, urban is the excluded category; Region, South is the excluded category.
a. $p < .05$;   b. $p < .01$;   c. $p < .001$.

With regard to health resource use (Table 10.3), several demographic factors are particularly salient as predictors (i.e., age, gender, urbanicity) in logistic regression analyses. The likelihood of having seen a doctor is lower among younger persons, men, persons with lower incomes and education, and those residing in rural areas. Use of a public health clinic is predicted by younger age, being fe-

Table 10.3

Logistic Regressions for Health Resource Utilization

Predictors	Private Physician	Public Health Clinic	Nurse Practitioner	Visiting Nurse	Outpatient Clinic	Emergency Room
Age	.029 (.005)[c]	−.02 (.00)[c]	−.02 (.00)[b]	−.01 (.00)	−.00 (.00)	−.02 (.00)[c]
Gender						
Men	−.92 (.13)[c]	−.38 (.10)[c]	.12 (.18)	−.98 (.25)[c]	−.29 (.10)[b]	−.39 (.11)[c]
Income	.08 (.01)[c]	−.07 (.01)[c]	.00 (.02)	−.02 (.02)	−.03 (.01)[a]	−.01 (.01)
Education	.09 (.02)[c]	−.03 (.01)	−.02 (.03)	−.07 (.03)	−.00 (.01)	−.03 (.01)
Marital Status						
Widowed	.23 (.24)	−.11 (.18)	.44 (.34)	.06 (.33)	−.20 (.18)	−.17 (.18)
Separated	.20 (.23)	.12 (.18)	−.08 (.35)	.33 (.31)	.01 (.18)	.22 (.20)
Divorced	.27 (.23)	.09 (.16)	−.12 (.33)	.06 (.31)	.10 (.16)	−.12 (.18)
Never married	−.19 (.17)	.29 (.14)[a]	.39 (.23)	−.28 (.30)	−.12 (.15)	−.43 (.15)[b]
Urbanicity						
Rural	−.65 (.15)[c]	−.04 (.13)	.20 (.23)	−.80 (.29)[b]	−.42 (.14)[b]	−.45 (.13)[b]
Region						
Northeast	.18 (.19)	.16 (.14)	.28 (.23)	−.28 (.27)	.49 (.14)[c]	.19 (.15)
North Central	−.07 (.17)	.07 (.13)	−.47 (.26)	−.23 (.25)	.54 (.13)[c]	.24 (.14)
West	.19 (.30)	.03 (.22)	.25 (.35)	−.68 (.53)	1.01 (.21)[c]	.44 (.24)
Chi-square	183.09	163.22	30.92	44.40	80.79	101.81
df	12	12	12	12	12	12

NOTE: For all health resource utilization variables, 0 = no, 1 = yes. Several predictors are represented by dummy variables; Gender, 0 = women, 1 = men; Marital status, married is the excluded category; Urbanicity, urban is the excluded category; Region, South is the excluded category.
a. $p < .05$; b. $p < .01$; c. $p < .001$.

male, lower income levels, and never having been married. The sole predictor of use of a nurse practitioner is age (younger individuals are more likely than older persons to use this resource); whereas use of a visiting nurse is predicted by being female and residing in an urban area. Use of an outpatient clinic is predicted by being female, lower income, living in an urban area, and residence in all regions except the South. Finally, emergency room use is less likely among older persons, men, persons who have never been married (as contrasted to married), and those residing in rural areas. Regressions for perceived effectiveness of health care resources (not shown) are significant in only two cases—physicians and emergency rooms. Being a woman, older, a resident of the South, and having higher levels of education are significant predictors of higher physician effectiveness ratings (R^2 = 3%). Negative assessments of emergency rooms are predicted by younger age, lower income, and residing in the North Central and Northeast regions (R^2 = 2%).

The regression for number of informal helpers (Table 10.1) indicates that younger persons, women and those with higher incomes have more helpers than their counterparts; those who are widowed and reside in the West, Northeast, or North Central regions have fewer helpers than do married persons and Southerners (R^2 = 6%). Persons who are younger and possess fewer financial and educational resources are significantly more likely to state that obtaining needed medical care is difficult for them (R^2 = 7.8%); further, persons who are never married feel that obtaining services is not difficult, whereas the opposite is true of widowed persons. Respondents with few financial and educational resources are more likely to state that they need more services than they currently receive, whereas older persons are less likely than younger persons to report unmet health care needs (see Table 10.2).

Summary and Discussion

These analyses demonstrated that age, gender, income, and education statuses were significantly related to and predictive of several self-report indicators of health among black Americans. Similar to other reports, women's poorer health status was reflected across a variety of indicators (i.e., number of problems, medicine use, resource use) and accompanied by reduced levels of overall satisfaction with health. Gender was not a significant predictor of average disability associated with health problems, despite the fact that women had more problems than did men. Bivariate relationships suggesting that women experienced more difficulty in receiving care and had unmet needs for health care were not significant when other factors were controlled. Women demonstrated a higher likelihood of using various health resources and rated their physicians' performance more positively than did men. Further, women were more likely than men to report multiple sources of informal assistance in the event of illness.

Age differences in these indicators demonstrate that older persons were more likely than young groups to be in poor health and to express dissatisfaction with their health status. Despite a greater tendency to experience recent health problems, older persons were not different from their young counterparts in terms of reported distress. Older persons were the most likely of all age groups to use a doctor and to rate his or her performance positively, but were less inclined to utilize other sources of health care. Although older persons were most likely to have health insurance coverage (bivariate analyses) and least likely to perceive a need for more services, they reported fewer informal help resources to assist them in the event of illness. Finally, increasing age was associated with the opinion that obtaining health and medical services was not difficult.

Consistent with other reports, income and education differences revealed better health was associated with higher position on these status factors. Surprisingly, both income and education were significant and positive predictors of number of health problems and average level of disability. However, only income was positively related to overall satisfaction with health. Although income was negatively related to the occurrence of a recent health problem, it bore no relation to the distress that such a problem might cause. Both education and income were related to whether respondents took medication, but neither was important with regard to adherence. Income and education were related to the differential use of various health care resources; higher status was associated with the use of exclusive (i.e., private physician) versus public sources of care (i.e., public health clinic, outpatient clinic). Surprisingly, there were no income or educational differences in the use of emergency rooms as a source of care, although persons with higher incomes rated emergency room assistance more favorably. Greater numbers of informal health resources were associated with higher levels of income and education. Persons from lower income and education groups tended to be uninsured, perceived greater need for additional medical services, and reported more difficulty in receiving care.

Although not the primary focus of this chapter, urbanicity, marital status, and region emerged as significant predictors in several of the multivariate analyses. The findings suggest that the use of informal and formal health resources, in particular, is related to the organizational and contextual circumstances associated with the distribution and use of health care resources. The use of various formal health care resources (i.e., physicians, outpatient clinic, emergency room) was most likely to occur in areas where such resources and facilities are concentrated, essentially in urban as opposed to rural settings. The pattern of findings for utilization support the observation that health care in rural areas is characterized by a shortage of primary health care personnel, services, and facilities. Interestingly, living in a rural area was not associated with poorer self-reported health, the perception that obtaining medical care was difficult, or the presence of unmet health care needs. To a lesser degree, the South demonstrated a similar differential pattern of utilization as compared to all other regions (i.e., reduced use of outpatient clinics). In the area of informal health resources, individuals who as a group possessed more informal social resources (i.e., married persons) were more likely than others to report greater numbers of persons who could assist during illness.

Particularly intriguing were those findings which suggested that, as compared to the South, residents of other regions of the country were in poorer health (i.e., number of health problems, the occurrence of and distress from a recent health problem), held more negative attitudes in regard to their health status and the agents which provide care (i.e., health satisfaction, physician and emergency room effectiveness), and had fewer resources to provide informal care (i.e., number of helpers). Continuing research is needed to address the nature of urbanicity and regional effects on health status, attitudes, and perceptions.

The primary objectives of this chapter were to investigate age, gender, income, and education differences in self-report measures of health status, health resource utilization, and health care perceptions. The collection of findings corroborates other sources in indicating that poorer health is associated with being older and female. Overall, more diverse resource use was found among women; men and older persons were disadvantaged with regard to the use of informal care. With the exception of private physicians, older respondents were less inclined to use health care resources and were less likely to perceive that they required additional care. Higher status on income and education was consistently related to better health among these respondents.

As might be anticipated, greater financial resources were associated with the use of exclusive versus public health care providers, the perception that obtaining care was not difficult, and reports that additional health care services were not required. However, the relative absence of informal health resources among the less economically advantaged suggests that, in addition to the scarcity of formal resources, they may be particularly vulnerable to the effects of sickness and disability. This finding runs counter to notions regarding the nature of the informal support networks of black Americans, in particular among those who are economically disadvantaged. The finding suggests that economic poverty is related to an impoverishment of social resources as well.

In this respect, older individuals similarly demonstrated poorer health, a reliance on physicians as a predominant source of care, and relatively few informal resources. However, in contrast to low income and education groups, older respondents reported that it was not difficult to obtain health services and that their current level of formal assistance was adequate for their needs. As has been suggested, the Medicare program has removed the financial barrier to health care among older adults. Important questions remain, however, as to the adequacy of that care relative to the health profiles (i.e., greater objective need for services) of older persons (Dutton, 1978). Further, changes in the management of health care costs associated with hospital stays implemented since the completion of the NSBA will place new demands on informal care networks that potentially jeopardize the health of persons with the least resources (i.e., the poor and the elderly).

Notes

1. Question wording for the NSBA health items is provided below.

HEALTH PROBLEM WITHIN PAST MONTH: Over the past month or so, have you had health problems? (If yes) How much did that upset you?—*a great deal* (4), *a lot* (3), *only a little* (2), or *not at all* (1)?

HEALTH PROBLEM LIST: I am going to read a list of health problems. After each one, please tell me whether a doctor has told you that you have that problem. (If yes) How much does this health problem keep you from working or carrying out your daily tasks? Would you say *a great deal* (3), *only a little* (2), or *not at all* (1)? The list of conditions include: (1) arthritis or rheumatism, (2) ulcers, (3) cancer, (4) hypertension or high blood pressure, (5) diabetes or "sugar," (6) a liver problem or "liver trouble," (7) a kidney problem or "kidney trouble," (8) stroke, (9) a nervous condition, (10) a blood circulation problem or "hardening of the arteries," and (11) sickle cell anemia.

HEALTH SATISFACTION: In general, how satisfied are you with your health? Would you say you are *very satisfied* (4), *somewhat satisfied* (3), *somewhat dissatisfied* (2), or *very dissatisfied* (1)?

MEDICINE USE: Have you taken any medicine in the past month or so that is supposed to be taken at a certain time—like every day or every so many hours? (If yes) Do you ever miss taking your medicine? (If yes) Why does this happen?

HEALTH RESOURCE USE: I'm going to read you a list of places where people go to get medical help. After I read each one, I'd like to know if you have gone to that place or person when you needed medical help. (If yes) How much help were you given—*a great deal, a lot, only a little,* or *none at all?* The list of places include: (1) private doctor, (2) a public health clinic, (3) a nurse in his or her own office, (4) a visiting nurse, (5) a hospital emergency room, and (6) a hospital outpatient clinic.

NONTRADITIONAL HEALERS: Here is a list of other people one might go to for help. Please tell me if you have gone to any of these people. The list included: (1) faith healer, (2) a person who does acupuncture, (3) a person who heals with roots and herbs, (4) a person who practices astrology or reads zodiac signs, and (5) a person who reads tea leaves, roots, or palms.

INFORMAL RESOURCES: Please look at this list of people. Is there anyone on this list who would give you help if you were sick or disabled? (Who is that?) The list included: (1) husband/wife/partner, (2) son, (3) daughter, (4) father, (5) mother, (6) brother, (7) sister, (8) other relative (please specify), (9) friend, (10) neighbor, (11) co-worker, and (12) other (please specify).

HEALTH INSURANCE COVERAGE: Are you presently covered by any health insurance plan like Blue Cross or Medicaid?

ACCESS TO MEDICAL TREATMENT: Overall, how hard has it been for you to get medical treatment or health services that you have needed? Would you say it has been *very hard, fairly hard, not too hard,* or *not hard at all?*

ADEQUACY OF MEDICAL CARE: Do you think that you need medical care or treatment that you are not getting now?

2. Disability values were summed across health problems, resulting in scores with a total possible range of 1 (which represented one health problem at the lowest level of disability) to 42 (indicating 14 health problems at the highest level of disability). The disability scores were then transformed by the addition of the value 1, resulting in a possible range of 2 to 43. Persons who were without health problems (and consequently without identified disabilities) were designated as the first level of the disability measure.

11

MENTAL HEALTH

Harold W. Neighbors

Studies focusing on the issue of race and mental health conclude that there is no clear evidence that African Americans are prone to higher rates of mental illness than whites (Neighbors, 1984a), despite the fact that African Americans are disproportionately exposed to social conditions considered to be antecedents of psychiatric disorder. Thus, the key epidemiologic issue is identifying factors that influence the occurrence of psychiatric morbidity in blacks. Research that examines rates of emotional distress, stressors African Americans face, and coping strategies used to adapt to those stressors is needed.

The Program for Research on Black Americans' fundamental premise has been that mental health models are of important practical significance. Particular health interventions are derived from the etiologic hypotheses suggested by the perspective employed. Because the concepts of mental health and mental illness are socially constructed on the basis of cultural conceptions of normality and abnormality, most groups hold differing perspectives on its psychopathology. Competing models of mental health and related phenomena are different in their underlying assumptions, implications, and intervention strategies. For reasons stated below, the National Survey of Black Americans (NSBA) investigated mental health issues through the use of a stress and adaptation perspective.

The concept of *stress* should be viewed as characterizing a discrepancy between demands impinging on a person and that individual's capacity to deal effectively with those demands and not to any one noxious thing or state (Mechanic, 1978). Such discrepancies are commonly assumed to be associated with psychological distress and the need felt for outside assistance.

There are two reasons why the stress and adaptation paradigm is a particularly useful framework within which to conceptualize issues related to African American mental health. First, this orientation places as much emphasis on environmental and situational factors as causes for psychological distress as it places on intrapsychic factors. This is especially important for African Americans (and other minorities) whose personal distress may be more a function of socially induced problems than individual predispositions toward mental illness. Second, the stress concept focuses attention on some of the more positive aspects of black coping—successful problem solving.

One of the aspects of the process by which African Americans cope with the stresses and strains of everyday life is seeking professional assistance in response to serious personal problems. The major impetus for the research comes from a review of the literature comparing rates of mental illness in blacks and whites (Fischer, 1969; Kramer & Rosen, 1973; Warheit, Holzer, & Arey, 1975). Despite extensive research, the epidemiologic literature is inconclusive in its assessment of black mental health status. The major reasons are the operational definition of the mental health/illness construct, mainly, the reliance on small unrepresentative samples, which contributes to the inability to analyze major population subgroups and the failure of studies to take black coping capacity into account (Kessler & Neighbors, 1986).

One method of investigating the issue of African American mental health status has been the comparison of how blacks and whites utilize public mental health facilities (Fischer, 1969). These utilization rates have been employed to argue that African Americans have higher rates of severe psychiatric disease than whites (Fried, 1975). Such conclusions are unwarranted. Rates derived from treatment figures only yield information about African Americans who have entered the professional health care system. Using utilization rates as estimates of the total prevalence of psychiatric illness contains the implicit assumption that morbidity is the equivalent of need for and eventual use of professional services. However, subjective symptomatology is not always defined as a psychiatric problem by the lay public. When the problem is defined in this manner, it still does not translate into the use of help, much less the demand for professional assistance (Rabkin, 1986). As a result, no definitive statement can be made about black mental health status based solely on utilization rate studies.

Treatment rate studies raise more questions about black help seeking than they answer about black mental health status. This is because admission to treatment is also related to a number of social factors affecting the help-seeking process. In fact, when it comes to African Americans, researchers have neglected the social processes that take place between the realization of a serious personal problem and actual entry into the professional helping system (McKinlay 1972, 1975). Thus, research on black help seeking must move toward investigating these intervening mechanisms. For example, it is generally accepted that health status or "need" is the major determinant of the decision to use professional services. As a result, to clarify why various population subgroups are more likely to use help, differential need must be taken into account. Although health status is important, its role should not be overemphasized to the exclusion of investigating other social and social psychological factors that may also have a significant impact on the use of professional help (Zola, 1973). These factors, which affect who seeks professional help and who does not, need further investigation to expand our understanding of African American help-seeking behavior and the meaning of official utilization statistics.

Given the amount of research on blacks, morbidity, and the use of help, much still is not known, especially about help-seeking differences within the African American population. One reason for this lack of knowledge is that most utilization studies focus only on race comparisons. Although in an exploratory sense it is important to know whether blacks and whites differ on various health behavioral measures, racial comparison studies that are not supplemented by more comprehensive investigations appear simplistic and limited. This is especially true if the goal is to advance knowledge about how African Americans cope with the distress they experience. To argue that it is enough to know whether blacks exhibit more or less of a specific behavior vis-a-vis whites is a naive assumption. The ability to describe the variability in help seeking within the black community is a major strength of the NSBA. By investigating African American help seeking in this manner, a more complete understanding of the various forces that influence how African Americans use professional help should be achieved.

The African American Help-Seeking Process

Theoretical Orientation

The majority of work on African Americans' use of professional services has been conceptualized within the sociodemographic approach, a research orientation that seeks to demonstrate that users of professional helping facilities have demographic characteristics that differ from nonusers (McKinlay, 1972). Although this approach has provided much useful information, such investigations have been criticized as being limited because they reveal only that demographic variables are associated with utilization measures and do not attempt to explain why the associations exist.

The social psychological approach to studying professional utilization is based on the view that individuals' health behaviors are dictated by the way they perceive the world. The present help-seeking study attempts to improve the shortcomings of the demographic approach by including two social psychological variables that influence the relationship between various demographic variables and professional help use.

Conceptual Model of Help Seeking

The section of the NSBA (1979–80) questionnaire designed to study help seeking was organized around the concept of a "stressful episode." The inquiry was based on the assumption that, although the majority of African Americans function at an adequate level, at some point they will experience a major life crisis, will be significantly upset by that problem, attempt to cope with it by various means, and in most instances return to their previous level of functioning. Instead of describing the mental health or illness of the African American population, the NSBA was more concerned with ascertaining the interplay of coping mechanisms and environmental stressors.

Taking such an orientation to the study of how African Americans cope with crises meant attempting to describe behaviors, which actually take place over a period of time. This is especially difficult when the analysis is confined to a cross-sectional dataset. The model used to guide the present analysis is based on a stage approach to help seeking. Although in many respects these stages are arbitrary delineations that overlap and blend with each other, the model is useful in helping order the analysis in a logical sequence corresponding to the typical stages that African Americans seeking assistance pass through.

There are a number of comprehensive help-seeking models described in the literature (Chrisman, 1977; Mechanic, 1978; Suchman, 1965). The NSBA (1979–80) relied most heavily on two particular models. Gurin, Veroff, and Feld (1960) developed an index designed to measure public commitment to the view that personal problems should be taken to specialized professional resources for treatment. This "readiness for self-referral" index was conceptualized as the following series of stages. (a) problem definition, (b) the decision to go for help, and (c) where to go for help. Kadushin (1958) also outlined a stage model of help seeking specifically having to do with the process of entering psychotherapy. To reach treatment, Kadushin stated that a person must (a) feel that an emotional problem exists, (b) decide whether to discuss the problem with others, (c) decide to seek professional help, (d) decide on a specific professional area, and (e) choose a particular therapist.

Based on a critical review and a synthesis of these two models, a stage model of black help seeking was developed and used as a general framework around which to organize data collection and analysis efforts pertaining to the use of professional helping resources among black Americans (Neighbors, 1982). The specific decision points corresponding to the stages used in this study were: (a) the realization that something is wrong, (b) the decision to get help, (c) the decision to seek professional help, and (d) the choice of a particular source of professional help. This chapter is concerned with the variables that impact on the decision to seek professional help and the choice of a specific professional help source.

Although the NSBA was greatly influenced by Kadushin's (1958) model and by the Gurin and colleagues (1960) index, certain modifications were made. Gurin's group was particularly interested in the public's acceptance of the idea that "personal" or "emotional" problems should be referred to professional resources for treatment. Although the NSBA was indeed interested in whether or not African Americans sought professional services in an effort to deal with their problems, it did not limit inquiries only to that area. In addition to the use of professional help, the NSBA was also interested in other coping responses used by blacks to adapt to personal problems. Therefore, it was decided not to take Gurin and associates' (1960) approach of asking people "if they had ever gone to a special place for handling personal problems" (p. 259). Instead, respondents were asked if they had ever experienced a serious personal problem and, if so, what they had done about it. Although other coping responses have been analyzed (Neighbors & Jackson, 1984; Neighbors & LaVeist, 1989), this chapter focuses only on the use of professional help.

Overview

The Variables

The two social psychological variables included in the present analyses are problem severity and problem type. Problem severity, which is viewed as an approximation of how much the personal problem interfered with the person's ability to perform his or her usual social obligations, is a dichotomous variable constructed from a set of five questions (Neighbors, 1985). Specifically, respondents who indicated that their problem brought them to the point of a nervous breakdown represent problems of "high" severity, whereas those who experienced their problem at some point "beneath" the nervous breakdown point represent "low" problem severity. To operationalize issues relevant to differential problem definition, each respondent who had experienced a problem was asked to tell about it. This question was designed to ascertain how the respondent conceptualized the nature of the distress experienced and the specific locus to which they attributed the cause of their personal distress. Responses were categorized into five problem categories: physical health problems, interpersonal difficulties, emotional adjustment problems, death of a loved one, and economic difficulties.

To measure professional help utilization, respondents were presented with a list of professional helping facilities and asked if they had gone to any of the places listed for help with their personal problem. This professional help list included the following places: hospital emergency room, medical clinic, social service agency or welfare agency, community mental health center, private mental health therapist (psychiatrist, psychologist), private physician, minister, lawyer, police, school, and employment agency.

Analysis Approach

It has been argued that utilization research should focus less on the simple bivariate relationships between sociodemographic variables and use and more on the multivariate relationships (Crandall & Duncan, 1981; McKinlay, 1972; Mechanic, 1975). One advantage of the NSBA is that the group studied comprises the first nationally representative probability sample ever drawn on the black population, resulting in the opportunity to utilize multivariate analysis techniques not possible in prior studies. Although bivariate relationships are reported, emphasis is placed on the multivariate structure of these data in order to clearly specify when a particular demographic relationship to help use is modified by some other variable.

The multivariate analysis approach is a multidimensional contingency table analysis using loglinear modeling procedures (Knoke & Burke, 1980). A more detailed explanation of this technique can be found in Neighbors (1984b) or Neighbors and Jackson (1984). This approach was chosen because it handles nominally scaled variables well, especially dichotomous dependent variables, and is sensitive to interactions among the independent variables, which is particularly relevant to the groups of variables to be analyzed below (Greenley & Mechanic, 1976). Loglinear analysis allows tests for the significance of partial association, regardless of the number of categories or level of measurement in the associated variables. In addition, it tests the significance of interactions where the control variable has many categories, including higher order interactions involving a combination of control variables (Davis, 1974; Veroff, Kulka, & Douvan, 1981).

Results

The help-seeking analysis results are presented in the following two sections. The first section focuses on the decision to seek professional help; the second focuses on respondents who sought professional help, specifically, how the demographic and social psychological variables relate to the use of four professional help resources, in particular medical organizations, physicians, human service organizations, and ministers. In each section, the bivariate relationships of problem severity and problem type to utilization are discussed first. Then, the sections report the bivariate associations between four sociodemographic variables (family income, education, gender, and age) and the use of help. Finally, the multivariate relationships among the variables are explored.

The reported results focus on 1,324 respondents, who reported experiencing a serious personal problem. Almost half (47.4%) of the respondents who experienced a problem felt it took them to the point of a nervous breakdown. The majority of these respondents (41.4%) defined their distress as being caused by an interpersonal difficulty, 21.6% were upset because of an economic problem, 16% were suffering from a physical health problem, 11.9% mentioned an emotional problem, and 9% said the death of a loved one caused them to be upset. A little less than half (48.7%, $n = 631$) of the respondents with a problem sought some form of professional help.

Findings From the National Survey of Black Americans

The Decision to Seek Professional Help

Following the conceptualization of help seeking as a decision-making process, the relationships of the demographic variables and the personal problem characteristics to the decision to seek some type of professional help will be analyzed. The decision to seek professional help was operationally defined by a dichotomous variable indicating the number of respondents with a problem who sought help from at least one of the following professional helping services: hospital emergency room, medical clinic, private physician, private mental health therapist, community mental health center, social services, minister, school, employment agency, and lawyer.

The relationships of problem severity and problem type to the decision to seek professional help are presented in Table 11.1 (column 1). Having experienced a problem at the nervous breakdown level increases the likelihood of seeking professional help. Table 11.1 also reveals that the type of problem experienced has an effect on the decision to seek professional help. Professional help use is most often reported by persons with physical health problems. For other types of personal problems, a little less than half of the respondents sought help.

Table 11.2 (column 1) presents the relationships between income, education, gender, age, and the decision to seek help. Neither income nor education is significantly related to the decision to seek professional help. On the other hand, gender and age do show relationships to professional help use. Women are more likely than men to seek help, while the younger (18–34 years old) age group is slightly less likely than the two older groups (35–54 and 55 years or older) to seek professional help.

Results of the loglinear analysis show that none of the four demographic variables is significantly related to the decision to seek pro-

Table 11.1
Bivariate Relationship of Personal Problem Characteristics to Help Seeking

Problem Characteristics	Deciding to Seek Help (%)	Using Medical Organization (%)	Using Private Physician (%)	Using Human Services (%)	Using Ministers (%)
Severity					
High	55.1[c]	27.3	39.9[a]	35.5[c]	32.3
Low	42.8	21.4	31.7	19.0	29.7
Type					
Physical	69.5[c]	51.5[c]	66.2[c]	23.8	22.3[c]
Interpersonal	48.9	17.9	29.6	27.1	35.0
Emotional	42.9	20.0	35.0	38.3	25.0
Death	43.8	21.7	34.8	21.7	54.3
Economic	45.7	14.7	18.1	35.3	24.1

NOTE: Percentages in column 1 are based on the 1,324 respondents with a personal problem. Percentages in columns 2 through 5 are based on the 631 respondents who sought professional help and are not mutually exclusive.
a. $p < .05$; b. $p < .01$; c. $p < .001$.

Table 11.2
Bivariate Relationship of Demographics to Help Seeking

Demographics	Deciding to Seek Help (%)	Using Medical Organization (%)	Using Private Physician (%)	Using Human Services (%)	Using Ministers (%)
Income					
Low	50.4	32.8[c]	36.2	33.8[b]	31.7
High	45.5	15.3	35.6	22.2	33.0
Education					
0 to 11 years	49.4	26.3	39.8	30.5	28.6
12 + years	48.2	23.3	33.2	26.0	33.0
Gender					
Male	42.4[c]	24.6	27.3[b]	21.9[a]	29.5
Female	51.8	24.6	39.7	30.4	31.7
Age					
18 to 34 years	44.4[a]	16.3[c]	22.1[c]	26.6	35.7
35 to 54 years	53.3	25.8	40.9	32.0	27.1
55 years or older	51.1	37.8	54.5	23.8	28.7

NOTE: Percentages in column 1 are based on the 1,324 respondents with a personal problem. Percentages in columns 2 through 5 are based on the 631 respondents who sought professional help and are not mutually exclusive.
a. $p < .05$; b. $p < .01$; c. $p < .001$.

fessional help when personal problem characteristics are taken into account. In all four instances, the best-fitting loglinear model contains a significant two-way effect for problem severity and a two-way effect for problem type. This is not surprising for income and education because these two factors were not related to use in the bivariate analysis. For gender and age, however, the bivariate associations with professional help use are eliminated when personal problem characteristics are taken into account.

Table 11.3 reveals that respondents whose problems brought them to the point of a nervous breakdown are about 1.6 times more likely to utilize some form of professional help, regardless of the type of problem they experienced. In addition, respondents with physical health problems are almost three times more likely than persons with economic problems to seek professional help. Respondents with other types of problems (interpersonal, emotional, and death) do not differ much from persons with economic problems in terms of help seeking. These effects are independent of problem severity.

Use of Specific Professional Help Sources

The relationship of professional help use to personal problem characteristics and the demographic variables among those people who did decide to seek professional help (n = 631) is explored

Table 11.3
Odds Ratios Describing the Effects of Problem Type and Problem Severity on the Decision to Seek Professional Help

Problem Characteristics	Sociodemographics			
	Income	Education	Gender	Age
Type				
Physical/Economic	2.74	2.86	2.84	2.87
Interpersonal/Economic	1.22	1.17	1.15	1.14
Emotional/Economic	.85	.90	.91	.90
Death/Economic	.92	1.00	.94	.98
Severity				
High/Low	1.66	1.66	1.66	1.66

NOTE: Preferred loglinear models: {TU} {SU} {ITS}; {TU} {SU} {ETS}; {TU} {SU} {GTS}; {TU} {SU} {ATS} where U = utilization; S = problem severity; T = problem type; I = income; E = education; G = gender; A = age.

through the use of four dichotomous (yes, no) variables: (a) medical organizations (which include hospital emergency rooms and medical clinics); (b) private physicians' offices; (c) human services organizations (community mental health centers, social services, and private mental health therapists), and (d) ministers. Persons who said they had sought professional help were allowed to mention as many as four places contacted. As a result, the analysis combines multiple mentions if a respondent had indeed contacted more than one professional help source. In coding the data in this manner, some multiple users may appear in the yes category more than once, depending on which particular professional help sources they contacted. Thus, a respondent who had contacted both a physician and a minister would be counted as using help during the analysis on physician use as well as when the use of ministers is analyzed (Neighbors, 1986; Neighbors & Taylor, 1985).

Medical Organizations

Table 11.1 (column 2) reveals that problem severity is not related to the use of medical organizations. Problem type, however, shows a strong relationship to use. As might be expected, persons with a physical health problem are much more likely to seek help from a medical organization than persons with other types of problems. Specifically, about half of the respondents with a physical health problem sought help, while only about one fifth of the people with other types of problems sought help.

Looking at the demographic variables' relationship to medical organization use, Table 11.2 (column 2) reveals that only income and age are related to the use of this professional help source. The poor are more likely than the rich to seek help; and the older one is, the higher the likelihood of using a medical organization for a personal problem. The results of the multivariate analysis indicate that income and age remain related to the use of medical organizations when problem severity and problem type are taken into account. The relationship of income to the use of medical institutions, however, is conditional on problem type. Table 11.4 shows that low income respondents are not very different from high income persons in the use of medical institutions for physical health and death problems. For economic and emotional problems, however, the low income group is 2.75 times more likely to use this particular professional help source. The income difference in the use of medical institutions for

Table 11.4

Odds Ratios Describing the Effects of Problem Type on the Use of Medical Organizations for Income and Age

Problem Type	Income (Low/High)	Age (Older/Younger)	Age (Middle/Young)
Physical	1.13	1.22	1.37
Interpersonal	4.60	1.46	1.06
Emotional	2.82	19.68	11.22
Death	1.19	.85	3.38
Economic	2.75	2.66	1.02

NOTE: Preferred loglinear models: {ITU} {ITS}; {ATU} {ATS} where U = utilization; S = problem severity; T = problem type; I = income; A = age.

interpersonal problems is particularly striking. Here, the low income group is more than 4.5 times more likely than the upper income group to utilize medical organizations.

The relationship of age to use is also affected by problem type (Table 11.4). Utilization of medical organizations does not differ by age for physical health problems or interpersonal problems. The oldest group is 2.5 times more likely than the 18- to 34-year-old age group to use medical institutions for economic problems. The middle age group (35–64 years old) does not differ from the youngest group in the use of medical organizations for economic problems. While the youngest and oldest age groups do not differ in the use of medical institutions for death problems, the middle-aged group is over three times more likely to use this professional help source for death problems than the youngest group and 2.5 times more likely than the oldest group. The largest age effect occurs for persons with emotional problems. Both the 35- to 54-year-old group and the 55 years or older group are much more likely than the youngest group to utilize medical organizations for this type of problem. Specifically, the oldest group is 19 times more likely to utilize them, while the middle group is 11 times more likely.

Private Physician

Table 11.1 (column 3) reveals that both problem severity and problem type are significantly related to seeking help from a private physician. People with a problem at the nervous breakdown level are more likely than respondents with less serious problems to utilize physician services. Persons with a physical health problem are the most likely to seek help, whereas people with economic problems are the least likely to take their problems to the doctor. About one third of the people with interpersonal, emotional, or death problems seek help from a physician.

Table 11.2 (column 3) shows that neither income nor education are associated with physician use. Gender and age, on the other hand, are significantly related to seeking help from physicians. Women are more likely than men to see the doctor, and physician use increases with age. Exploring physician use for the demographic subgroups, taking problem severity and type into account, reveals that gender and age remain significantly related to the use of the doctor, regardless of problem severity or problem type (Table 11.5). Women are almost twice as likely as men to contact a physician. The older group (55 years or older) is 2.5 times more likely to see the doctor than the 18 to 34 year olds, regardless of problem type or problem severity. Those between the ages of 35 and 54 years old are almost twice as likely as the youngest age group (18–34 years old) to contact a physician. Again, neither problem type nor problem severity make a difference in this relationship.

Table 11.5
Odds Ratios Describing the Effects of Gender, Age, Problem Type, and Problem Severity on the Use of Physicians

	Gender	*Age*
Problem Type		
Physical/Economic	9.10	7.22
Interpersonal/Economic	1.70	1.83
Emotional/Economic	2.22	2.11
Death/Economic	2.11	2.16
Problem Severity		
High/Low	1.48	1.62
Gender		
Female/Male	1.85	
Age		
Older/Young		2.62
Middle/Young		1.92

NOTE: Preferred loglinear models: {SU} {TU} {GU} {STG}; {SU} {TU} {AT} {ATG} where U = utilization; S = problem severity; T = problem type; G = gender; A = age.

Human Services

Table 11.1 (column 4) shows that although problem severity is related to the use of human services, problem type is not. As has been the case, the more serious the problem, the more likely help will be sought. Table 11.2 (column 4) reveals that only two demographic variables, income and gender, are significantly related to the use of human services in the bivariate sense. Persons with low family incomes are more likely to utilize human service organizations than respondents with high incomes, and women are more likely than men to seek help from human service organizations.

Some interesting patterns emerge when looking at the multivariate analysis. Although income remains related to human services use, net of the effects of problem severity, or problem type, the bivariate association between gender and use is eliminated. Furthermore, the relationship of age to the use of human service organizations is conditional on problem severity. Table 11.6 shows that low income respondents are a little more than 1.5 times more likely to utilize human services than high income persons, regardless of the seriousness or the type of problem. Looking at age (Table 11.7), among those respondents categorized as high problem severity, the young (18-34 years old) and middle groups (35-54 years old) are 1.7 times more likely to utilize human service organizations than the older group. On the other hand, for low problem severity, the middle and older groups do not differ from each other. Here, the youngest group (18-34 years old) is distinctive, using human services at a rate 55% less than the middle and older groups.

Minister

Table 11.1 (column 5) reveals that problem severity is not related to the use of ministers. Problem type, however, is related to seeking help. Persons who experienced the death of a loved one are most likely to seek help, while about one third of those with interpersonal problems seek help from a minister. Not more than one quarter of the respondents with other types of personal problems (physical health, emotional, and economic) utilize ministers.

Turning next to the demographic variables, Table 11.2 (column 5) shows that neither income, education, gender, nor age is related to seeking help from ministers. In all cases, no demographic subgroup differs very much from the marginal utilization rate of about 32%. The multivariate analysis revealed that education, gender, and age

Table 11.6
Odds Ratios Describing the Effects of Income, Problem Type, and
Problem Severity on the Use of Human Service Organizations

	Odds Ratio
Income	
Low/High	1.66
Problem Type	
Interpersonal/Physical	.95
Emotional/Physical	2.13
Death/Physical	.71
Economic/Physical	1.57
Problem Severity	
High/Low	2.25

NOTE: Preferred loglinear model: {SU} {TU} {IU} {STI} where U = utilization; S = problem severity; T = problem type; I = income.

Table 11.7
Odds Ratios Describing the Effects of Age and Problem Severity
on the Use of Human Service Organizations

| | Age | |
Problem Severity	Younger/Older	Middle/Older
High	1.81	1.73
Low	.45	1.16

NOTE: Preferred loglinear model: {ASU} {AST} where U = utilization; S = problem severity; T = problem type; A = age.

remain unrelated to the use of ministers. Income, however, is related to the use of ministers, but this relationship is conditional on problem type (Table 11.8). High income respondents are about 40% more likely than low income respondents to use ministers for a physical health problem and 25% more likely to use them for interpersonal problems. On the other hand, low income respondents are about 30% more likely than high income respondents to seek help from ministers for economic problems, 40% more likely for emotional problems, and four times more likely to contact a minister for death problems.

Table 11.9 provides an overall summary of the results on African American help seeking from the NSBA. This table shows that although none of the four demographic variables was significantly related to the decision to seek professional help, both problem severity and problem type were. Specifically, experiencing a problem at the nervous breakdown level and interpreting distress as caused by a physical health problem increased the likelihood of turning to a professional for assistance. Table 11.9 indicates that neither problem severity nor problem type is related to the use of medical organizations (in the bivariate sense), and problem type interacts with both

Table 11.8

Odds Ratios Describing the Effects of Income and Problem Type on the Use of Ministers

Problem Type	Income (Low/High)
Physical	.58
Interpersonal	.77
Emotional	1.38
Death	4.22
Economic	1.29

NOTE: Preferred loglinear model: {ITU} {ITS} where U = utilization; S = problem severity; T = problem type; I = income.

Table 11.9

Summary of Multivariate Findings on Help Seeking

	Decision to Seek Help	Medical Organization	Private Physician	Human Services	Minister
Problem Characteristics					
Severity	{SU}		{SU}	{SU}	
Type	{TU}		{TU}	{TU}	
Demographic Variables					
Income		{ITU}		{IU}	{ITU}
Education					
Gender			{GU}		
Age		{ATU}	{AU}	{ASU}	

NOTE: U = utilization; S = problem severity; T = problem type; I = income; E = education; G = gender; A = age.

age and income in predicting medical utilization. Low income respondents were more likely to seek this form of professional help for emotional, economic, and interpersonal problems. Middle-aged (35–55 years old) and older respondents (55 years or older) were more likely than younger respondents (18–34 years old) to use medical organizations for emotional, economic, and death problems.

Summarizing the findings on physician use, Table 11.9 shows that high problem severity and physical health problems significantly increased the likelihood of professional help utilization. Women and the two older age groups (34–55 and 55 years or older) were more likely to use physicians than men and the young (18–34 years old), respectively. Problem type and problem severity were also significantly related to the use of human services. Respondents experiencing problems at the nervous breakdown level, as well as those with interpersonal and economic difficulties, were the most likely to use human services facilities. Finally, Table 11.9 shows that low-income African Americans were more likely to consult ministers for interpersonal, death, and economic problems, whereas high-income African Americans were more likely to seek the help of a minister for physical and interpersonal problems.

By focusing on the multivariate structure of these data, this chapter has clarified when a particular demographic relationship is robust and when it is either eliminated or modified by intervening social psychological processes. In so doing, a number of new research questions have been raised. Why are the black poor so inclined to make use of medical organizations for nonmedical problems? Why are older people more likely to use human services for very serious personal problems, but not for those that are less severe? What explains the fact that the poor are more likely to contact ministers for certain types of problems (emotional, death, and economic) but not others? (See Chatters, Taylor, & Neighbors, 1989; Neighbors, 1984b, 1985, 1986; Neighbors & Howard, 1987; Neighbors & Jackson, 1984; Neighbors & Taylor, 1985.)

┌───────┐
│ 12   │
└───────┘

RACE IDENTITY

James S. Jackson
Wayne R. McCullough
Gerald Gurin
Clifford L. Broman

This chapter explores the nature and interrelationships among in-group and intergroup orientations and particularly whether collective commitments to the ingroup derive more from ingroup or intergroup aspects of group identity. Several recent articles (e.g., Demo & Hughes, 1990; Denton & Massey, 1989; Hughes & Hertel, 1990) document the continuing importance of race in comtemporary American society. These persistent racial cleavages raise significant questions about how ingroup and outgroup sentiments affect and are affected by racial group identity of oppressed groups (Gurin, Hatchett, & Jackson, 1989).

A secondary issue addressed is the relationship of reported childhood socialization messages regarding race to the development of ingroup and outgroup orientations. The relationship that minority group members, and specifically Americans of African descent, have with their racial group has received extensive attention over the last three-and-one-half decades (Gurin et al., 1989; McCullough, Gurin, & Jackson, 1981). Some researchers have focused on effects of minority status or membership (e.g., Clark & Clark, 1940, 1947; Grier & Cobbs, 1968; Jackson, McCullough, & Gurin, 1988); others have fo-

AUTHORS' NOTE: This chapter is based on analyses originally presented at the 1981 Annual Convention of the American Psychological Association, Los Angeles, CA.

cused on either the transformation to a positive social identity or the development of collective commitments to redress societal inequalities (Brown, Allen, & Dawson, 1991; Cross, 1971; Gurin & Epps, 1975; Gurin, Miller, & Gurin, 1980).

In a previous chapter (Jackson et al., 1988) we noted that over the last 50 years or so much of the social psychological literature on black Americans has dealt, directly or indirectly, with issues of group identification and consciousness. Several researchers have stressed the theoretical independence of the relationship between self and social group identity (Cross, 1985; Harrison, 1985; Jackson et al., 1988; Krause, 1983; McAdoo, 1985; Peters, 1985; Porter & Washington, 1979, 1989; Rosenberg, 1985, 1989; Semaj, 1985). This literature highlights the serious measurement limitations (e.g., Banks, 1976; Semaj, 1985) and conceptual confusion in the definitions of personal and group identity and consciousness, as well as the inadequate formulation of the conceptual links among the concepts (Harrison, 1985). Based on the recent literature (e.g., Cross, 1985; McAdoo, 1985; Porter & Washington, 1979; Spencer, 1985), we have argued that the development of group and personal identity are separable phenomena and may be tied only under certain socialization conditions (Jackson et al., 1988).

Previous research of the National Survey of Black Americans (NSBA) has defined and documented the existence of a strong sense of group identification among black Americans (e.g., Broman, Neighbors, & Jackson, 1988; McCullough et al., 1981) as well as a unique system of personal beliefs related to the life circumstances of Americans of African descent (Allen, Dawson, & Brown, 1989; Allen & Watkins, 1991; Brown, Allen, & Dawson, 1990). Theoretically this belief system has been suggested to contain, and empirically shown to consist of, five related constructs: (a) Closeness to mass groups, defined as the emotional bonds to one's racial group, growing out of a sense of common fate; (b) closeness to elite blacks, reflecting an individual belief that one's political self-worth and that of the group can best be served by supporting black leaders; (c) positive stereotypic beliefs, indicating the extent of assignment of positive values to group traits; (d) negative stereotypic rejection, reflecting one's dismissal of negative images about the group; and (e) black autonomy, reflecting one's ideological beliefs that African Americans should build and support independent black institutions based on the cultural values and interests of the group. Previous research has documented the nature of this African American belief system (Allen et al., 1989) and the fact that its structure is fairly invariant across socioeconomic status and gender (Allen & Watkins, 1991; Brown et al., 1990).

Theoretically an African American belief system should reflect several different components of one's life circumstances. Prior work has been couched within the context of three major theoretical arguments to account for the existence of invariance or differences in this African American belief system among Americans of African descent who occupy different socioeconomic and structural positions and who differ in important sociodemographic characteristics. Intragroup polarization theory suggests that the increasing economic diversity among blacks should lead to different levels of attachment to the group. In this way individual self-interest becomes more tied to other group loyalties (e.g., white middle-class) or to self-interest (Wilson, 1978). The existence of such differences has not received wide empirical support (Allen & Watkins, 1991; Gurin et al., 1989).

Both group interest and group conflict theories (Allen & Watkins, 1991; Bobo, 1984; Jackman & Muha, 1984) posit that the existence of race group polarization and categorical racial group treatment should lead to greater solidarity and a commonality of beliefs among African Americans. All three theories are predicated on the nature of the position of African Americans in the American opportunity structure and to changes in this position with the passage of time. Intragroup polarization theory is based on a growing division among African Americans in socioeconomic fortunes. In this case, for example, among middle-class blacks self-interest and intraracial group interest should lead to the emergence of an active schema that predicates different actions for individual and group success than those of lower class blacks. Thus, the interest of different stratum blacks should diverge, and this divergence should lead to increasing conflict among blacks and, by extension, to an increase in a sense of attachment and common fate with the white middle class by the black middle class (Gurin et al., 1989).

Intraracial group polarization, real group conflict, and group self-interest theories operate from a similar underlying dynamic. In the case of African Americans, they are all based on the extent to which mobility is constrained by subordinate group status defined by racial group membership. To the extent that individual and family economic mobility is operative, intragroup polarization should become a reality. As individuals join other important group categories (middle class, for example), their group interests change, and they should perceive less of a tie to other members of their racially subordinate group who do not share these same interests.

All three theoretical positions are based on the assumption that positive changes occur over time in the fortunes of the group. And these changes result in greater individual and family opportunity, the capability to seize these opportunities, and the social and political mobility to capitalize on newfound economic fortunes. In the case of European ethnic groups this underlying assumption has been true (although differences do exist among these groups). And in fact real-group conflict and interest group theories have been predicated on the experience of such ethnics; intragroup polarization theory has been built on the experiences of one particular ethnic/religious group, Americans of Jewish descent. We argue that the experiences of Americans of African descent have been fundamentally different and thus theoretical models of group mobility and the consequences of this mobility may be different.

In-depth studies of the last five decades (Jaynes & Williams, 1989; Myrdal, 1944; National Advisory Commission on Civil Disorders, 1968) have all pointed to the continued subjugation and comparatively slow individual and family mobility of Americans of African descent. These same studies, however, document that significant economic, social, and political gains have occurred. We argue that even with such advances, the nature of the general American racial belief system has not undergone fundamental change over the years. Schuman, Steeth, and Bobo (1989) point to the increased positive attitudes of the white public toward African Americans over the last 50 years. But their work also shows a lack of change in the willingness of these same Americans to endorse specific and general policies that would in reality ameliorate the deleterious effects of the subordinate status of African Americans. In a recent article we argued and empirically demonstrated that the juxtaposition of socially acceptable driven changes in white attitudes, and the failure to endorse and evoke true ameliorative policies, results in a consistent and unchanging set of beliefs among Americans of African descent in different age cohorts (Allen, Chadiha, & Jackson, 1991; McCullough, 1982). This is true even though we found in earlier analyses that racial identification is strongest among older blacks and the least educated who live in urban areas, although income and gender show no relationships to racial group identification (Broman et al., 1988; McCullough et al., 1981).

Ingroup and Outgroup Orientations

In the literature on group identity, there has been interest in exploring the possible interdependence between identification with the ingroup and attitudes toward the outgroup (Tajfel, 1978, 1982; Turner, 1982). Controversy exists over the relationship between "ingroup favoritism" and "outgroup dislike" (Gurin et al., 1989). These ingroup and outgroup attitudes are presumed by some to be inversely related even when there has been little intergroup contact (Sherif, 1953). On the other hand, others have found that ingroup bias does not necessarily lead toward outgroup antagonism (Dion, 1973; Gurin et al., 1989; Wilson & Kayatani, 1968). More recent studies have sought to make the development of positive bias toward the ingroup dependent to some degree on the level of disaffection with the outgroup. Others have proposed that ingroup cohesion and outgroup attitudes are linked under conditions of high external threat (e.g., Dion, 1979).

Because so much of the prior work has focused on ingroup/outgroup attitudes in experimental settings, the relationship for "natural" groups in the social environment is unclear. In this chapter we examine the relationship between ingroup affiliation and outgroup orientations in one such natural setting, the group identifications and intergroup attitudes of a representative national sample of African American adults. Prior research has also been limited in that it has focused almost exclusively on the relationship between ingroup and outgroup orientations. We view both intragroup and intergroup orientations as aspects of group identity and explore some of their determinants and consequences (Thornton & Taylor, 1988a, 1988b).

Specifically, this chapter has three primary aims: (a) to examine the extent to which black identity includes both ingroup and intergroup elements; (b) to explore the implications of both these aspects of identity for the political mobilization of black Americans, particularly whether collective commitments derive more from ingroup or intergroup aspects of identity; and (c) to explore the antecedents of these two aspects of identity in the socialization messages imparted by parents on what it means to be black and how to deal with the white world.

The Measures

The measures of ingroup orientations in this study followed the approach of other studies on group identification in the National

Survey of Black Americans (i.e., Broman et al., 1988; McCullough et al., 1981). In earlier studies (e.g., Gurin, Miller, & Gurin, 1980) the major measure of identification has been one that asked respondents their feelings of "closeness" to the group, with closeness defined in terms of similarity to other group members in ideas and feelings about things. Previous work has suggested that such a question would get little variance if asked about blacks as a group; as measured in this way, almost all blacks feel identified. In the present study, therefore, the measure of closeness was applied to non-American black groups because we felt this would provide a more differentiated measure of the respondents' identification with blacks (Thornton & Taylor, 1988a). Specifically, respondents were asked how close they felt to West Indians and how close they felt to black people in Africa, with the responses combined into an index of the respondents' identification as black.

There were two central measures of intergroup orientations. One was directed toward the respondents' actual intergroup behavior. Respondents' were asked: "Do you know any white person who you think of as a good friend; that is, someone to whom you can say what you really think?" A second measure tapped a broader cognitive orientation toward intergroup relations; it asked the respondents: "Do you think most white people want to see blacks get a better break, or do they want to keep blacks down, or don't they care one way or the other?" Thus, positive intergroup orientations were measured by having a close white friend and by the perception that white people are generally supportive of black people's interests.

Two other questions in the questionnaire had elements of both intergroup and ingroup orientations. These questions presented a choice between ingroup and outgroup identifications. One question asked: "Who do you feel closer to: black people in Africa or white people in America?" The other question phrased the outgroup less specifically as "whites" and more generally as "Americans"; it asked: "Which would you say is more important to you, being black or being American, or are both equally important to you?"

In conceptualizing the political mobilization of identity, we have focused on the two concepts that have been central in the work on group consciousness: system blame and collective orientations. For groups of lower status and power in a society, one central element in the development of political group consciousness is the adherence to an ideology of system blame; that is, that the causes of the group's lower status lie in the system rather than the defects of the individual group members. A second critical element in the politicalization of group consciousness is that group members see collective group action, rather than individual mobility, as the means of redressing their lower power position. In this study, system blame was measured by two forced choice questions which counterposed individual and systemic explanations for lower status of black Americans. Collective orientation was measured by two different questions. The first counterposed collective and individual action as the way for blacks to improve their position in America. The second asked respondents whether they felt what happened to them depended more on what happens to blacks as a group or what they did themselves.

Analyses of Ingroup and Outgroup Orientations

The seven items and indices described above were factor analyzed. The analysis was restricted to a two-factor solution, corresponding to the expected distinction between ingroup and outgroup orientations in order to determine how the perception of political mobilization measures loaded on these two factors. The results of the factor analysis appear in Table 12.1. Both factors are strong, each explaining the same proportion of the total variance.

As indicated in Table 12.1, the two main measures of intergroup orientations, whether the respondent has a close white friend and

Table 12.1
Factor Analysis of Measures of Ingroup and Outgroup Orientations

Measure of Orientation	Outgroup Orientation	Ingroup Orientation
Has close white friend	.6449	.0948
Whites support black interests	.7120	−.0273
Closeness to non-American blacks	.2269	.8007
Identification with black Africans vs. white Americans	−.2231	.6905
Identification as black vs. American	−.4212	.2785
System blame	−.4966	.2034
Collective orientations	−.1399	.4509
Percent total variance	20.97	20.71
Percent common variance	50.30	49.70

whether white people are seen as supportive of blacks, have the largest loadings on one factor; and the ingroup measure of feelings of closeness to non-American blacks has the largest loading on the second factor. Moreover, the other four measures load in opposite ways on these two factors. Having a white friend and seeing whites as supportive seem to be related to identifying as American and with white Americans, viewing the causes of blacks' lower status as individually rather than systemically determined, and advocating individual rather than collective action. Feeling close to non-American blacks appears more closely related to choosing black and black African identifications over American and white American ones and with belief in system blame and collective action. Moreover, the loadings on these two factors tend to be very different, suggesting further implications of the distinction between ingroup and intergroup orientations among American blacks.

The question that forced a choice of identification between being black or being American loads fairly equally on both, although slightly more on the intergroup orientation factor. However, the other question which forced a choice between ingroup and intergroup identifications, blacks in Africa or whites in America, loads on the ingroup factor. This question apparently captures the respondents' worldwide identification as black, more than their rejection of white Americans.

It is also interesting that the two measures of the development of group identification into political consciousness load differently on the two factors. System blame has a fairly high negative loading on the intergroup factor, indicating a common thread in intergroup orientations that ties reactions to whites at the personal friendship level to ideological views of the system where whites have exercised control. Having a white friend goes with individual rather than system blame. Collective orientations, on the other hand, which measure the sense of common fate and the need to act collectively, load primarily on the ingroup orientation factor. Work on gender identity has noted that identification as a woman does not necessarily imply commitment to collective action; it does so only when that identification has become politicized ideologically. Among blacks, as some previous research (Gurin, Miller, & Gurin, 1980) has suggested, identification as black at this stage of history in America automatically implies some sense of common fate and collective commitment (Gurin et al., 1989).

To summarize, the data suggest that the measures of ingroup and outgroup orientations are separate components of identity, and that, for American blacks, they have different implications for the development of group political consciousness. Although ingroup and outgroup orientations are clearly separate, the question on the nature of their relationship remains. We noted at the beginning of this chapter that controversy exists in the literature on whether or not positive identification with the ingroup necessarily involves at least some degree of antagonism toward the outgroup. We would expect some such negative relationship to exist in any group that, like American blacks, has suffered a long history of discrimination and limited power. In such low power groups we expect that positive orientations toward their own group would be related to negative orientations toward the group that exercised the power and constraints.

This expectation is not supported by the data when we examine the correlation between the ingroup identification measure on closeness to non-American blacks and the question on whether or not the respondent has a close white friendship. There is only a correlation of 0.03 between positive identification with non-American blacks and not having any close white friend. The correlation does increase somewhat, however, as one moves from the interpersonal to ideological expression of intergroup orientations. Thus, there is a correlation of 0.08 between positive identification with non-American blacks and the feeling that whites want to keep blacks down, and a correlation of 0.13 (low but significant) between positive identification with non-American blacks and feeling that the system, not individual blacks, is to blame for the condition of blacks in America. Thus, for American blacks, positive ingroup orientations do not seem to imply rejection of the outgroup on the personal level, but do imply some outgroup antagonism on the ideological level.

The Development of Ingroup and Outgroup Orientations

Having determined the nonindependence of the broad measures of ingroup and outgroup orientations, we now address the issue of how individuals may be influenced to arrive at these particular orientations through parental socialization. The literature on political socialization strongly suggests that there is high correspondence between parents' and children's political orientations and attitudes toward the system (Gurin et al., 1989; Jennings & Niemi, 1968; Pitts, 1975). This literature and the well-documented oppression of minority group members by the larger society lead us to believe there may be a substantial impact of these parental messages on the ingroup and outgroup orientations of African Americans.

The family is the important agent of socialization for blacks, for it is within the family context that the individual first becomes aware of and begins to grapple with the significance of racism and discrimination (Alejandro–Wright, 1985; Peters, 1985; Washington, 1976). The intra-familial socialization of group and personal identity has considerable bearing on personal functioning in a society that cultivates negative conceptions of minority group members through direct interaction, the media, and institutional barriers (Allen & Hatchett, 1986). An important social structural factor discussed in this chapter is racial homogeneity or heterogeneity of the socialization environment. How do such environments differentially affect the development and compartmentalization of group and personal identity and consciousness? Our concern is not only the degree of racial homogeneity of the socialization environment, but also the timing of socialization and the elements of group and personal identity that are transmitted across generations.

In a previous chapter (Jackson et al., 1988) we pointed out that there is little systematic evidence regarding the protective functions and the identity nurturant roles served by the black family in fostering group or personal identity among blacks (Lipscomb, 1975; Taylor, 1976). We also noted that the coping strategies and situational adaptations derived from this identity and fostered in the familial context have only recently begun to receive theoretical and empirical attention (Bowman & Howard, 1985; McCullough, 1982; Peters, 1985; Spencer, 1985).

We also have proposed that the racially homogeneous home environment may also serve an important insulating function in the personal identity development of black children (Jackson et al., 1988). We have suggested that self-worth and self-conceptions are formed under the auspices of the family (Rosenberg, 1989). We have suggested that in the homogeneous racial environment there are fewer occasions than in the heterogeneous environment for negative messages regarding group membership to directly impinge upon personal identity development. And, thus, the homogeneous environment can help to foster a high degree of individual compartmentalization. Once the development of self is established, integrating conceptions of one's relationship to the group and understanding the group's status in society can be achieved through exposure to images through art, stories, history, and culture as well as direct parental socialization.

We believe that parental ideologies provide the filter through which the external world is presented to the developing child (Jackson et al., 1988; Jackson et al., 1989; Lipscomb, 1975; Peters, 1985). For example, Bowman and Howard (1985) in an analysis of the Three-Generation Family Study data (Jackson & Hatchett, 1986) found positive effects on personal efficacy and academic achievement in black youth who reported receiving strong black socialization messages. The suggestion that the socialization environment may have a bearing on the development of identity has some empirical grounding. The optimal environments to foster independent identity development are suggested by the findings of several studies (Bowman & Howard, 1985; McAdoo, 1985; McCullough, 1982; Porter & Washington, 1979; Wellman, 1970). For example, Hare (1977) found that home and peer self-esteem were not significantly different by racial group; however, school self-esteem was significantly higher among whites. For blacks, only home area specific esteem accounted for a significant amount of variance in general self-esteem. These data suggest both differences in racial groups and the influence of the socialization environment in the development of group and personal identity.

In a recent study using NSBA data, Broman, Jackson, and Neighbors (1989) found that sociocultural context of upbringing (notably grade schools and neighborhood) had significant effects on racial identification in adulthood. Notably, it was found that black racial contexts in grammar school, junior and senior high, and neighborhood of upbringing were significantly related to reports of heightened racial identification. On the other hand, a black racial context in one's place of worship and mixed racial contexts in high school, college, and present workplace were associated with reports of increased racial identification. Although these findings were very complex, they do suggest that sociocultural context of socialization and current contextual experiences have significant influences on racial identification.

In one of the few direct socialization studies, Lipscomb (1975) examined the child rearing practices of mothers of 5- and 6-year-old children. She hypothesized that the mothers' background characteristics (education, income) affect mothers' attitudes (toward the system) which, in turn, affect the socialization practices they employ in rearing their children. She further hypothesized a direct effect of socialization practices on the children's ingroup orientation. A causal analysis supported this socialization sequence. Although her measures of ingroup and outgroup orientations are not directly comparable to the measures here, they were ascriptions of positive and negative stereotypes to ingroup and outgroup members by the children.

The underlying conception guiding this chapter also proposes a model comparable in many respects to that outlined by Lipscomb (1975). To assess the impact that socialization practices may have had on the development of ingroup and outgroup orientations, respondents were asked two major questions relative to the socialization they received. As in the identification measures, the socialization measures separated socialization practices relevant to ingroup and intergroup orientations. The first question asked: "What did your parents or the people who raised you teach you to help you know what it is to be black?" The second asked: "What did your family teach you about how to get along with white people?" The open-ended responses for each of these questions were categorized into one of six response categories: nothing, those who noted receiving no message relative to the question; individually focused messages, which had little or no emphasis on the individual's connection to the racial group and tended to stress coping with the living environment or individual achievement orientations, in the educational and occupational arenas; positive group orientations, which include messages that stress the noninferiority of and the equality of blacks with all others, or specifically mention racial pride and the black heritage; negative affect responses, which embodied themes of fear and distrust of whites and negative messages about the racial group; acceptance responses, which reflected a lack of assertiveness with respect to whites and may have stressed the status of intergroup relations as acceptable, good, or changing for the better; and challenge messages, which stressed standing up for self and for group rights and the awareness of social structural blockages.

As indicated in Figure 12.1, the number of respondents mentioning these six different response categories varied for the two different socialization questions. As Figure 12.1 shows, sizeable proportions of the sample did not recall receiving any notable message from their parents on each of the two questions. Positive group and individual themes were the most prevalent messages for those who were told about what it means to be black. Themes of acceptance and positive

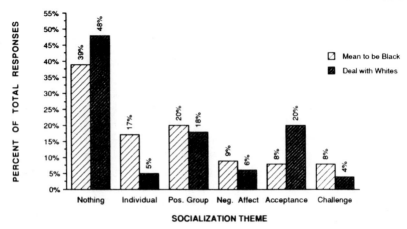

Figure 12.1. Proportion of Messages Received by Socialization Question

group orientations were those most often stressed on how to deal with whites.

Analyses were conducted to test for differential effects of socialization on each of the seven measures of group identification and consciousness. Unvaryingly, respondents who did not receive any socialization message relative to what it means to be black or how to deal with whites were less identified with the group and significantly less likely to have white friends. The trend is also evidenced in the other associated indices of identification and consciousness.

The two socialization questions, designed to tap highly overlapping socialization practices, were initially thought to have similar outcomes. The socialization questions and their emergent themes, however, have somewhat different effects. Some socialization themes seem to lead to the development of pro-ingroup orientations, whereas others seem to play a role in facilitating intergroup relations. These effects are discussed separately in the next two sections.

What It Means To Be Black

In the development of ingroup identification we found the major difference was between those who received the acceptance socialization message and those who were recipients of any of the remaining five messages. The two political consciousness measures (collective orientation and system blame) were similar in that those who received no socialization messages were significantly least likely to be collectively oriented or system blaming than all other socialization orientations combined. One of the more distinguishing findings is the greater collective orientations of respondents who were socialized with positive group messages in comparison with those who were socialized to an individual or even a challenge perspective. Respondents who received no socialization message were significantly less collective than those who received positive group or negative affect themes. Negative affect and challenge orientations lead to significantly more system blaming than the no-message orientation.

The measures of intergroup attitudes (having a white friend and perceiving whites as wanting a better break for blacks) have little internal differentiation by the particular messages received. Respondents who were socialized to individual, positive group, negative affect, acceptance, and challenge messages are more likely to have a white friend than those with no socialization to blackness. There were no socialization distinctions regarding the perceptions of whites wanting a better break for blacks.

These particular socialization trends suggest several important considerations in the development of group identity, system blame, and collective orientations. First, challenge and positive group orientations are most prominently implicated in the development of group identity and system blame orientations. The collective orientation is more strongly induced by the socialization to positive group and negative affect themes. Intergroup attitudes and interaction appear to be little influenced by socialization to "what it means to be black."

How To Deal With Whites

This question appears to differentiate those socialization themes that lead to better intergroup attitudes better than the previous question did. As was evidenced with the prior question no reported socialization was the least likely to result in having a white friend. Unexpectedly, however, it was significantly less positive in this regard than the challenging, acceptance, or positive group themes. Respondents who were socialized with positive group themes were, in fact, significantly more likely to have a white friend than those who were socialized to individual or acceptance themes. For the perception that whites want a better break for blacks, those socialized to positive group orientations were significantly more positive about whites' intergroup attitudes than those socialized to acceptance or no messages. Unexpectedly, this group was significantly more positive than even those reared to acceptance.

For collective orientation, respondents who were socialized to acceptance were significantly more collective than those who received no messages. The most anomalous finding is that respondents socialized to positive group orientations with regard to how to deal with whites were significantly less system blaming than those raised with individual, acceptance, or no messages.

Overall this question led to more differentiation in intergroup attitudes than those messages about socialization to blackness. This pattern of results suggest that being socialized to challenge inequities somehow more fully integrates one into the system and results in closer intergroup relations.

Summary and Conclusions

These data from the National Survey of Black Americans provide evidence that ingroup and outgroup orientations may be inversely related. In exploring the degree to which parental socialization accounts for these ingroup and outgroup orientations, we have found that they are not the result of a singular monolithic message, but rather are derived from separate socialization messages, resulting in separate ends. The only differential thematic effects in socialization to what it means to be black were found in ingroup measures (except having a white friend where receiving any message produced more intergroup friendship than receiving nothing). Conversely, the only overall differential effects found for how to deal with whites were in the intergroup measures. As a group, and almost without exception, those who report not receiving socialization messages relative to what it means to be black or how to deal with whites also report the relatively weakest ingroup and outgroup orientations.

Those who were reared with themes of challenge and positive group orientations to blackness clearly exhibit the most positive ingroup orientation profile. Those who were socialized to challenge are the most highly identified and most system blaming group. Socialization to positive group orientations seems to produce the next highest level of group identification and the highest level of collective orientation. Unexpectedly, these same two themes, challenge and positive group orientations, led to the highest levels of outgroup orientations. Recipients of these themes were the most likely to report having close white friends and to feel that whites wanted to see blacks get a better break.

In summary, the analyses conducted for this chapter suggest that the measures of ingroup and outgroup orientations are separate components of racial identity and that they have different implications for the development of political consciousness among African Americans. Although complicated, the findings indicated that ingroup and outgroup socialization messages were differentially related to the strength of racial identification and consciousness in black adults.

POLITICAL ACTION

Ronald E. Brown

Black Americans are a socioeconomically disadvantaged but politically active group (Dawson, Brown, & Allen, 1990; Miller, Gurin, Gurin, & Malachuck, 1981; Shingles, 1981; Verba & Nie, 1972). On one hand, black Americans in comparison to whites are more likely to have lower levels of formal education (Jones, 1981), lower median family incomes (Allen & Simms, 1988; Edelman, 1987), and lower employment rates (Pettigrew, 1981; Wilson & Neckerman, 1986). In addition, because of the higher percentage of female-headed households, poverty is significantly higher among blacks in comparison to whites (Edelman, 1987; Wilson, 1986). Furthermore, blacks are more likely than whites to reside in communities where there are limited employment opportunities (Wilson, 1980). On the other hand, Shingles (1981) states that a large number of studies, using a variety of indicators and samples, report black activism at levels significantly above those which would be expected, given the average level of education, income, and occupational prestige of the racial group.

Black political participation rates violate the socioeconomic hypothesis. In general, college-trained individuals and those with high incomes have higher levels of political interest and efficacy (Verba & Nie, 1972). So, individuals from high status groups have high rates of political activism. Individuals from low status groups feel more isolated and alienated from the political system (Zipp, Landerman, & Luebre, 1982) and have lower political participation rates.

A group-based political mobilization strategy motivates black Americans to participate in the political process (see McAdam, 1982;

Morris, 1984; Nelson & Meranto, 1977). The subordinate status of African Americans and the natural in group favoritism (Yancey, Ericksen, & Juliani, 1976) which flows from frequent patterns of association creates the necessity and the conditions for group-based resources and mobilization. One of these resources is racial common fate identification. A common fate perspective implies that one has made a cognitive decision to identity with a group with which one shares a common history, kinship, and destiny. A belief in group fate means that blacks think that a collective effort will be effective in bringing about social change (Brown, 1984; Nelson & Meranto, 1977; Tate, 1989). A common fate orientation is demonstrated when blacks vote for candidates whom they think will best represent the race (Campbell, Converse, Miller, & Stokes, 1960; Tate, 1989).

Community-based organizations (McAdam, 1982; Morris, 1984; Morris, Hatchett, & Brown, 1989) are also group-based political resources which boost the political participation rates of black Americans. Churches, block clubs, and local branches of national black organizations are vehicles for political mobilization because individuals realize that their common interests are advanced through a collective effort (Brown, 1984; McAdam, 1982; Morris, 1984). Brown and Jackson's (1989) analyses on the 1984 National Black Election Study demonstrate this point. They found that membership and involvement in black civil-rights organizations were highly correlated with involvement in traditional campaign activities. They also reported that exposure to political information in a church setting was highly correlated with church-based campaign activism.

The political mobilization of black Americans over the past several decades has had the greatest impact on the "Civil Rights Generation" (Jennings & Niemi, 1981). These are individuals who reached political maturation during the struggle for racial equality between 1954 and 1968. Black students enrolled at predominantly black colleges and universities participated in direct actions that resulted in the destruction of legal segregation in the South (Branch, 1988; Gurin & Epps, 1975; Matthew & Prothro, 1966; McAdam, 1982; Morris, 1984). These students were also instrumental in encouraging sharecroppers and illiterate black farmers to register and vote during this era (Branch, 1988). Young blacks were also in the forefront of the black power movement (Caplan, 1970; Gurin & Epps, 1975; Matthew & Prothro, 1966) and were participants in the urban riots (Sears & McConahay, 1973).

Empirical investigations of black voting reveal that the civil-rights generation of blacks votes at about the same rate as do older blacks (Brown, 1984; *Current Population Reports,* 1985; Tate, Brown, Hatchett, & Jackson, 1988) but are more active in protest activities (see Issac, Murtran, & Stryker, 1980; Morris et al., 1989).

Mannheim's (1972) concept of "generation" explains the mobilization of this subgroup. According to Mannheim, a generation is an aggregate of individuals who reach political maturation during a period of rapid social change. Members within the generation must be aware that they share a sense of commonality (Delli Carpini, 1989) and it is this awareness which can motivate members to become political activists. As cited above, black adults undergoing political maturation during the mid to late 1950s and 1960s were significantly involved in the struggle for black equality.

One should not overlook the possibility that protest politics in the 1950s and 1960s resocialized elderly black Americans. Although this age group reached political maturation while blacks had limited political opportunities and power, the efficacy of the Civil Rights Movement may have changed their political orientations. The influence of the Civil Rights Movement on these individuals is noted in a number of works. Brown and Jackson (1989) report that over 90% of the respondents in the 1980 National Survey of Black Americans (NSBA) stated that the Civil Rights Movement had improved the quality of their lives. In addition, when asked to name the most important "thing which had happened to you," elderly blacks overwhelmingly mentioned civil-rights events. Schuman and Scott (1989) also report similar findings. Regardless of age, blacks were more likely than whites to mention the Civil Rights Movement as the most important historical event that had occurred in their lifetime. Moreover, elderly blacks (aged 60 to 69) mentioned the Civil Rights Movement more than any other age group.

Older blacks were no doubt resocialized by black churches, media outlets, and community-based organizations. Mass meetings, citizenship schools, and editorials were employed to raise the racial consciousness of black Americans (see Morris et al., 1989). McAdam's (1982) study on black insurgency demonstrates the influence of these socializing agents. He shows that black churches, local chapters of the National Association for the Advancement of Colored People (NAACP), and student groups were all part of a communication network which coordinated protest activities between 1955 and 1960.

Older black Americans may be politically active in the current era because of their exposure to these "resocialization" agents. They may feel competent to participate fully in political affairs. Therefore, being able to perform one's civic duty may be more important and have more intrinsic value for this age group in comparison to young age groups. In sum, older blacks may be activists because of resocialization.

Despite the efficacy of a collective mobilization process and its impact on the civil-rights generation and older age groups, young and poor blacks are not an integral part of this collective mobilization effort. Registration efforts in the 1980s by the Democratic Party and by the Jackson campaign in 1984 and 1988 have had only a marginal effect on increasing voting turnout among these subgroups (*Detroit Free Press,* 1988; Reed, 1986). Why is this the case?

One explanation could be that the post-civil-rights age group does not hold as intense feelings about voting as do their elders. Young black adults lack a collective memory of legal segregation. And unlike their parents or grandparents, few have to observe social customs which remind blacks as individuals of their subordinate status. Therefore, few feel the urgency to use the ballot to secure justice and liberty. Being socialized during a very cynical period could also contribute to low political interest. Watergate, the assassination of Martin Luther King, Jr., and the ascendency of conservatives to national office may have contributed to decreased political interest. Finally, younger blacks may lack political interest because of more pressing social concerns, for example, finding a mate, stable employment, and a community to reside in. In essence, life cycle forces may make them less likely to be activists (Verba & Nie, 1972).

These findings on age and voting lead to the hypothesis that voting will be highest among blacks in the pre-civil-rights and civil-rights age groups and lowest among blacks in the post-civil-rights age group. A different set of concerns explain why poor people do not vote. Day-to-day survival needs may influence how much interest poor people have in political affairs (see Schlozman & Verba, 1979). For these individuals, time spent on politics may take away from managing meager family budgets and keeping children away from drug pushers and crime. Poor people may not have the energy to devote to politics. Trying to keep one's family from destructive forces may be all that such individuals can handle.

Taking care of family needs is not the only factor that prohibits poor blacks from becoming political activists. The lack of organizational affiliation is equally important. In general, poor people and, in our case, poor blacks are less likely to be members of churches and local organizations (see Brown, 1989). Inasmuch as blacks are more likely than whites to use the church as a political resource (Brown & Jackson, 1988; Wald, 1987), the absence of poor blacks from such institutions may have devastating consequences. By not being in church, poor people will not be exposed to political information, nor will they develop organizational skills which can be used in the world of politics. Parenti (1972) argues that it is rational for poor people not to vote. He argues that conventional political involvement by poor people rarely results in governmental polices that directly attack and reduce the causes of poverty. Thus, poor people make the right calculus when they stay away from the polls. These findings lead to the hypothesis that personal resources—for example, adequate economic resources and education—will correlate positively with voting.

Although poor and young blacks exhibit low levels of involvement in electoral politics, they are among the strongest advocates for the creation of a black political party. Brown, Jackson, and Bowman's (1982) analysis of the 1980 National Survey of Black Americans showed that of the 53% of blacks who have less than a high school education, those between the ages of 18–26 years old, felt that blacks should create their own political party. Their data also revealed that 48% of the civil-rights generation believed that blacks should form their own party. Tate and colleagues' (1988) analysis on the 1984 National Black Election Study yields similar findings. In this study, only 38% of low income and younger black adults state that blacks should form their own political party. The presidential aspirations and campaign of the Reverend Jesse Jackson and his call for a "Rainbow Coalition" may have dampened the cry for a black party among the poor and the young. Even if this is true, the fact remains that a significant proportion of the black electorate believes that there is a need for a grass-roots organization that will represent their political interests.

These findings suggest that there are two black electorates—voters and those who would vote if there was a black political party. If we are to increase our understanding of a group-based process of electoral mobilization, there must be a more systematic examination of how resource availability affects the decision to vote and the call for the creation of a black party. We will empirically investigate these issues in the remainder of this chapter.

Dependent Variables

Voting

Respondents were asked if they had voted in the last presidential election and the last state or local election. Fifty-five percent of the respondents reported voting in the last presidential election and 40% reported voting in the last state or local election. These variables were recoded and combined into an index ranging from 1 to 3, with 1 being low and 3 being high. The mean level of voting is 2.00.

Black Party Support

Respondents were asked if they thought that blacks should form their own political party and if they would join if such a party existed. These two variables were combined and ranged from low to high, with low meaning that respondents do not think that blacks should form a party and high meaning that respondents would join such a party if one existed. Thirty-five percent of the respondents stated that blacks should form their own party and that they would join such a party if one existed; 9% think that blacks should form their own party, but they would not join; and 57% do not think that blacks should form their own party. The mean score for black party support is 1.82.

Independent Variables

Racial Common Fate Identification

This variable was operationalized by asking respondents whether their life chances were dependent on what happens to blacks as a group, on what they did themselves, or both. A dummy variable was created; respondents who stated that group outcomes affect them were coded as 1 and all others were coded as 0. Thirty-five percent of the respondents had high common fate scores.

Organizational memberships were represented by two variables. Membership in black national organizations was one measure, with 14% of the sample in such organizations. Seventy-five percent of organizational memberships were with civil-rights organizations.

Church-Based Activism

Two variables are combined to make up this index. Respondents were asked about their level of church attendance and the level of their involvement in church activities besides regular church services. The categories ranged from "involved every day" to "never involved." The index ranges from a low of 1 to a high of 5. The mean for church-based activism is 2.93.

Poverty

This is an income/needs ratio that takes into account the ratio of family income to family needs. The Panel Study of Income Dynamics' definition of family needs is used. This measure takes into account the size of the household, gender of the respondents, and age of the respondents in the household. Respondents who are coded 1 (10% of the respondents) or 2 (17% of the respondents) do not have incomes that meet the economic needs of the family. Respondents who are coded 3 to 5 have incomes which are above the needs category. About 16% are in category 3, 22% are coded 4, and 35% are coded as 5. The mean for the poverty variable is 3.05.

Education

This variable ranges from less than a high school education to a college degree. Respondents with less than a high school degree are coded as 1; 41% are in this group. Respondents with a high school degree are coded as 2; 33% are in this category. Respondents with some college education are coded as 3; 17% are in this group. Finally, college graduates are coded as 4; 10% are in this group. The mean for education is 1.81.

Generational Membership/Age

The age variable was created from responses to the question, "What is your date of birth?" These classifications reflect both age of early socialization and position in the life cycle. These age groups are as follows:

1. New Deal, respondents who were at least 16 years of age in 1930;

2. Before Brown, respondents who were at least 16 years of age before the Brown versus Topeka Supreme Court case;
3. Civil rights, respondents who were 16 years of age between 1954 and 1968; and
4. Post-civil-rights, respondents who were 16 years of age between 1969 and 1977.

Resource Mobilization and Voting

As expected, black voters are integrated into the social fabric of the African-American community (see Table 13.1). They are active church and community organization members and feel that their individual fate and that of the group are interwoven. The betas for poverty and education equal those for organizational memberships, which implies that marked improvement in the socioeconomic status of the group will have a drastic impact on voter turnout.

The age findings reveal that both the New Deal (65 years old and older) and the Before Brown (42–64 years old) age groups have higher mean levels of voting than the civil-rights (27–41 years old) age group. As expected, the civil-rights age group has a higher mean level of voting than the post-civil-rights (18–26 years old) age group. Why do older black Americans show a higher mean level of voting than the civil-rights age group? These differences may be the result of controlling for schooling and poverty levels. By controlling for the

Table 13.1
Voting Activism by Individual and Group Based Resources

Predictor	Beta	Partial R
Common fate	.05[a]	.06
Church activism	.13[b]	.13
Organizational membership	.14[b]	.14
New Deal age group	−.27[b]	−.26
Before Brown age group	−.16[b]	−.16
Post-civil rights age group	.10[b]	.09
Poverty ratio	.16[b]	.16
Education	.18[b]	.17

NOTE: Age is treated as a dummy variable with the civil rights age group excluded.
$R^2 = .23$; a. $p \geq .01$; b. $p \geq .001$.

influence of these personal resources, the true effect of age may have been more accurately shown. This pattern of age results is consistent with other research findings on the general population (Strate et al., 1989; Verba & Nie, 1972). These findings may also be the result of re-socialization. Older blacks may be active voters because of their position in the life cycle and because of the intrinsic importance of the vote.

Black Party Support

The data in Table 13.2 show black party supporters as having low financial resources and lacking a high school education. Moreover, the civil-rights age group has a statistically significant higher level of support for a black party than do the older age groups. However, the mean level of support for a black party is the same for the civil-rights and post-civil-rights age groups. This is not surprising given the protest tradition of the former age group.

The correlation between racial common fate and black party support leads one to speculate that a segment of the African American community longs for the creation of a political organization that pursues a much more black nationalistic agenda. Our poverty, education, and age findings indicate that these individuals are the poor and the members of the civil-rights and post-civil-rights age groups.

Although the findings in Table 13.2 imply that members of churches and national black organizations will not be in the forefront of a

Table 13.2

Black Party Support by Individual and Group Based Resources

Predictor	Beta	Partial R
Common fate	.10[b]	.10
Church activism	−.03	−.03
Organizational membership	.01	.01
New Deal age group	.15[b]	.13
Before Brown age group	.12[b]	.11
Post-civil rights age group	−.03	−.03
Poverty ratio	.07[a]	.07
Education	.17[b]	.14

NOTE: Age is treated as a dummy variable with the civil rights age group excluded.
$R^2 = .06$; a. $p > .01$; b. $p > .001$.

black party movement, some national organizational members would join such a party. This speculation is based on the absence of a significant correlation between national organizational membership and black party support. Some organizational activists may see the need for both voting and protest-demand activities. The latter may include boycotting party conventions, staging protest marches and demonstrations at party conventions, or running third party candidates for major political offices. These types of actions in combination with voting activities may be what is needed to mobilize the nonvoting segment of the black population.

Conclusion

Frequent and free elections are a barometer of democracy because citizens can use the ballot to put officials in office who will represent their interests. The findings in this chapter show that African Americans who are older, who have adequate personal and organizational resources, and who feel that their fate and the group are linked are more likely to vote.

If black voting is to increase, community organizers and scholars must come to grips with the strong commitment toward a black party among the poor and the civil-rights and post-civil-rights age groups. The challenge that confronts political leaders who wish to mobilize this group is to convince them that they must work through the two major parties and existing black organizations. Should strong black party supporters become involved, their challenge will be to push and pressure these organizations to recruit and involve the poor and young. Until strong black party supporters become integrated into mainstream partisan politics or a black party movement emerges, they will remain in a state of readiness to be politically mobilized.

BLACK AMERICAN
LIFE COURSE

James S. Jackson

I have given this final chapter a title that raises for me a fundamental question for citizens of African descent in the United States of America: To what extent are blacks attaining the reality of the rights guaranteed to all citizens in the Constitution of the United States (Gurin, Hatchett, & Jackson, 1989)? The facts of exclusion are demonstrated in the cold, hard statistical data reflecting the historical and continuing race differentials in economic and employment statuses, poverty, morbidity, mortality, schooling, and housing (Jaynes & Williams, 1989; Myrdal, 1944; National Advisory Commission on Civil Disorders, 1968). Although the form of exclusion has changed, few would deny that living in black America has been, and continues to be, detrimental to one's life chances, social integration, upward mobility, opportunities in the world of politics, and physical and mental health functioning (Farley & Allen, 1987; Jaynes & Williams, 1989; Myrdal, 1944). Consequently, as we have suggested in this volume exclusion from the mainstream American opportunity structure is played out in many other ways in the social and psychological nature of black neighborhood, family, and individual life. While the structural conditions of life for African Americans have long been known and documented (Farley & Allen, 1987; Jaynes & Williams, 1989; Myrdal, 1944; National Advisory Commission on Civil Disorders, 1968), national data on the physical, social, and psychological concomitants of these structural conditions have been largely absent in the scientific literature.

The findings in this book provide support for an evolving individual and group life-course framework for interpreting and understanding the reactions and responses of Americans of African descent to their continued unequal status (Bowman, 1989; Gibson, 1982a; Jackson, Antonucci, & Gibson, 1990). The analyses in the preceding chapters provide unassailable evidence that the status and position of different segments of the black population in the larger opportunity structure are linked in explicable and predictable ways to differential levels of social, psychological, and health outcomes.

Coping and Adaptation Over the Individual and Group Life Course: An Evolving Framework for Research on African Americans

A major focus of the research reported in this book has been on the stress, internal and external coping capacities, resiliency and adaptability, and mental and physical health, and functioning of blacks at various ages, points in the life-course, and role positions (e.g., youth, parents, workers, retirees; the married, divorced, and separated; women who head households; those in and out of poverty; adult children and their aged parents, the middle-aged, and the elderly). We have focused a considerable portion of our research effort on examining the nature and measurement of status inequality and the responses of Americans of African descent to this unequal status.

We have been concerned with the assessment of social, political, and economic sources of race inequality, black reactions to these perceived status-based differences, and possible mediating factors like race identity, race consciousness, perceived efficacy, and perceived legitimacy of status (Chapters 12 and 13). Work has included the examination of the effects of race identity and racially based treatment on well-being, and the role of social status, poverty, and inequality generally in coping and adaptation and physical and mental well-being. Generally, analyses of the 1980 NSBA respondents suggest differences in exposure to stressors, responses to these stressors, and consequent adaptations which are linked to age group, life-cycle stage, and position in the social structure (Chapters 4, 7, 8, and 9).

One useful way of understanding the empirical results in the present volume is to place them in the context of a resource-based framework. Milburn and Bowman's results in Chapter 3 point to the importance of neighborhood organizations in maintaining a sense of community. However, only one third of all black Americans have access to such organizations, and of these only 20% are actually involved. The lack of access to and involvement in community organizations has serious political consequences. As Brown points out in Chapter 13, members of national black organizations and churches are more likely to report voting. Black organizations, especially at the grass-roots level, have the potential for off-setting the lack of socioeconomic resources that hamper the activism level of individual blacks. Hatchett, Cochran, and Jackson's findings in Chapter 4 continue a similar theme, pointing to important support functions available through the family but simultaneously describing family systems that are weakened by lack of financial resources and formal support systems. In Chapter 5 Hatchett examines the resources that women and men bring to their partnerships. Not unexpectedly she finds that marital discord and negative expectations of marriage and other permanent relationships are affected by structural conditions and that age and socioeconomic level play critical roles. Men and women have different perspectives on the value of close personal relationships, with women valuing the instrumental aspects of conjugal relationships more than men. Taylor and Chatters' findings in Chapter 6 provide empirical confirmation that black Americans are very religious in both private and public dimensions of spiritual life. Religion and religious participation appear to function as important resources for the expression of group values and beliefs, for exercising black rights, and as an important source of support for families and individuals.

The results of Bowman's analyses in Chapters 7 and 8 clearly point to the negative implications of secondary sector job placement and to the deleterious social and psychological consequences of joblessness. Since the official statistics continue to portray serious macroeconomic conditions that seriously impede the work possibilities for sizable numbers of young (and increasingly middle-aged as well) blacks, it is clear that these problems will remain of central importance for the foreseeable future.

Extending the difficulties related to work and opportunities for work, Gibson's analyses in Chapter 9 point out how work and nonwork experiences at earlier periods in the life course negatively influence the retirement experiences of black Americans. The problems that lead to less-than-successful retirement are sowed in earlier periods of the life course among successive age cohorts. Thus, we can predict with unfortunate but unerring precision that future cohorts of retirement-age blacks will continue to evince the problems from which these analyses show older cohorts are now suffering.

We also find differences due to age and life-cycle stage in the ways in which internal and external resources, individual coping, sense of personal efficacy, self-esteem, informal support, and "religiosity" buffer or insulate against stress (Antonucci & Jackson, 1987; Gibson & Jackson, 1978). Informal support, in fact, may operate differently on the relationship between stress and effective functioning for blacks at different points in the individual life course (Gibson, 1991a).

Age may also change the strength of the ties between physical and mental health. Stress, for example, seems to play less of a role in the physical health of younger and very old blacks than in the health of older blacks (Chapters 10 and 11; Gibson, 1986a). Perhaps not so co-incidentally, the death rate from stress-related diseases is also the highest for blacks during these years. Age and life-cycle stage may also make a difference in the epidemiology of health and mental health disorders (Jackson et al., 1990). A given disease, in fact, may manifest itself differently among the young and old. For example, in-dividuals at mid-life, in contrast to those at older ages, are at higher risk for stress reactions and perhaps depression due to major life losses like divorce (Gibson, 1982a).

Stressful events, responses, and consequent adaptation and the ways in which these factors are interrelated also differ across cohort and age. It might be tentatively concluded that age group, aging, and cohort membership have special effects on the well-being and func-tioning of blacks. Thus, age and cohort are clearly pivotal in the in-terpretation of any model of stress and adaptation. The model, in fact, could vary at different ages or points in the life span, among dif-ferent cohorts, and in different socio-historical periods (Gibson, 1991a). This makes it clear that the functioning of African Ameri-cans must be examined within a theoretical model that takes a life-span perspective (Bowman, 1989; Jackson et al., 1990).

We are beginning to identify race and life-stage differences in stressors, responses to stressors, and consequent adaptation. Blacks and whites in middle and late life respond differently to distress, par-ticularly in their use of prayer and help-seeking in the informal net-work (Chapter 6; Gibson, 1982a). Measures of religion and religios-ity as coping mechanisms, in fact, differ among young and old blacks and whites. Two arguments as yet unresolved in the literature are concerned with the ways in which race and social positions change the relationship between chronic stressors and well-being and effective functioning. Being a worker in old age seems to decrease the mental health of blacks, whereas the worker role seems to increase the mental health of older whites (Chapter 9; Jackson & Gibson, 1985).

Another important area is social support, religiosity, and the family support system as a buffer against environmental stressors (Chapters 4 and 6). Our present concern with family and social networks is preceded by a long line of work emphasizing the importance of social networks as buffers of stress (Bowman & Jackson, 1983; Taylor 1986b), sources of stress (Antonucci, 1990), and sources of support in times of physical and mental health crises (Chapters 10 and 11). Little research has focused specifically on the nature of black American support networks (Taylor & Chatters, 1986b) or their function as stress buffers (Chatters, Taylor, & Jackson, 1985, 1986).

Extensive research on black women at two life points, mid- and late life, has centered on: (1) the stresses of multiple roles; (2) the interrelatedness of informal support, physical functioning, and social and mental health; (3) relationships among stressors and responses to these stressors in terms of frequency, magnitude, and level of social impairment; (4) effects of stressors on physical health; and (5) effects of stressful life events on use of informal and formal networks (Gibson, 1986a). We have also analyzed differences due to race, comparing black and white women who are heads of households on anxiety, achievement orientation, and effects of stressful life events on internal resources, and comparing older black men and women workers and retirees with their white counterparts on measures of well-being and the influence of mental health status on retirement (Gibson, 1991c).

Previous and current research on health conditions among blacks and their changes over time demonstrate that the black population, age for age, tends to be sicker than the general population; morbidity and mortality indicators reveal great disparities (Chapter 10; J. J. Jackson, 1981; J. S. Jackson, 1988). Although little work has been done on the issue, we believe the nature of these ill-health conditions is possibly related to the co-occurrence of mental health problems (Kessler, Tessler, & Nycz, 1983). Physical health problems may (a) directly affect mental health as preceding or co-occuring conditions (Lawson, 1986), (b) have indirect effects by first affecting coping capacities, or (c) interfere with the use of informal networks and mental health services (Shapiro, 1984). Under the World Health Organization conceptualization, health is a state of complete physical, mental, and social well-being, not merely the absence of disease or infirmity (World Health Organization, 1958). Our work in this area has centered on the interplay of these three dimensions, most often conceptualizing mental health as a construct that, in and of itself, incorporates a variety of well-being indicators: chronic stressors, responses to stressors, coping effectiveness, self-esteem, efficacy, general and specific life satisfactions, and happiness. Social health is conceived not only as social participation, involvement, and commitment, but also as the quality of family and social network exchanges. In this sense, the health and well-being and family and social support areas have some convergence (Gibson, 1991a).

In our analyses of the NSBA and other datasets, we have found physical, mental, and social health to be tied in intricate ways (Jackson, 1988) and have examined physical health in relation to its structure, meaning, and measurement (Gibson, 1991b); self-esteem (Antonucci & Jackson, 1983); efficacy (Antonucci & Jackson, 1987); mental health status of the elderly (Jackson, Chatters, & Neighbors, 1982); serious personal problems (Neighbors, Jackson, Bowman, & Gurin, 1983); size and composition of the helping network (Chatters et al., 1985, 1986); physical functioning among the elderly (Gibson & Jackson, 1987); and mental health and physical functioning among the oldest old (Gibson & Jackson, 1991).

Some work also suggests that the strength of the relationship between physical and mental health is different for various age groups of blacks. In an analysis of the NSBA data, stress was more intricately tied to physical health among respondents aged 65 to 74 than in any other age group (Gibson, 1986b). Other investigators have also found mental and physical health to be more related among the elderly (Kasl & Berkman, 1981). An argument as yet unsettled in the literature is whether poor mental health is a cause, an effect, or both of poor physical health. Problems of ill health, in fact, are magnified among older blacks (Jackson, 1988), and because this group is the fastest growng segment of the black population, it is an important population segment in which to study the links between physical and mental health and illness (Jackson, Chatters, & Neighbors, 1982). Future work in this area will involve greater focus on the nature of blacks' poor physical health and issues of co-morbidity (Chapter 10).

Concerns with family and social support and health and well-being overlap to the extent that both assume a tripartite structure of the health construct: family and social support as a social health dimension and health and well-being as physical and mental dimensions (Gibson, 1991b). Our work in this area has examined the patterns of size, composition, frequency, choices, and correlates of helper networks (Chatters et al., 1985, 1986; Taylor, 1986; Taylor & Chatters, 1986a, 1986b) and the juxtaposition of informal and formal help-seeking (Neighbors & Jackson, 1984). We have also examined the importance of religion and church member support in the lives of blacks (Taylor, 1986, 1988; Taylor & Chatters, 1986a, 1986b) and intergenerational exchanges between adult children and parents (Taylor, 1985), adult children and the black elderly (Gibson & Jackson, 1987), and adult children and the black oldest old (Gibson & Jackson, 1991). Research on family and social support as buffers of, contributors to, or alleviators of stress among black Americans (Allen & Stukes, 1982) will continue.

Finally, we believe that there must be renewed emphasis on the nature of social environment and contextual factors and their relationships to well-being and effective functioning among blacks. Social and economic inequality have been important topics of research (Allen & Britt, 1983; Cannon & Locke, 1977; Dohrenwend & Dohrenwend, 1974; Hollingshead & Redlich, 1958). The role of social and economic status in the nature of social and psychological functioning, particularly issues of selection and causation, and social change and social mobility, are still unresolved (Allen & Britt, 1983; Chapter 11). Many questions regarding the role of social status and social mobility relate to appropriate conceptualization, measurement, and interpretation of major constructs like social change, social mobility, and socioeconomic status (Jackson, Chatters, & Neighbors, 1982; Kessler & Neighbors, 1986). Thus, we view the study of the nature of social status, social mobility, and black reactions to economic and political circumstances as being important topics in their own right and also as having significant implications for the social and psychological functioning of Americans of African descent (Allen & Britt, 1983; Jackson, Chatters, & Neighbors, 1982).

Summary

We believe that the findings presented in this volume point to a coherent life-course framework within which the nature of the social and psychological life of black Americans can be comprehended and explained in the context of structural disadvantage and blocked mobility opportunities. The National Survey of Black Americans was designed to scientifically explore the nature of African Americans' reactions to their unequal status in the United States. This research is essentially social psychological in nature, focused on understanding the factors that facilitate a highly physically definable and historically disparaged group in overcoming sparse social and physical resources in the face of racial intolerance and hatred.

Specifically, the research findings presented in this volume have attempted to address the question of how structural disadvantage in the environment is translated into physical, social, and psychological aspects of group and self, such as self-esteem, personal efficacy, close personal and social relationships, neighborhood and family integration, sustained work, physical and mental health, group solidarity, and political participation. Our work differs from much of the social science research on race-related issues in the sense that it starts from a different basis than most. It begins with the question, "Why have black Americans done as well as they have in the face of what are unquestionably severe structural disadvantages and impediments?" rather than the traditional social science question, "Why do black Americans suffer from so much psychological and social pathology?"

The work that resulted in this book has been predicated on a set of assumptions that race is first and foremost a summary social construct that "stands in" for other structural, social, and psychological statuses. We have been concerned with how blacks as an oppressed racial group actually do as well as they do in the face of severe structural, political, and social constraints, and we have written numerous papers that have addressed the coping skills capacity and the adaptability of Americans of African descent at different points in the life course.

We have also argued that the type of data needed to assess the adaptability and resiliency of Americans of African descent has been sorely lacking. Previous work and speculation lead us to believe that the most important race effects, if they do occur, are probably in the form of interactions with other ethnic, structural, or cultural factors, for example, socioeconomic status, religion, or world views, relating more to differences between blacks and whites in underlying mediating processes than in average differences. Thus, although blacks and whites may show similar (or dissimilar in some cases) levels of functioning, the processes that underlie important outcomes like self-esteem, personal efficacy, religiosity, or family solidarity may be unique for different racial groups. This interpretation is consistent with our general model of coping and adaptation which suggests that blacks may utilize, over the individual life course, different mechanisms than whites to maintain adequate levels of well-being and effective functioning. Finally, we have been concerned with the general tendency in the social science literature to paint Americans of African descent in monochromatic tones, suggesting a large degree of homogeneity among the population in values, motives, social and psychological statuses, and behaviors. While categorical treatment must result in some degree of behavioral uniformity and belief congruence (Allen et al., 1991; Gurin et al., 1989), it has always been clear to us that the rich heterogeneity among blacks in this society is worthy of study in its own right. Thus, we have eschewed the need for race comparative studies without necessarily discarding the comparative framework (Jackson et al., 1990; Markides, Liang, & Jackson, 1990; Taylor, Chatters, Tucker, & Lewis, 1991).

We believe that comparative research needs to be applied vigorously to the heterogeneity among African Americans themselves (Jackson et al., 1990; Markides et al., 1990). The data from our national survey show blacks residing in all areas of the country but in disproportionately large numbers in America's declining inner cities; they have varying family arrangements but are disproportionately female headed; they live in widely disparate neighborhoods but disproportionately in dilapidated housing stock; their socioeconomic fortunes are different but they disproportionately live in poverty; they have varying historical family circumstances but overwhelmingly have little in family wealth; many hold responsible managerial positions, while others have never worked; many are formally retired, while others do not have this luxury; many are in excellent health, while others suffer from a wide variety of physical and mental disorders; many adhere to a strong sense of racial self, while others are more distant; they run the political party gamut, although predominately Democratic; many are active participants in the political process, while others watch from the sidelines.

In other words black Americans span the same spectrum of structural circumstances, psychological statuses, and social beliefs as millions of other Americans of different ethnic and racial backgrounds. Lack of parental advantages, past and current discrimination, and lack of the personal and structural resources needed to seize the paucity of available opportunities all serve to place disproportionate numbers of Americans of African descent in the United States at risk for social, physical, and psychological harm. It is this harm that is represented in the grim statistics that face us daily: a continuing, and perhaps, increasing gap in mortality rates; disintegrating neighborhoods; growing numbers living in poverty, particularly women and children; and continued increases in impoverished single-parent households, joblessness, and unemployment. In this volume we have attempted to examine the heterogeneity in major life domains of importance to black Americans in the face of these daunting physical realities.

In addition to the inherent scientific value and contribution to our theoretical understanding, a focus on the heterogeneity among black Americans reveals important areas of needed public policy changes and private and government interventions. Because of our attempts to cover a broad spectrum of life in black America we have had to treat each of the life domains in less detail than they deserve. It is our intention in subsequent work to focus more specifically on each of the major life areas initially explored in this volume.

Thus far, however, our findings show African Americans to be a diverse and heterogeneous group possessing a wide array of group and personal resources with an overarching adaptability and resilience in the face of long-standing, imposing environmental, social, and resource constraints. Our continuing tasks as social scientists are to explore how these environmental stressors affect and interact with group and personal resources to impede and facilitate the health and effective functioning of successive cohorts of African Americans over the individual and group life course.

REFERENCES

Abbott, J. (1977). Socioeconomic characteristics of the elderly: Some black-white differences. *Social Security Bulletin, 40*, 16–42.

Akbar, N. (1985). Our destiny: Authors of a scientific revolution. In H. McAdoo & J. McAdoo (Eds.), *Black children* (pp. 17–32). Beverly Hills, CA: Sage.

Alejandro-Wright, M. (1985). The child's conception of racial classification: A social-cognitive developmental model. In M. B. Spencer, G. K. Brookens, & W. R. Allen (Eds.), *Beginnings: The social and affective development of black children* (pp. 185–200). Hillsdale, NJ: Lawrence Erlbaum.

Allen, J. E., & Simms, M. C. (1988). No income gains for blacks. *Focus: Joint Center for Political Studies, 16*, 5–6.

Allen, L. R., & Britt, D. W. (1983). Social class, mental health, and mental illness: The impact of resources and feedback. In D. Felner, L. A. Jason, J. N. Moritsuko, & S. Farber (Eds.), *Preventive psychology*. Elmsford, NY: Pergamon.

Allen, R. L., Chadiha, L., & Jackson, J. S. (1991, under review). Generational differences in the structure of an African American belief system.

Allen, R. L., Dawson, M. C., & Brown, R. E. (1989). A schema based approach to modeling an African American racial belief system. *American Political Science Review, 83*, 421–442.

Allen, R. L., & Hatchett, S. J. (1986). The media and social reality effects: Self and system orientations of blacks. *Communications Research, 13*, 97–123.

Allen, R. L., & Watkins, S. C. (1991, under review). An African American racial belief system, gender and social structural relationships: A test of invariance.

Allen, W. R. (1978a). Black family research in the United States: A review, assessment and extension. *Journal of Marriage and the Family, 28*(4), 421–439.

Allen, W. R. (1978b). Black family research in the United States: A review, assessment and extension. *Journal of Comparative Family Studies, 9*, 167–189.

Allen, W. R., & Farley, R. (1985). The shifting social and economic tides of black America, 1950–1980. *Annual Review of Sociology, 12*, 277–306.

Allen, W. R., & Stukes, S. (1982). Black family lifestyles and the mental health of black Americans. In F. U. Munoz & R. Endo (Eds.), *Perspectives on minority group mental health*. Washington, DC: University Press of America.

America, R. F., & Anderson, B. (1978). *Moving ahead: Black managers in American business*. New York: McGraw-Hill.

Anderson, B. E. (1982). Economic patterns in black America. In J. D. Williams (Ed.), *The state of black America*. New York: National Urban League.

Angel, R., & Tienda, M. (1982). Determinants of extended household structure: Cultural patterns or economic model? *American Journal of Sociology, 87,* 1360–1383.

Antonucci, T. C. (1990). Social supports and social relationships. In L. K. George & R. H. Binstock (Eds.), *Handbook of aging and the social sciences* (3rd ed., pp. 205–226). New York: Academic Press.

Antonucci, T. C., & Jackson, J. S. (1983). Physical health and self-esteem. *Family and Community Health, 6*(2), 1–9.

Antonucci, T. C., & Jackson, J. S. (1987). Social support, interpersonal efficacy and health. In L. L. Cartensen & B. R. Edelstein (Eds.), *Handbook of clinical gerontology* (pp. 291–311). Elmsford, NY: Pergamon.

Argyle, M., & Beit-Hallahmi, B. (1975). *The social psychology of religion.* Boston: Rutledge & Keagen Paul.

Aschenbrenner, J. (1978). Continuities and variations in black family structure. In D. Shimpkin, E. Shimpkin, & D. Frate (Eds.), *The extended family in black societies.* Chicago: Aldine.

Ash, P. (1972). Job satisfaction differences among women of different ethnic groups. *Journal of Vocational Behavior, 2,* 495–507.

Atchley, R. C. (1976). *The sociology of retirement.* New York: Schenkman.

Atchley, R. C. (1982a). The process of retirement: Comparing women and men. In M. Szinovacz (Ed.), *Women's retirement.* Beverly Hills, CA: Sage.

Atchley, R. C. (1982b). Retirement: Leaving the world of work. *The Annals of the American Academy, 464,* 120–131.

Auletta, K. (1982). *The underclass.* New York: Random House.

Babchuck, N., & Thompson, R. (1963). Voluntary associations of Negroes. *American Sociological Review, 27,* 647–655.

Banks, W. C. (1976). White preference in blacks: A paradigm in search of a phenomenon. *Psychological Bulletin, 83,* 1179–1186.

Barfield, R. E., & Morgan, J. N. (1969). *Early retirement: The decision and the experience and a second look.* Ann Arbor: University of Michigan Press.

Barnes, A. (1979). An urban black voluntary association. *Phylon, 40,* 264–269.

Bartel, A. P. (1981). Race differences in job satisfaction: A reappraisal. *Journal of Human Resources, 16,* 294–303.

Barth, M. C. (1982). Dislocated workers. *Journal of Socioeconomic Studies, 7,* 23.

Bartlett, R. L., & Poulton-Callahan, C. (1982). Changing family structures and the distribution of family income: 1951 to 1976. *Social Science Quarterly, 63,* 28–38.

Bass, B. (1984). The black minority in high-technology organizations: Interpersonal relationships, management and supervision. In *Minorities in High Technology Organizations* Symposium at Office of Naval Research, Pensacola, FL.

Beck, S. H. (1982). Adjustment to and satisfaction with retirement. *Journal of Gerontology, 37*(5), 616–624.

Becker, G. S. (1975). *Human capital.* Chicago: University of Chicago Press.

Bernard, J. (1966). Marital stability and patterns of status variables. *Journal of Marriage and the Family, 28*(4), 421–439.

Bianchi, S. M. (1981). *Household composition and racial inequality.* New Brunswick, NJ: Rutgers University Press.

Bianchi, S. M., & Farley, R. (1979). Racial differences in family living arrangements and economic well-being: An analysis of recent trends. *Journal of Marriage and the Family, 41,* 537–551.

Bianchi, S. M., & Spain, S. (1986). *American women in transition.* New York: Russell Sage.

Bielby, W. T. (1987). Modern prejudice and institutional barriers to equal employment for minorities. *Journal of Social Issues, 43,* 79–84.

Billingsley, A. (1968). *Black families in white America.* Englewood Cliffs, NJ: Prentice-Hall.

Billingsley, A., & Giovannoni, J. (1972). *Children of the storm: Black children and American welfare.* New York: Harcourt Brace Jovanovich.

Blau, P. M., & Duncan, O. D. (1967). *The American occupational structure.* New York: John Wiley.

Blazer, D., & Palmore, E. (1976). Religion and aging in a longitudinal panel. *The Gerontologist, 16,* 82–85.

Blechman, E. (1982). Are children with one parent at psychological risk? A methodological review. *Journal of Marriage and the Family, 44,* 179–198.

Bloom, R., & Barry, J. R. (1967). Determinants of work attitudes among Negroes. *Journal of Applied Psychology, 51,* 291–294.

Bluestone, B., & Harrison, B. (1982). *The deindustrialization of America.* New York: Basic Books.

Bobo, L. (1988). Group conflict, prejudice, and the paradox of contemporary racial attitudes. In P. A. Katz & D. A. Taylor (Eds.), *Eliminating racism: Profiles in controversy* (pp. 85–114). New York: Plenum.

Bock, E. W. (1969). Farmers daughter effect: The case of the Negro female professional. *Phylon, 30,* 17–26.

Boskin, M. J. (1977). Social security and retirement decisions. *Economic Inquiry, 15,* 1–25.

Bould, S. (1980). Unemployment as a factor in early retirement decisions. *American Journal of Economics and Sociology, 39*(2), 123–136.

Bowman, P. J. (1980). Toward a dual labor market approach to black-on-black homicide. *Public Health Reports, 95,* 555–556.

Bowman, P. J. (1983). Significant involvement and functional relevance: Challenge to survey research. *Social Work Research, 19,* 21–27.

Bowman, P. J. (1984). A discouragement-centered approach to studying unemployment among black youth: Hopelessness, attributions and psychological distress. *International Journal of Mental Health, 13,* 68–91.

Bowman, P. J. (1988). Post-industrial displacement and family role strains: Challenges to the black family. In P. Voydanof & L. C. Majka (Eds.), *Families and economic distress.* Newbury Park, CA: Sage.

Bowman, P. J. (1989). Research perspectives on black men: Role strain and adaptation across the adult life cycle. In R. L. Jones (Ed.), *Black adult development and aging* (pp. 117–150). Richmond, CA: Cobb & Henry.

Bowman, P. J. (1990a). Toward a cognitive adaptation theory of role strain: Relevance of research on black fathers. In R. Jones (Ed.), *Advances in black psychology.* Richmond, CA: Cobb & Henry.

Bowman, P. J. (1990b). Naturally occurring psychological expectancies: Theory and measurement in black populations. In R. L. Jones (Ed.), *Handbook of tests and measurements for black populations.* Richmond, CA: Cobb & Henry.

Bowman, P. J. (1990c). Organizational psychology. In R. L. Jones (Ed.), *Black psychology.* Richmond, CA: Cobb & Henry.

Bowman, P. J., Gurin, G., & Howard, C. (1984). *A longitudinal study of black youth: Is-*

sues, scope and findings. Ann Arbor: Institute for Social Research, University of Michigan.

Bowman, P. J., & Howard, C. (1985). Race related socialization, motivation, and academic achievement: A study of black youths in three-generation families. *Journal of the American Academy of Child Psychiatry, 24,* 134–141.

Bowman, P. J., & Jackson, J. S. (1983). *Familial support and life stress among jobless black Americans.* Paper presented at the national meeting of the American Association for the Advancement of Science, Detroit, MI.

Bowman, P. J., Jackson, J. S., Hatchett, S. J., & Gurin, G. (1982). Joblessness and discouragement among black Americans. *Economic Outlook U.S.A.,* 85–88.

Boykin, A. W., Franklin, A. J., & Yates, F. (Eds.). (1980). *Research directions of black psychologists* (pp. 131–145). New York: Russell Sage.

Boykin, A. W., & Toms, F. D. (1985). Black child socialization: A conceptual framework. In H. McAdoo & J. McAdoo (Eds.), *Black children* (pp. 33–52). Beverly Hills, CA: Sage.

Bradburn, N. (1969). *The structure of psychological well-being.* Chicago: Aldine.

Branch, T. (1988). *Parting the waters: America in the King years 1954–63.* New York: Simon & Schuster.

Brenner, O. C., & Tomkiewicz, J. (1982). Job orientation of black and white college graduates in business. *Personnel Psychology, 35,* 89–103.

Brimmer, A. F. (1973). *Employment and income in the black community: Trends and outlook.* Los Angeles: UCLA Institute for Government Affairs.

Brimmer, A. F. (1976). Economic growth, employment and income trends among black Americans. In E. Ginzberg (Ed.), *Jobs for Americans* (pp. 142–163). Englewood Cliffs, NJ: Prentice-Hall.

Brimmer, A. F. (1984). Reagonomics: A report card. *Black Enterprise, 14,* 43–46.

Brimmer, A. F. (1985). *Trends, prospects, and strategies for black economic progress.* Washington, DC: Joint Center for Political Studies.

Broman, C. L., Jackson, J. S., & Neighbors, H. W. (1989). Sociocultural context and racial group identification among black adults. *Revue Internationale de Psychologie Sociale, 2,* 367–378.

Broman, C. L., Neighbors, H. W., & Jackson, J. S. (1988). Racial group identification among black adults. *Social Forces, 67,* 146–158.

Brown, R. E. (1984). *Determinants of black political participation.* Unpublished doctoral dissertation, University of Michigan, Ann Arbor.

Brown, R. E. (1989). *Church-based process of political action among black women.* (National Science Foundation Proposal SES-8821681). Ypsilanti: Eastern Michigan University.

Brown, R. E., Allen, R. L., & Dawson, M. C. (1991, under review). *A racial belief system: An examination of gender differences.*

Brown, R. E., & Jackson, J. S. (1988). *Church-based determinants of black campaign participation.* Unpublished manuscript, University of Michigan, Ann Arbor.

Brown, R. E., & Jackson, J. S. (1989, April 13–15). *Age, class and gender dimensions of black public opinion.* Paper presented at the 47th Annual MidWest Political Science Association Meeting, Chicago, IL.

Brown, R. E., Jackson, J. S., & Bowman, P. J. (1982). *Racial consciousness and political mobilization of black Americans.* Paper presented at the American Political Science Association, Denver, CO.

Campbell, A. (1981). *The sense of well-being in America.* New York: McGraw-Hill.

Campbell, A., Converse, P. E., Miller, W. E., & Stokes, D. E. (1960). *The American voter.* New York: John Wiley.

Cannon, M., & Locke, B. (1977). Being black is detrimental to one's mental health. *Phylon, 38,* 408–428.

Caplan, N. (1970). The new ghetto man: A review of recent empirical studies. *Social Issues, 26*(1), 59–73.

Carp, F. M. (Ed.). (1972). *Retirement.* New York: Behavioral Publications.

Chadiha, L. A. (1989). *Narrating black newlywed courtships: A structural functional and interactive-situational approach.* Unpublished doctoral dissertation, University of Michigan. Ann Arbor, MI: University Microfilms.

Chatters, L. C. (1986). *Health satisfaction or satisfaction with God: Results of a random probe in the National Survey of Black Americans.* Unpublished manuscript. Brandeis University, Boston.

Chatters, L. M., & Taylor, R. J. (1989a). Age differences in religious participation among black adults. *Journal of Gerontology: Social Sciences, 44,* S183–189.

Chatters, L. M., & Taylor, R. J. (1989b). Life problems and coping strategies of older black adults. *Social Work, 34,* 313–319.

Chatters, L. M., Taylor, R. J., & Jackson, J. S. (1985). Size and composition of the informal helper networks of elderly blacks. *Journal of Gerontology, 40,* 605–614.

Chatters, L. M., Taylor, R. J., & Jackson, J. S. (1986). Aged blacks' choices for an informal helper network. *Journal of Gerontology, 41,* 94–100.

Chatters, L. M., Taylor, R. J., & Neighbors, H. W. (1989). Size of the informal health network mobilized in response to serious personal problems. *Journal of Marriage and the Family, 51,* 667–676.

Chirikos, T., & Nestel, G. (1983). *Economic aspects of self-reported work disability.* Columbus: Center for Resource Research, Ohio State University.

Chrisman, N. (1977). The health seeking process: An approach to the natural history of illness. *Culture, Medicine and Psychiatry, 1,* 351–377.

Clark, K., & Clark, M. P. (1940). Skin color as a factor in racial identification of Negro preschool children. *Journal of Social Psychology, 11,* 159–169.

Clark, K. B., & Clark, M. P. (1947). Racial identification and preference in Negro children. In T. M. Newcomb & E. L. Hartley (Eds.), *Readings in social psychology.* New York: Holt, Rinehart & Winston.

Cone, J. H. (1969). *Black theology and black power.* New York: Seabury Press.

Cone, J. H. (1985). Black theology in American religion. *Journal of the American Academy of Religion, 53,* 755–771.

Crandall, L., & Duncan, R. (1981). Attitudinal and situational factors in the use of physician services by low income persons. *Journal of Health and Social Behavior, 22,* 64–77.

Cross, W. E. (1985). Black identity: Rediscovering the distinction between personal identity and reference group orientation. In M. B. Spencer, G. K. Brookins, & W. R. Allen (Eds.), *Beginnings: The social and affective development of black children* (pp. 152–172). Hillsdale, NJ: Lawrence Erlbaum.

Cross, W. E., Jr. (1971). Negro-to-black conversion experience: Toward a psychology of black liberation. *Black World, 20,* 13–27.

Crovits, E., & Steinmann, A. (1980). A decade later: Black-white attitudes toward women's familial role. *Psychology of Women Quarterly, 5*(2), 170–176.

Current Population Reports. (1985). *Voting and registration in the election of November 1984* (Series P-20, No. 397). Washington, DC: Bureau of the Census.

D'Amico, R. (1984). Industrial feudalism reconsidered: The effects of unionization on labor mobility. *Work and Occupations, 11*(4), 407–437.

Davis, J. (1974). Hierarchical models for significance tests in multivariate contingency tables: An exegesis of Goodman's recent papers. In *Sociological methodology, 1973–1974.* San Francisco: Jossey-Bass.

Dawson, M., Brown, R. E., & Allen, R. E. (1990). Racial belief systems, religious guidance, and African American political participation. *National Political Science Review, 2,* 22–44.

Delli Carpini, M. X. (1989). Age and history: Generations and sociopolitical change. In R. Sigel (Ed.), *Political learning in adulthood.* Chicago: University of Chicago Press.

Demo, D. H., & Hughes, M. (1990). Socialization and racial identity among black Americans. *Social Psychology Quarterly, 53,* 364–374.

Denton, N. A., & Massey, D. S. (1989). Racial identity among Caribbean Hispanics: The effect of double minority status on residential segregation. *American Sociological Review, 54,* 790–808.

Department of Health and Human Services. (1985). *Report of the secretary's task force on black and minority health.* Rockville, MO: Public Health Service.

Dill, B. T. (1988). Our mother's grief: Racial ethnic women and the maintenance of families. *Journal of Family History, 13,* 412–431.

Dion, K. L. (1978). Cohesiveness as a determinant of ingroup-outgroup bias. *Journal of Personality and Social Psychology, 28,* 163–171.

Dion, K. L. (1979). Intergroup conflict and intragroup cohesiveness. In W. G. Austin & S. Worchel (Eds.), *The social psychology of intergroup relations.* Monterey, CA: Brooks/Cole.

Dohrenwend, B. P., & Dohrenwend, B. S. (1974). Social and cultural influences on psychopathology. *Annual Review of Psychology, 2S,* 417–452.

Dowd, J., & Bengston, V. (1978). Aging in minority populations: An examination of the double jeopardy hypothesis. *Journal of Gerontology, 28,* 497–502.

Drake, St. C., & Cayton, H. (1945). *Black metropolis.* New York: Schocken.

Duncan, G. J., & Morgan, J. N. (1980). Five thousand American families—patterns of economic progress. (Vol. 10). *Analysis of the first thirteen years of the Panel Study of Income Dynamics.* Ann Arbor, MI: Survey Research Center.

Duncan, O. D. (1967). *Patterns of occupational mobility among negro men.* Ann Arbor, MI: Population Studies Center.

Duncan, O. D. (1968). Inheritance of poverty or inheritance of race? In D. P. Moynihan (Ed.), *On understanding poverty.* New York: Basic Books.

Duncan, O. D., Schuman, H., & Duncan, B. (1973). *Social changes in a metropolitan community.* New York: Russell Sage.

Duster, T. (1988). Social implications of the "new" black underclass. *Black Scholar, 19,* 2–9.

Dutton, D. (1978). Explaining the low use of health services by the poor: Costs, attitudes or delivery systems? *American Sociological Review, 43,* 348–368.

Edelman, M. W. (1987). *Families in peril: An agenda for social change.* Cambridge, MA: Harvard University Press.

Elder, G. H. (1985). Household, kinship, and the lifecourse: Perspectives on black families and children. In M. B. Spencer, G. K. Brookens, & W. R. Allen (Eds.), *Beginnings: The social and affective development of black children*. Hillsdale, NJ: Lawrence Erlbaum.

Ellison, D. L. (1968). Work, retirement, and the sick role. *The Gerontologist, 8,* 189–192.

English, R. (1974). Beyond pathology: Research and theoretical perspectives on black family life. In L. E. Gary (Ed.), *Social research and the black community: Selected issues and priorities.* Washington, DC: Institute for Urban Affairs, Howard University.

Epps, E. (1969). Correlates of academic achievement among northern and southern urban Negro students. *Journal of Social Issues, 25,* 55–70.

Epstein, L. (1966). Early retirement and work life experience. *Social Security Bulletin, 29,* 3–10.

Erbe, B. M. (1975). Black occupational change and education. *Psychology of Work and Occupations, 2,* 156–158.

Farley, R., & Allen, W. R. (1987). *The color line and the quality of American life.* New York: Russell Sage.

Feagin, J. F. (1987). Changing black Americans to fit a racist system. *Journal of Social Issues, 43,* 85–89.

Feather, N. T., & Davenport, P. R. (1981). Unemployment and depressive affect: A motivational and attributional analysis. *Journal of Personality and Social Psychology, 41,* 422–436.

Ferman, L. A., Kornbluh, J. L., & Miller, J. A. (1968). *Negroes and jobs.* Ann Arbor: University of Michigan.

Fichter, J. H., & Maddox, G. L. (1965). Religion in the south old and new. In J. C. McKinnwey & E. T. Thompson (Eds.), *The south in continuity and change.* Durham, NC: Duke University Press.

Fillenbaum, G. (1971). On the relation between attitude to work and attitude to retirement. *Journal of Gerontology, 26,* 244–248.

Fischer, J. (1969). Negroes and whites and rates of mental illness: Reconsideration of a myth. *Psychiatry, 32,* 428–446.

Forgionne, G. A., & Peters, V. E. (1982). Differences in job motivation and satisfaction among male and female managers. *Human Relations, 35,* 101–118.

Frazier, E. F. (1974). *The negro church in America.* New York: Schocken.

Freeman, R. B. (1973). *Brookings papers on economic activity. I. Changes in the labor market for black Americans, 1948-1972.* Washington, DC: Brookings Institution.

Fried, M. (1975). Social differences in mental health. In J. Kosa & I. Zola (Eds.), *Poverty and health.* Cambridge, MA: Harvard University Press.

Fryer, D. (1986). Employment deprivation and personal agency during underemployment. *Social Behaviour, 1,* 3–24.

Gary, L., Brown, D., Milburn, N., Ahmed, F., & Booth, J. (1989). *Depression in black American adults: Findings from the Norfolk area health study* (Final Report). Washington, DC: Institute for Urban Affairs and Research.

Gary, L., Brown, D., Milburn, N., Thomas, V., & Lockley, D. (1983). *Pathways: A study of black informal support networks* (Final Report). Washington, DC: Institute for Urban Affairs and Research.

Gary, L. E. (Ed.). (1981). *Black men.* Newbury Park, CA: Sage.

George, H. (1988). Black America, the "underclass" and the subordination process. *Black Scholar, 19,* 44–53.

George, L. K., & Maddox, G. L. (1977). Subjective adaptation to loss of the work role: A longitudinal study. *Journal of Gerontology, 32*(4), 456–462.

Gibson, R. C. (1982a). Blacks at middle and late life: Resources and coping. *Annals of the Americans Academy of Political and Social Science, 464,* 79–90.

Gibson, R. C. (1982b). Race and sex differences in the work and retirement patterns of older heads of households. *Scripps Foundation Minority Research Conference Monograph,* pp. 138–184.

Gibson, R. C. (1982c). Race and sex differences in retirement patterns. *Quarterly Contact, 5*(2), 5–8.

Gibson, R. C. (1983). Work patterns of older black female heads of household. *Journal of Minority Aging, 8*(2), 1–16.

Gibson, R. C. (1986a). *Blacks in an aging society* (pp. 1–41). New York: The Carnegie Corporation.

Gibson, R. C. (1986b). Blacks in an aging society. *Daedalus, 115*(1), 349–371.

Gibson, R. C. (1986c). Perspectives on the black family. In A. Pifer & D. L. Bronte (Eds.), *Our aging society: Paradox and promise.* New York: Norton.

Gibson, R. C. (1987a). Reconceptualizing retirement for black Americans. *The Gerontologist, 27*(6), 691–698.

Gibson, R. C. (1987b). Defining retirement for black Americans. In D. E. Gelfand & C. Barresi (Eds.), *Ethnicity and aging* (pp. 224–238). New York: Springer.

Gibson, R. C. (1988). The work, retirement, and disability of older black Americans. In J. S. Jackson (Ed.), *The black American elderly: Research on physical and psychosocial health* (pp. 304–324). New York: Springer.

Gibson, R. C. (1989). Minority aging research: Opportunity and challenge. *Journal of Gerontology, 44*(1), 52–53.

Gibson, R. C. (1991a). Age-by-race differences in health and functioning of elderly persons. *Journal of Aging and Health.*

Gibson, R. C. (1991b). Race and the self-reported health of elderly persons. *Journal of Gerontology.*

Gibson, R. C. (1991c). The subjective retirement of black Americans. *Journal of Gerontology.*

Gibson, R. C., & Jackson, J. S. (1987). The health, physical functioning and informal supports of the black elderly. In D. Willis (Ed.), Currents of health policy and impact on black Americans. *Milbank Memorial Fund Quarterly, 65* (Suppl. 2), 1–34. Reprinted 1989 in D. P. Willis (Ed.), *Health policies and black Americans.* New Brunswick, NJ: Transaction Press.

Gibson, R. C., & Jackson, J. S. (1991). The health, physical functioning and informal supports of the black elderly. In R. Suzman, D. Willis, & K. Manton (Eds.), *The oldest old.* New York: Oxford University Press.

Glasgow, D. G. (1980). *The black underclass.* San Francisco, CA: Jossey-Bass.

Glick, P. C. (1988). Demographic pictures of black families. In H. P. McAdoo (Ed.), *Black families.* Newbury Park, CA: Sage.

Glock, C. Y., Ringer, B. R., & Babbie, E. E. (1967). *To comfort and to challenge.* Berkeley: University of California Press.

Gordon, T. (1973). Notes on black and white issues. *Journal of Social Issues, 29,* 87–96.

Gorsuch, R. L. (1988). Psychology of religion. *Annual Review of Psychology, 39,* 201–221.

Goudy, W., Powers, E., & Keith, P. (1975). Work and retirement: A test of attitudinal relationship. *Journal of Gerontology, 30,* 193–198.

Greeley, A. M. (1979). Ethnic variations in religious commitment. In R. Wuthnow (Ed.), *The religious dimension: New direction in quantitative research.* New York: Academic Press.

Greenley, J., & Mechanic, D. (1976). Social selection and seeking help for psychological problems. *Journal of Health and Social Behavior, 17,* 249–262.

Grier, W., & Cobbs, D. (1968). *Black rage.* New York: Basic Books.

Gump, J. P. (1975). Comparative analysis of black women's and white women's sex-role attitudes. *Journal of Consulting and Clinical Psychology, 43*(3), 858–863.

Gump, J. P. (1977). Reality and myth: Employment and sex role ideology in black women. In J. A. Sherman & F. L. Denmark (Eds.), *Psychology of Women: Future directions in research* (pp. 349–380). New York: Psychological Dimensions.

Gurin, G., Veroff, J., & Feld, S. (1960). *Americans view their mental health.* New York: Basic Books.

Gurin, P., & Epps, E. (1975). *Black consciousness, identity and achievement: A study of students in historically black colleges.* New York: John Wiley.

Gurin, P., Hatchett, S. J., & Jackson, J. S. (1989). *Hope and independence: Blacks' response to electoral and party politics.* New York: Russell Sage.

Gurin, P., Miller, A. H., & Gurin, G. (1980). Stratum identification and consciousness. *Social Psychology Quarterly, 43*(1), 30–47.

Guttman, R. (1983). Job training partnership act: New help for the unemployed. *Monthly Labor Review, 106,* 3–10.

Hackman, J. R., & Oldham, G. R. (1976). Motivation through the design of work: Test of a theory. *Organizational Behavior and Human Performance, 16,* 250–279.

Hare, B. R. (1977). Racial and socioeconomic variations in preadolescent area-specific and general self-esteem. *International Journal of Intercultural Relations, 1,* 1–59.

Harrison, A. O. (1985). The black family's socializing environment: Self-esteem and ethnic attitude among black children. In H. P. McAdoo & J. L. McAdoo (Eds.), *Black children* (pp. 174–193). Beverly Hills, CA: Sage.

Harrison, B. (1972). *Education, training, and the urban ghetto.* Baltimore: Johns Hopkins University.

Harrison, B., & Sum, A. (1980). Data requirements for dual or "segmented" labor market research. In *Counting the labor force* (Vol. 1, Appendix). Washington, DC: National Commission on Employment and Unemployment.

Hatchett, S., & Quick, A. D. (1982). Correlates of sex role attitudes among black men and women: Data from a national survey of black Americans. *Urban Research Review, 9*(2), 1–11.

Hatchett, S., Veroff, J., & Douvan, E. (in press). Factors influencing marital instability among black and white couples. In B. Tucker & C. Mitchell–Kernan (Eds.), *The decline of black marriages.* New York: The Ford Foundation.

Heller, K., Price, R. H., Reinlare, S., Riger, S., & Wandersman, A. (1984). *Psychology and community change.* Homewood, IL: Dorsey.

Hershey, M. R. (1978). Racial differences in sex role identities and sex role stereotyping: Evidence against a common assumption. *Social Science Quarterly, 58*(4), 583–596.

Herzog, E., & Sudia, C. E. (1968). Fatherless homes: A review of research. *Children, 15*(5), 177–182.

Hess, I. (1985). *Sampling for social research surveys: 1947–1980.* Ann Arbor: Institute for Social Research, University of Michigan.

Hill, M. S. (1983). Trends in the economic situation of U.S. families and children. In R. L. Nelson & F. Skidmore (Eds.), *American families and the economy.* Washington, DC: National Academy Press.

Hill, R. (1971). *Strengths of black families.* New York: Emerson Hall.

Hill, R. (1977). *Informal adoption.* Washington, DC: National Urban League.

Hill, R. (1981). *The state of black America.* New York: National Urban League.

Hill, R. (1988). Cash and non-cash benefits among poor black families. In H. P. McAdoo (Ed.), *Black families* (2nd ed.). Newbury Park, CA: Sage.

Hoffman, E. (1985). The effect of race-ratio composition on the frequency of organizational communication. *Social Psychology Quarterly, 48,* 17–26.

Hollingshead, A. B., & Redlich, F. C. (1958). *Social class and mental illness.* New York: John Wiley.

Houghland, J., Jr., Kyong–Dong, K., & Christenson, J. (1979). The effects of ecological and socioeconomic status variables on membership and participation in voluntary organizations. *Rural Sociology, 44*(3), 602–612.

Hughes, M., & Hertel, B. R. (1990). The significance of color remains: A study of life chances, mate selection, and ethnic consciousness among black Americans. *Social Forces, 68*(4), 1105–1120.

Hunter, A. (1975). The loss of community: An empirical test through replication. *American Sociological Review, 40*(5), 537–552.

Inglis, K. M., Groves, R. M., & Heeringa, S. G. (1985, August). *Telephone sample designs for the black household population.* Proceedings of the survey section, Conference of the American Statistical Association, Washington, DC.

Irelan, L. M., & Bell, D. B. (1972). Understanding subjectively defined retirement: A pilot analysis. *The Gerontologist, 12,* 354–356.

Israel, B. A., House, J. S., Schurman, S. J., Heaney, C. A., & Mero, R. P. (1989). The relation of personal resources, participation, influences, interpersonal relationships, and coping strategies to occupational stress, job strains and health: A multivariate analysis. *Work and Stress, 3,* 163–194.

Issac, L., Murtran, E., & Stryker, S. (1980). Protest orientations among white and black adults. *American Sociological Review, 45,* 191–213.

Jackman, M. R., & Muha, M. J. (1984). Education and intergroup attitudes: Moral enlightenment, superficial democratic commitment or ideological refinement? *American Sociological Review, 49,* 751–769.

Jackson, J. J. (1980). *Minorities and aging.* Belmont, CA: Wadsworth.

Jackson, J. J. (1981). Urban black Americans. In A. Harwood (Ed.), *Ethnicity and medical care.* Cambridge, MA: Harvard University Press.

Jackson, J. J. (1983). Contemporary relationships between black families and churches in the United States: A speculative inquiry. In W. D. Antonio & J. Aldous (Eds.), *Families and religion: Conflict and change in modern society.* Beverly Hills, CA: Sage.

Jackson, J. S. (1985). *Community surveys of black mental health.* Invited address, American Psychological Association Annual Convention, Los Angeles.

Jackson, J. S. (Ed.). (1988). *The black American elderly: Research on physical and psychosocial health.* New York: Springer.

Jackson, J. S. (1989). Methodological issues in survey research on older minority adults. In M. P. Lawton & A. R. Herzog (Eds.), *Research methods in gerontology* (pp. 137–161). Farmingdale, NY: Baywood.

Jackson, J. S. (in press). Survey instruments in national studies of blacks. In R. L. Jones (Ed.), *Handbook of tests and measurements for black populations.* Richmond, CA: Cobb & Henry.

Jackson, J. S., Antonucci, T. C., & Gibson, R. C. (1990). Cultural, racial and ethnic minority influences on aging. In J. E. Birren & K. W. Shaie (Eds.), *Handbook of the psychology of aging* (3rd ed., pp. 103–123). New York: Academic Press.

284   LIFE IN BLACK AMERICA

Jackson, J. S., Bacon, J. D., & Peterson, J. (1977/1978). Life satisfaction among black
    urban elderly. *Aging and Human Development, 8,* 169–179.
Jackson, J. S., Chatters, L. M., & Neighbors, H. W. (1982). The mental health status of
    older black Americans: A national survey. *Black Scholar, 13*(1), 21–35.
Jackson, J. S., & Gibson, R. C. (1985). Work and retirement among the black elderly.
    In Z. Blau (Ed.), *Current perspectives on aging and the life cycle.* Greenwich, CT:
    JAI Press.
Jackson, J. S., Gurin, P., & Hatchett, S. J. (1984). *The National Black Election Study.* Un-
    published manuscript. Institute for Social Research, University of Michigan,
    Ann Arbor.
Jackson, J. S., & Hatchett, S. J. (1983). *Finding black respondents in low density areas: The
    Wide Area Screening Procedure.* Unpublished manuscript. Institute for Social Re-
    search, University of Michigan, Ann Arbor.
Jackson, J. S., & Hatchett, S. J. (1986). Intergenerational research: Methodological
    considerations. In N. Datan, A. L. Green, & H. W. Reese (Eds.), *Intergenerational
    relations* (pp. 51–75). Hillsdale, NJ: Lawrence Erlbaum.
Jackson, J. S., McCullough, W. R., & Gurin, G. (1988). Family, socialization environ-
    ment and identity development in black Americans. In H. P. McAdoo (Ed.),
    Black families (pp. 242–256). Newbury Park, CA: Sage.
Jackson, J. S., Tucker, M. B., & Bowman, P. J. (1982). Conceptual and methodological
    problems in survey research on black Americans. In W. T. Liu (Ed.), *Methodologi-
    cal problems in minority research.* Chicago: Pacific/Asian American Mental
    Health Research Center. (Reprinted in R. L. Jones [Ed.], *Advances in black psy-
    chology* [pp. 5–29]. Richmond, CA: Cobb & Henry.)
Jackson, J. S., Tucker, M. B., & Gurin, G. (1987). *National survey of black Americans,
    1979–80.* Ann Arbor, MI: Inter-University Consortium for Political and So-
    cial Research.
Jackson, M., & Wood, J. (1976). *The black aged.* Washington, DC: The National Coun-
    cil on the Aged.
Jackson, P. R. (1986). Toward a social psychology of unemployment. *Social Behaviour,
    1,* 33–40.
Jahoda, M. (1982). *Employment and underemployment: A sociopsychological analysis.*
    New York: Cambridge University.
Jameson, I. (1973). *A study of the influence of neighborhood associations on the public
    schools of an urban school district.* Unpublished doctoral dissertation, Temple Uni-
    versity, Philadelphia.
Jaynes, G. D., & Williams, R. M. (1989). *A common destiny: Blacks and American society.*
    Washington, DC: National Academy Press.
Jennings, M. K., & Niemi, R. (1968). The transmission of political values from parent
    to child. *American Political Science Review, 62,* 169–184.
Jennings, M. K., & Niemi, R. E. (1974). *Generations and politics: A panel study of young
    adults and their parents.* Princeton, NJ: Princeton University Press.
Jones, A. P., & Demaree, R. G. (1975). Family disruption, social indices, and problem
    behavior: A preliminary study. *Journal of Marriage and the Family, 37*(3), 497–502.
Jones, F. (1981). External cross currents and internal diversity: An assessment of black
    progress, 1960–1980. *Daedulus, 2,* 71–101.
Jones, F. C. (1977). *The changing mood in America: Eroding commitment?* Washington,
    DC: Howard University.
Jones, R. (Ed.). (1980). *Black psychology* (2nd ed.). New York: Harper & Row.

Kadushin, C. (1958). Individual decisions to undertake psychotherapy. *Administrative Science Quarterly, 3,* 379–411.

Kahn, R. (1981). *Work and health.* New York: John Wiley.

Kasl, S. V., & Berkman, L. F. (1981). Some psychosocial influences on the health status of the elderly: The perspective of social epidemiology. In J. McCaugh & S. Kiesler (Eds.), *Aging: Biology and behavior.* New York: Academic Press.

Katz, I. (1970). Experimental studies of Negro-white relationships. In L. Berkowitz (Ed.), *Advances in experimental social psychology* (Vol. 5). New York: Academic Press.

Kaul, M. (1976). Block clubs and social action: A case study in community conflicts. *Journal of Sociology and Social Welfare, 3*(4), 437–450.

Keith, V. M., & Smith, D. P. (1988). The current differential in black and white life expectancy. *Demography, 25,* 625–632.

Kelvin, P., & Jarrett, J. E. (1983). *Unemployment: Its social psychological effects.* London, UK: Cambridge University.

Kessler, L. G., Tessler, R. C., & Nycz, G. R. (1983). Co-occurrence of psychiatric and medical morbidity in primary care. *The Journal of Family Practice, 16,* 319–324.

Kessler, R., & Neighbors, H. (1986). A new perspective on the relationships among race, social class and psychological distress. *Journal of Health and Social Behavior, 27,* 107–115.

Kimmel, D. C., Price, K. F., & Walker, J. W. (1978). Retirement choice and retirement satisfaction. *Journal of Gerontology, 33*(4), 575–585.

Kinder, D. R. (1986). The continuing American dilemma: White resistance to racial change 40 years after Myrdal. *Journal of Social Issues, 42,* 151–171.

King, D. K. (1988, Autumn). Multiple jeopardy, multiple consciousness: The context of black feminist ideology. *Signs, 14,* 42–72.

Kingson, E. R. (1980). *Disadvantaged very early labor force withdrawal.* Paper presented at the 33rd annual meeting of the Gerontological Society, San Diego, CA.

Kish, L. (1965). *Survey sampling.* New York: John Wiley.

Knoke, D., & Burke, P. (1980). *Log-linear models.* Beverly Hills, CA: Sage.

Kramer, M., & Rosen, B. (1973). Definitions and distributions of mental disorders in a racist society. In C. Willie, B. Kramer, & B. Brown (Eds.), *Racism and mental health.* Pittsburgh: University of Pittsburgh Press.

Krause, N. (1983). The racial context of black self-esteem. *Social Psychology Quarterly, 46,* 98–107.

Krause, N., & Tran, T. V. (1989). Stress and religious involvement among older blacks. *Journal of Gerontology: Social Sciences, 44,* S4–13.

Ladner, J. (1968). On becoming a woman in the ghetto: Modes of adaptation. *Dissertation Abstracts, 29,* 6A.

Ladner, J. (1971). *Tomorrow's tomorrow: The black woman.* Garden City, NY: Doubleday.

Lamb, H. R., & Rogawski, A. S. (1978). Supplemental security income and the sick role. *American Journal of Psychiatry, 135,* 1221–1224.

Lambing, M. L. B. (1972a). Leisure-time pursuits among retired blacks by social status. *The Gerontologist, 12,* 363–364.

Lambing, M. L. B. (1972b). Social class living patterns of retired Negros. *The Gerontologist, 12,* 285–288.

Landry, B. (1988). *The new black middle class.* Berkeley: University of California Press.

Lawson, W. B. (1986). Racial and ethnic factors in psychiatric research. *Hospital and Community Psychiatry, 37,* 50–54.

Lee, G. R. (1980). Kinship in the seventies: A decade review of research and theory. *Journal of Marriage and the Family, 43,* 193–204.

Lenski, G. E. (1961). *The religious factor: A sociological study of religion's impact on politics, economics, and family life.* Garden City, NY: Doubleday.

Levine, D. M., & Bane, M. J. (1975). *The "inequality" controversy: Schooling and distributive justice.* New York: Basic Books.

Liebow, E. (1967). *Tally's corner: A study of street corner men.* Boston: Little, Brown.

Lipscomb, L. (1975). *Socialization factors in the development of black children's racial self-esteem.* Paper presented at the Annual Meeting of the American Sociological Association, San Francisco.

Litwak, E. (1965). Extended kin relations in an industrial society. In E. Shanas & G. Strieb (Eds.), *Social structure and the family: Generational relations* (pp. 290–323). Englewood Cliffs, NJ: Prentice-Hall.

Locke, E. A. (1983). The nature and causes of job satisfaction. In M. D. Dunnette (Ed.), *Handbook of industrial and organizational psychology.* Chicago, IL: Rand McNally.

Lopata, H. Z. (1969). Loneliness: Forms and components. *Social Problems, 17*(2), 248–252.

Lopata, H. Z. (1986). Becoming and being a widow: Reconstruction of the self and support systems. *Journal of Geriatric Psychiatry, 19*(2), 203–214.

Loury, G. C. (1981). Intergenerational transfers and the distribution of earnings. *Econometrics, 49,* 843–867.

Ludwig, A. (1981). The disabled society? *American Journal of Psychotherapy, 35,* 5–15.

Macklin, E. D. (1980). Nontraditional family forms: A decade of research. *Journal of Marriage and the Family, 43,* 175–192.

Mannheim, K. (1972). The problem of generations. In R. S. Laufer (Ed.), *The new pilgrims.* New York: David McKay.

Markides, K., Liang, J., & Jackson, J. S. (1990). Race, ethnicity and aging: Conceptual and methodological issues. In L. K. George & R. H. Binstock (Eds.), *Handbook of aging and the social sciences* (3rd ed., pp. 112–129). New York: Academic Press.

Martin, E., & Martin, J. (1978). *The black extended family.* Chicago, IL: University of Chicago Press.

Matthew, D., & Prothro, J. W. (1966). *Negroes and the new southern politics.* New York: Harcourt & Brace.

McAdam, D. (1982). *Political process and the development of black insurgency, 1930–1970.* Chicago, IL: University of Chicago Press.

McAdoo, H. P. (1978). Factors related to stability in upwardly mobile black families. *Journal of Marriage and the Family, 40,* 762–778.

McAdoo, H. P. (1985). Racial attitude and self-concept of young black children over time. In H. P. McAdoo & J. L. McAdoo (Eds.), *Black children* (pp. 213–242). Beverly Hills, CA: Sage.

McAdoo, H. P. (Ed.). (1988). *Black families* (2nd ed.). Newbury Park, CA: Sage.

McCullough, W. R. (1982). *The development of group identification in black Americans.* Unpublished doctoral dissertation, University of Michigan, Ann Arbor.

McCullough, W. R., Gurin, G., & Jackson, J. S. (1981). *Racial identity and consciousness: The socialization of ingroup and outgroup orientations.* Paper presented at the annual meeting of the American Psychological Association. Los Angeles, CA. (ERIC Document Reproduction Service No. ED 212 687.)

References   287

McGahan, P. (1972). The neighbor role and neighboring in a highly urban area. *Sociological Quarterly, 13*(3), 397–408.

McGahey, R., & Jeffries, J. (1985). *Minorities and the labor market: 20 years of misguided policy.* Washington, DC: Joint Center for Political Studies.

McGrath, J. (1983). Stress and behavior in organizations. In M. D. Dunnette (Ed.), *Handbook of industrial and organizational psychology* (pp. 1351–1396). Chicago: Rand McNally.

McKinlay, J. (1972). Some approaches and problems in the study of the use of services: An overview. *Journal of Health and Social Behavior, 13,* 115–152.

McKinlay, J. (1975). The help seeking behavior of the poor. In J. Kosa & I. Zola (Eds.), *Poverty and health.* Cambridge, MA: Harvard University Press.

McLean, A. (1979). *Work stress.* Reading, MA: Addison-Wesley.

McPherson, J. (1977). Correlates of social participation: A comparison of the ethnic community and compensatory theories. *Sociological Quarterly, 18,* 197–208.

Mechanic, D. (1978). *Medical sociology.* New York: Free Press.

Melton, W., & Thomas, D. L. (1976). Instrumental and expressive values in mate selection of black and white college students. *Journal of Marriage and the Family, 38*(3), 509–517.

Merton, R. K. (1957). *Social theory and social structure.* New York: Free Press.

Milburn, N. (1982). *Individual, organizational and individual-organizational fit characteristics and their relationship to participation in neighborhood associations.* Unpublished doctoral dissertation, University of Michigan, Ann Arbor.

Miller, A. H., Gurin, P., Gurin, G., & Malanchuk, O. (1981). Group consciousness and political participation. *American Journal of Political Science, 25,* 494–511.

Millham, J., & Smith, L. E. (1981). Sex role differentiation among black and white Americans: A comparative study. *Journal of Black Psychology, 1*(2), 77–90.

Mills, D. Q. (1983). The human resource consequences of industrial revitalization. In M. L. Wachter & S. M. Wachter (Eds.), *Toward a new U.S. industrial policy?* Philadelphia: University of Pennsylvania.

Miner, J. B., & Brewer, J. F. (1983). The management of ineffective performance. In M. D. Dunnette (Ed.), *Handbook of industrial and organizational psychology* (pp. 995–1030). Chicago: Rand McNally.

Mitchell, J., & Register, J. C. (1986). An exploration of family interaction with the elderly by race, socioeconomic status, and residence. In L. E. Troll (Ed.), *Family issues in current gerontology.* New York: Springer.

Montaga, P. D. (1977). *Occupations and society.* New York: John Wiley.

Morgan, J. N. (1980a). Retirement in prospect and retrospect. In G. J. Duncan & J. N. Morgan (Eds.), *Five thousand American families* (Vol. 8). Ann Arbor: Institute for Social Research, University of Michigan.

Morgan, J. N. (1980b). Occupational disability and its economic correlates. In G. J. Duncan & J. N. Morgan (Eds.), *Five thousand American families* (Vol. 8). Ann Arbor: Institute for Social Research, University of Michigan.

Morgan, J. N. (1981). Antecedents and consequences of retirement. In M. S. Hill, D. H. Hill, & J. N. Morgan (Eds.), *Five thousand American families* (Vol. 9). Ann Arbor: Institute for Social Research, University of Michigan.

Morris, A. (1984). *The origins of the civil rights movement: Black communities organizing for change.* New York: Free Press.

Morris, A., Hatchett, S., & Brown, R. E. (1989). The Civil Rights Movement and black political socialization. In R. S. Sigel (Ed.), *Political learning in adulthood* (pp. 272–

303). Chicago: University of Chicago Press.

Moynihan, D. P. (1986). *Family and nation.* New York: Harcourt Brace Jovanovich.

Muller, J. (1971). *Community organization, neighborhood redevelopment, and local politics: The East Tremont neighborhood association.* Unpublished doctoral dissertation, Fordham University, New York.

Murray, C. (1986). *Losing ground: American social policy, 1950–1980.* New York: Basic Books.

Murray, J. (1979). Subjective retirement. *Social Security Bulletin, 42*(11), 20–25, 43.

Mutran, E., & Reitzes, D. C. (1981). Retirement, identity and well-being: Realignment of role relationships. *Journal of Gerontology, 36*(6), 733–740.

Myers, L. J. (1985). Transpersonal psychology: The role of the afrocentric paradigm. *Journal of Black Psychology, 12,* 31–42.

Myers, V. (1977). Survey methods in minority populations. *Journal of Social Issues, 33,* 11–19.

Myrdal, G. (1944). *An American dilemma: The Negro problem and modern democracy* (2 vols.). New York: Harper & Bros.

National Advisory Commission on Civil Disorders. (1968). *Report of the National Advisory Commission on Civil Disorders.* New York: Bantam.

Neighbors, H. (1982). *Socioeconomic status and the use of professional help: A national study of black illness behavior.* Unpublished doctoral dissertation, University of Michigan, Ann Arbor.

Neighbors, H. W. (1984a). The distribution of psychiatric morbidity: A review and suggestions for research. *Community Mental Health Journal, 20,* 5–18.

Neighbors, H. W. (1984b). Professional help use among black Americans: Implications for unmet need. *American Journal of Community Psychology, 12,* 551–566.

Neighbors, H. W. (1985). Seeking professional help for personal problems: Black Americans' use of health and mental health services. *Community Mental Health Journal, 21,* 156–166.

Neighbors, H. W. (1986). Ambulatory medical care among adult black Americans: The hospital emergency room. *Journal of the National Medical Association, 78,* 275–282.

Neighbors, H. W., & Howard, C. S. (1987). Sex differences in professional help use among adult blacks. *American Journal of Community Psychology, 15,* 403–417.

Neighbors, H. W., & Jackson, J. S. (1984). The use of informal and formal help: Four patterns of illness behavior in the black community. *American Journal of Community Psychology, 12,* 629–644.

Neighbors, H. W., & Jackson, J. S. (1986). Uninsured risk groups in a national survey of black Americans. *Journal of the National Medical Association, 78*(10), 979–983.

Neighbors, H. W., & Jackson, J. S. (1987). Barriers to medical care among adult blacks: What happens to the uninsured? *Journal of the National Medical Association, 79*(5), 489–493.

Neighbors, H. W., Jackson, J. S., Bowman, P. J., & Gurin, G. (1982). Stress, coping and black mental health: Preliminary findings from a national study. *Prevention in Human Services, 2,* 5–29.

Neighbors, H. W., & LaVeist, T. (1989). Socioeconomic status and psychological distress: The impact of material aid on economic problem severity. *Journal of Primary Prevention, 10,* 149–165.

Neighbors, H. W., & Taylor, R. J. (1985). The use of social service agencies among black Americans. *Social Service Review, 59,* 258–268.

Nelsen, H. M., & Nelsen, A. K. (1975). *Black church in the sixties.* Lexington: University Press of Kentucky.

Nelsen, H. M., Yokley, R. L., & Nelson, A. K. (1971). *The black church in America.* New York: Basic Books.

Nelson, W. E., & Meranto, P. J. (1977). *Electing black mayors: Political action in the black community.* Columbus: Ohio State University Press.

Norton, A. J., & Glick, P. C. (1986). One parent families: A social and economic profile. *Family Relations, 35*(1), 9-17.

Ogbu, J. (1986). The consequences of the American caste system. In U. Neisser (Ed.), *The school achievement of minority children: New perspectives.* Hillsdale, NJ: Lawrence Erlbaum.

Ogbu, J. U. (1988). Black education: A cultural-ecological perspective. In H. P. McAdoo (Ed.), *Black families* (2nd ed.). Newbury Park, CA: Sage.

Olson, M. (1970). Social and political participation of blacks. *American Sociological Review, 35*(4), 682-697.

Ondeck, C. (1978, October). Discouraged workers' link to jobless rate reaffirmed. *Monthly Labor Review,* pp. 40-42.

Orchowsky, S. (1979). *Life satisfaction of blacks and whites: A lifespan perspective.* Unpublished paper. Richmond: Department of Sociology and Anthropology, Department of Gerontology, Virginia Commonwealth University.

Ortega, S., Crutchfield, R., & Rushing, W. (1983). Race differences in elderly personal well-being: Friendship, family, and church. *Research on Aging, 5*(1), 101-118.

Palmore, E. B., Fillenbaum, G. G., & George, L. K. (1984). Consequences of retirement. *Journal of Gerontology, 39,* 109-116.

Palmore, E. B., George, L. K., & Fillenbaum, G. G. (1982). Predictors of retirement. *Journal of Gerontology, 37*(6), 733-742.

Parenti, M. (1972). Power and pluralism: A view from the bottom. In P. Kimbell (Ed.), *The discontented.* New York: Columbia University Press.

Parnes, H. D. (1982). *Unemployment experiences of individuals over a decade.* Kalamazoo, MI: W. E. Upjohn Institute for Employment Research.

Parnes, H. S., & Nestel, G. (1981). The retirement experience. In H. S. Parnes (Ed.), *Work and retirement.* Cambridge, MA: MIT Press.

Parsons, T. (1944). The social structure of the family. In R. Anslen (Ed.), *The family: Its function and destiny* (pp. 173-201). New York: Harper & Row.

Peters, M. F. (1985). Racial socialization of young black children. In H. P. McAdoo & J. L. McAdoo (Eds.), *Black children* (pp. 159-173). Beverly Hills, CA: Sage.

Pettigrew, T. F. (1981). Race and class in the 1980's: An interactive view. *Daedulus, 2,* 233-236.

Pettigrew, T. F., & Martin, J. (1987). Shaping the organizational context for black Americans. *Journal of Social Issues, 43,* 41-78.

Piore, M. J. (1977). The dual labor market: Theory and implications. In D. M. Gordon (Ed.), *Problems in political economy: An urban perspective.* Lexington, MA: Heath.

Pitts, J. (1974). The study of race consciousness: Comments on new directions. *American Journal of Sociology, 80,* 665-687.

Pitts, J. (1975). Self-direction and the political socialization of black youth. *Social Science Quarterly, 80,* 93-104.

Porter, J. (1974). Race, socialization and mobility in educational and early occupational attainment. *American Sociological Review, 39,* 303-316.

Porter, J. R., & Washington, R. E. (1979). Black identity and self-esteem: A review of studies of black self-concept. *Annual Review of Sociology, 5,* 53–74.

Porter, J. R., & Washington, R. E. (1989). Developments in research in black identity and self-esteem: 1979–1988. *Revue Internationale de Psychologie Sociale, 2,* 341–353.

Prince, E. (1978). Welfare status, illness, and subjective health definition. *American Journal of Public Health, 68,* 865–871.

Quinn, J. F. (1977). Microeconomic determinants of early retirement: A cross-sectional view of white married men. *Journal of Human Resources, 12,* 329–436.

Quinn, J. F. (1979). Wage determination and discrimination among older workers. *Journal of Gerontology, 34*(5), 728–735.

Quinn, R. P. (1972). *Locking-in as a moderator of the relationships between job satisfaction and mental health.* Ann Arbor, MI: Survey Research Center.

Quinn, R. P., & Shepard, L. J. (1974). *The 1972–73 quality of employment survey.* Ann Arbor: Institute for Social Research, University of Michigan.

Rabkin, J. (1986). Mental health needs assessment: A review of methods. *Medical Care, 24,* 1093–1109.

Raelin, J. A. (1980). *Building a career: The effects of initial jobs experiences and related work attitudes on later employment.* Kalamazoo, MI: Upjohn Institute for Employment Research.

Reed, A. L., Jr. (1986). *The Jesse Jackson phenomenon.* New Haven, CT: Yale University Press.

Reno, V. (1976). Why men stop working before age 65. In *Reaching retirement age* (Research Report No. 47). Washington, DC: Government Printing Office, Office of Research and Statistics, Social Security Administration.

Riger, S., & Lavrakas, P. (1981). Community ties: Patterns of attachment and social interaction in urban neighborhoods. *American Journal of Community Psychology, 9*(1), 55–66.

Rosen, R. (1978). Sex roles, family and society. The seventies and beyond. *International Journal of Women's Studies, 1,* 544–554.

Rosenberg, M. (1985). Summary. In M. B. Spencer, G. K. Brookins, & W. R. Allen (Eds.), *Beginnings: The social and affective development of black children* (pp. 231–236). Hillsdale, NJ: Lawrence Erlbaum.

Rosenberg, M. (1989). Old myths die hard: The case of black self-esteem. *Revue Internationale de Psychologie Sociale, 2,* 355–365.

Rumberger, R. W. (1983). The changing skill requirements of jobs in the U.S. economy. *Industrial and Labor Relations Review, 34,* 578–590.

Sasaki, M. S. (1979). Status inconsistency and religious commitment. In R. Wuthnow (Ed.), *The religious dimension: New directions in quantitative research.* New York: Academic Press.

Scanzoni, J. (1971). *The black family in modern society.* Boston, MA: Allyn & Bacon.

Scanzoni, J. (1975). Sex roles, economic factors, and marital solidarity in black and white marriages. *Journal of Marriage and the Family, 37*(1), 130–144.

Scanzoni, J. (1976). Gender roles and the process of fertility control. *Journal of Marriage and the Family, 38*(4), 677–691.

Scanzoni, J. (1978). Sex-role influences on married women's status attainments. *Journal of Marriage and the Family, 41*(4), 793–800.

Scanzoni, L., & Scanozi, J. (1981). *Men, women, and change: A sociology of marriage and the family.* New York: McGraw-Hill.

Schlozman, K. L., & Verba, S. (1979). *Injury to insult: Unemployment, class, and political response.* Cambridge, MA: Harvard University Press.

Schmidt, F. L., & Lappin, M. (1980). Race and sex as determinants of the mean and variance of performance ratings. *Journal of Applied Psychology, 65,* 428–435.

Schuman, H. (1966). The random probe: A technique for evaluating the validity of closed questions. *American Sociological Review, 41,* 224–235.

Schuman, H., & Kalton, G. (1985). Survey methods. In G. Lindzey & E. Aronson (Eds.), *Handbook of social psychology* (Vol. 3, pp. 635–697). New York: John Wiley.

Schuman, H., & Scott, J. (1989). Generations and collective memories. *American Sociological Review, 54,* 359–381.

Schuman, H., Steeth, C., & Bobo, L. (1985). *Racial attitudes in America: Trends and interpretations.* Cambridge, MA: Harvard University Press.

Sears, D. O., & McConahay, J. B. (1973). *The politics of violence.* Boston: Houghton Mifflin.

Semaj, L. T. (1985). Afrikanity, cognition and extended self-identity. In M. B. Spencer, G. K. Brookins, & W. R. Allen (Eds.), *Beginnings: The social and affective development of black children* (pp. 173–184). Hillsdale, NJ: Lawrence Erlbaum.

Shapiro, S. (1984). Utilization of health and mental health services: Three epidemiologic catchment area sites. *Archives of General Psychiatry, 41,* 971–978.

Sherif, M. (1953). The concept of reference groups in human relations. In M. Sherif & M. O. Wilson (Eds.), *Group relations at the crossroads.* New York: Harper.

Shimpkin, D., Shimpkin, E., & Frate, D. (Eds.). (1978). *The extended family in black societies.* Chicago, IL: Aldine.

Shingles, R. (1981). Black consciousness and political participation: The missing link. *American Political Science Review, 75,* 76–91.

Siaughter, D. T., & McWorter, G. A. (1985). Social origins and early features of the scientific study of black American families and children. In M. B. Spencer, G. K. Brookens, & W. R. Allen (Eds.), *Beginnings: The social and affective development of black children.* Hillsdale, NJ: Lawrence Erlbaum.

Smith, A. W. (1987). Problems and progress in the measurement of black public opinion. *American Behavioral Scientist, 30,* 441–455.

Smith, C., & Freedman, A. (1972). *Voluntary associations: Perspectives on the literature.* Cambridge, MA: Harvard University Press.

Social Security Administration. (1969–1979). *Retirement history longitudinal survey* [Machine readable data file]. Ann Arbor, MI: Inter-University Consortium for Political and Social Research (Distributor).

Spencer, M. B. (1985). Cultural cognition and social cognition as identity correlates of black children's personal-social development. In M. B. Spencer & G. K. Brookins (Eds.), *Beginnings: The social and affective development of black children* (pp. 215–230). Hillsdale, NJ: Lawrence Erlbaum.

Sproat, K. V., Churchill, H., & Sheets, C. (1985). *The national longitudinal surveys of labor market experience: An annotated bibliography of research.* Lexington, MA: Lexington Books.

St. John, N. H. (1975). *School desegregation: Outcome for children.* New York: John Wiley.

Stack, C. (1974). *All our kin.* New York: Harper & Row.

Stanford, E. P. (1983). A minority perspective. *The Gerontologist, 23,* 215.

Staples, R. (1971). Towards a sociology of the black family: A theoretical and methodological assessment. *Journal of Marriage and the Family, 33,* 19–138.

Staples, R. (1973). Male-female sexual variations: Functions of biology or culture. *Journal of Sex Research, 9*(1), 11–20.

Staples, R., & Mirande, A. (1980). Racial and cultural variations among American families: A decennial review of the literature on minority families. *Journal of Marriage and the Family, 42,* 157–173.

State GOP likes look of '90 race. (1988, November 10). *Detroit Free Press.*

Stein, P. J. (Ed.). (1981). *Single life: Unmarried adults in social context.* New York: St. Martin's.

Strate, J. M., Parrish, C. J., Elder, C. D., & Ford III, C. (1989). Life span civic development and voting participation. *The American Political Science Review, 83*(2), 443–464.

Streib, G. F., & Schneider, C. J. (1971). *Retirement in American society.* Ithaca, NY: Cornell University Press.

Suchman, E. (1965). Stages of illness and medical care. *Journal of Health and Human Behavior, 6,* 114–128.

Sudarkasa, N. (1980). African and Afro-American family structure: A comparison. *The Black Scholar, 11,* 37–60.

Sudarkasa, N. (1988). Interpreting the African heritage in Afro-American family organizations. In H. P. McAdoo (Ed.), *Black families* (2nd ed.). Newbury Park, CA: Sage.

Sutherland, L. E. (1989). *Sex-role attitudes and behaviors among black and white newlyweds.* Unpublished manuscript, University of Michigan.

Sweet, J. A., & Bumpass, L. L. (1987). *American families and households.* New York: Russell Sage.

Swinton, D. H. (1988). Economic status of black Americans. In J. Deward (Ed.), *The state of black America* (pp. 9–40). New York: National Urban League.

Swinton, D. H. (1989). Economic status of blacks 1987. In J. Dewart (Ed.), *The state of black America 1988.* New York: National Urban League.

Tajfel, H. (1978). The psychological structure of intergroup relations. In H. Tajfel (Ed.), *Differentiation between social groups: Studies in the social psychology of intergroup relations.* London: Academic Press, European Monographs in Social Psychology.

Tajfel, H. (Ed.). (1982). *Social identity and intergroup relations.* Cambridge, UK: Cambridge University Press.

Tate, K. (1989). *Black politics as a collective struggle: The impact of race and class in 1984.* Unpublished doctoral dissertation, University of Michigan, Ann Arbor.

Tate, K., Brown, R. E., Hatchett, S., & Jackson, J. S. (1988). *The 1984 National Black Election Study: A sourcebook.* Ann Arbor: Institute for Social Research, University of Michigan.

Taylor, R. J. (1985). The extended family as a source of support for elderly blacks. *The Gerontologist, 26,* 488–495.

Taylor, R. J. (1986a). Religious participation among elderly blacks. *The Gerontologist, 26,* 630–636.

Taylor, R. J. (1986b). Receipt of support from family among black Americans: Demographic and familial differences. *Journal of Marriage and the Family, 48,* 67–77.

Taylor, R. J. (1988a). Correlates of religious non-involvement among black Americans. *Review of Religious Research, 30,* 126–139.

Taylor, R. J. (1988b). Structural determinants of religious participation among black Americans. *Review of Religious Research, 30,* 114–125.

Taylor, R. J. (1988c). Aging and supportive relationships among black Americans. In J. S. Jackson (Ed.), *The black American elderly: Research on physical and psychosocial health* (pp. 259–281). New York: Springer.

Taylor, R. J., & Chatters, L. M. (1986a). Church-based informal support among elderly blacks. *The Gerontologist, 26,* 637–642.

Taylor, R. J., & Chatters, L. M. (1986b). Patterns of informal support to elderly black adults: Family, friends, and church members. *Social Work, 31,* 432–438.

Taylor, R. J., & Chatters, L. M. (1988). Church members as a source of informal social support. *Review of Religious Research, 30,* 193–203.

Taylor, R. J., & Chatters, L. M. (1991). Non-organizational religious participation among elderly blacks. *Journal of Gerontology: Social Science.*

Taylor, R. J., Chatters, L. M., Tucker, M. B., & Lewis, E. (1990). Developments in research on black families: A decade in review. *Journal of Marriage and the Family, S2,* 993–1014.

Taylor, R. J., Jackson, J. S., & Quick, A. D. (1982). The frequency of social support among black Americans: Preliminary findings from the National Survey of Black Americans. *Urban Research Review, 8*(2), 1–4.

Taylor, R. J., & Taylor, W. H. (1982). The social and economic status of the black elderly. *Phylon, 42,* 295–306.

Taylor, R. J., Thornton, M. C., & Chatters, L. M. (1987). Black Americans' perception of the socio-historical role of the church. *Journal of Black Studies, 18,* 123–138.

Taylor, R. L. (1976). Black youth and psychosocial development: A conceptual framework. *Journal of Black Studies, 6,* 35–72.

Thornton, M., & Taylor, R. (1988a). Intergroup perceptions: Black American feelings of closeness to black Africans. *Ethnic and Racial Studies, 11,* 139–150.

Thornton, M., & Taylor, R. (1988b). Intergroup attitudes: Black American perceptions of Asian Americans. *Ethnic and Racial Studies, 11*(4), 474–488.

Tomeh, A. (1974). Formal voluntary organizations: Participation, correlates, and inter-relationships. In M. P. Effrat (Ed.), *The community: Approaches and application.* New York: Free Press.

Troll, L. E. (Ed.). (1986). *Family issues in current gerontology.* New York: Springer.

Troll, L. E., & Bengtson, V. L. (1979). Generations in the family. In W. Burr, G. Nye, R. Hill, & I. Reiss (Eds.), *Contemporary theories about the family* (pp. 127–161). New York: Free Press.

Tucker, M. B., & Taylor, R. J. (1989). Demographic correlates of relationship status among black Americans. *Journal of Marriage and the Family, 51,* 655–666.

Turner, J. C. (1982). Towards a cognitive redefinition of the social group. In H. Tajfel (Ed.), *Social identity and intergroup relations.* Cambridge, UK: Cambridge University Press.

Unger, D., & Wandersman, A. (1983). Neighboring and its role in block organizations: An exploratory report. *American Journal of Community Psychology, 11*(3), 291–300.

U.S. Bureau of the Census. (1983). Americans in transition. An aging society. *Current Population Reports,* Series P-23, No. 128. Washington, DC: Government Printing Office.

U.S. Bureau of Labor Statistics. (1980). *Employment in perspective: Minority workers.* Washington, DC: Government Printing Office.

U.S. Department of Commerce (1980). *Current population survey: Annual demographic file, 1980.* (Machine-readable file). Washington, DC: U.S. Department of Com-

294   LIFE IN BLACK AMERICA

merce, Bureau of the Census (Producer). Ann Arbor, MI: Inter-University Consortium for Political and Social Research (Distributor).

Vatter, H. G., & Palm, T. (1972). *The economics of black America.* New York: Harcourt Brace Jovanovich.

Verba, S., & Nie, N.H. (1972). *Participation in America: Political democracy and social equality.* New York: Harper & Row.

Verbrugge, L. M. (1985). Gender and health: An update on hypotheses and evidence. *Journal of Health and Social Behavior, 26,* 156–182.

Verbrugge, L. M., & Madans, J. H. (1985). Social roles and health trends of American women. *Milbank Memorial Fund Quarterly/Health and Society, 63,* 691–735.

Veroff, J., Kulka, R., & Douvan, R. (1981). *Mental health in America: Patterns of help seeking from 1957–1976.* New York: Basic Books.

Wald, K. (1987). *Religion and politics in the United States.* New York: St. Martin's.

Wandersman, A. (1981). A framework of participating in community organizations. *Journal of Applied Behavioral Sciences, 17,* 27–58.

Wandersman, A., Jakubs, J., & Giamartino, G. (1981). Participation in block organizations. *Community Organization,* 40–47.

Warheit, G., Holzer, C., & Arey, S. (1975). Race and mental illness: An epidemiologic update. *Journal of Health and Social Behavior, 16,* 243–256.

Warren, D. (1975). *Black neighborhoods: An assessment of community power.* Ann Arbor: University of Michigan Press.

Washington, V. (1976). Learning racial identity. In R. C. Granger & J. C. Young (Eds.), *Demythologizing the inner-city child* (pp. 85–98). Silver Springs, MD: National Association for the Education of Young Children.

Watson, J. G., & Barone, S. (1976). The self-concept, personal values, and motivational orientations of black and white managers. *Academy of Management Journal, 19,* 36–48.

Watson, W. (1983). *Stress and old age: A case study of black aging and transplantation shock.* New Brunswick, NJ: Transaction Books.

Weaver, C. N. (1978). Black-white correlates of job satisfaction. *Journal of Applied Psychology, 63,* 255–258.

Weiner, B. (1985). An attribution theory of achievement motivation and emotion. *Psychological Review, 92,* 548–573.

Weiss, C. H. (1977). Survey researchers and minority communities. *Journal of Social Issues, 33,* 20–35.

Wellman, B. (1970). Social identities in black and white. *Sociological Inquiry, 41,* 57–66.

Wielgosz, J. B., & Carpenter, S. (1983). *The effectiveness of job search and job finding methods of young Americans.* Columbus: Center for Human Resource Research, Ohio State University.

Wilson, W., & Kayatani, M. (1968). Intergroup attitudes and strategies in games between opponents of the same or a different race. *Journal of Personality and Social Psychology, 9,* 24–30.

Wilson, W. J. (1978). *The declining significance of race: Blacks and changing American institutions.* Chicago, IL: University of Chicago Press.

Wilson, W. J. (1980). *The declining significance of race: Blacks and changing American institutions* (2nd ed.). Chicago, IL: University of Chicago Press.

Wilson, W. J. (1987). *The truly disadvantaged: The inner city, the underclass, and public policy.* Chicago, IL: University of Chicago Press.

Wilson, W. J., & Neckerman, K. M. (1986). Poverty and family structure: The widening gap between evidence and public policy issues. In S. Danzinger & D. Weinberg (Eds.), *Fighting poverty.* Cambridge, MA.: Harvard University Press.

Wirth, L. (1938). Urbanism as a way of life. *American Journal of Sociology, 44,* 3–24.

Woodson, C. G. (1939). The Negro church: An all-comprehending institution. *Negro History Bulletin, 3,* 7–15.

Wool, H. (1978). *Discouraged workers, potential workers, and national employment policy.* Washington, DC: National Commission for Manpower Policy.

Word, C. O. (1977). Cross-cultural methods of survey research in black urban areas. *Journal of Black Psychology, 3,* 72–87.

Work in America: Report of a special task force to the Secretary of Health, Education, and Welfare. (1973). Cambridge, MA: MIT Press.

World Health Organization (1958). *The first ten years of the World Health Organization.* Geneva: Author.

Yancey, W. L., Ericksen, E., & Juliani, R. N. (1976). Emergent ethnicity: A review and reformulation. *American Sociological Review, 41,* 391–403.

Zipp, J. F., Landerman, R., & Luebre, P. (1982). Political participation: A re-examination of the standard socio-economic model. *Social Forces, 60,* 1140–1151.

Zola, I. (1973). Pathways to the doctor: From person to patient. *Social Science and Medicine, 7,* 677–689.

AUTHOR INDEX

SUBJECT INDEX

Adoption, informal, 58, 61
Affirmative action policies, 128, 154,
    178
Atlanta: NSBA field coordinators in,
    20, 26; NSBA training sessions in,
    21

Baltimore, NSBA field coordinators in,
    26
Black American Elderly, The, 200
Black Americans: African Methodist
    Episcopal, 108; African Methodist
    Episcopal Zion, 108; agnostics,
    108; atheists, 108; Baptists, 107,
    108, 110, 118; Catholics, 107, 108,
    118; causes of death among, 199;
    Colored Methodist Episcopal, 108;
    elderly, 30; family life and, 10,
    46–83; Holiness, 108; Jehovah's
    Witnesses, 108; joblessness and,
    10, 156–178; life expectancy of,
    199; marital patterns among, 10,
    84–104; mental health of, 11,
    221–237; Methodists, 107, 108, 110;
    national samples of, 22–28;
    neighborhood life and, 9, 31–45;
    physical health of, 11, 199–220;
    racial identification among, 11,
    238–253; religiosity of, 10, 105–123;
    retirement and, 10–11, 179–198;
    social support for, 9, 31–263;
    voting and, 11, 254–263; work life
    of, 10, 124–178

Boston: NSBA field coordinators in,
    20, 26
Bowman, P. J., 9, 10
Broman, C. L., 11
Brown, R. E., 11

Carnegie Corporation, 5
Center for the Study of Minority
    Group Mental Health, 3
Chatters, L. M., 10, 11
Chicago: NSBA retraining sessions in,
    21; NSBA training sessions in, 21
Civil rights generation, 255, 256, 257,
    258, 261, 263
Civil Rights Movement, 128, 130, 135,
    151, 196, 256
Cochran, D., 10
Current Population Surveys (CPS),
    125, 127, 135, 154, 157, 160

Dallas: NSBA field coordinators in,
    20; NSBA training sessions in, 21
Decennial Census, 125, 127
Depression, Great, unemployment
    during, 158, 160
Detroit: NSBA field coordinators in,
    20; NSBA pretests in, 15; NSBA
    training sessions in, 21
Duncan, G., 155

Employment in Perspective, 154

ABOUT THE AUTHORS

Phillip J. Bowman, Ph.D., is Assistant Professor of Psychology with the University of Illinois at Urbana-Champaign. He completed his doctoral work in Social Psychology at the University of Michigan in 1977; he worked as a National Research Council/Ford Foundation Postdoctoral Scholar from 1988-1989. He has published on many topics, including the black family, unemployment, and life-course development.

Clifford L. Broman, Ph.D., is Assistant Professor of Sociology at Michigan State University. In 1983, he received his doctoral degree in Sociology from the University of Michigan. He was a National Institute of Mental Health Postdoctoral Scholar from 1984-1985. He conducts research and publishes primarily in the areas of mental health, help seeking, and racial group identification among African Americans.

Ronald E. Brown, Ph.D., is Associate Professor of Political Science at Eastern Michigan University and Adjunct Faculty Associate with the Institute for Social Research, University of Michigan. Upon receiving his doctoral degree in Political Science from the University of Michigan in 1984, he accepted the Rockefeller Postdoctoral Scholar position for 1984-1985. His current research interests center around the role of religion and the church in the political action of African Americans.

Linda M. Chatters, Ph.D., is Assistant Professor in the Health Behavior-Health Education Department of the School of Public Health and Faculty Associate with the Institute for Social Research at the University of Michigan. After earning her doctorate in Psychology at the University of Michigan, she completed postdoctoral study supported by the Rockefeller Foundation and the National Institute on Aging. As a recipient of a First Independent Research Support and Transition (FIRST) Award from the National Institute on Aging, she is investigating issues related to the use of survey data among diverse groups of black Americans.

Donna L. Cochran, M.S.W., is a graduate student in the Department of Social Work and Social Psychology at the University of Michigan. Her research interests include issues that effect black families, such as shades of skin color, racial identity, self-esteem, multigenerational households, and early grandparenthood. Her specialization is in gerontology and mental health.

Anderson James Franklin, Ph.D., is a Professor and the Director of the Clinical Psychology Program at the City College and Graduate School of the City University of New York. He is a past member of the New York State Board of Psychology and has a long history of research, writing, and involvement in issues of mental health in black populations. He began his long history of work with the Program for Research on Black Americans as a member of the original Advisory Panel in 1977, and over the past several years has been involved with analyses and writing from the various PRBA data sets.

Rose C. Gibson, Ph.D., is Associate Professor in the School of Social Work and Faculty Associate at the Institute for Social Research at the University of Michigan. A former National Institute on Aging Postdoctoral Fellow in statistics, survey research design, and methodology on minority populations, she has participated in pioneering national surveys. She is the author of *Blacks in an Aging Society* and serves on the editorial boards of several journals in the field of aging. Her major research interests are in the area of sociocultural factors in aging.

Gerald Gurin, Ph.D., is Professor of Higher Education at the University of Michigan's School of Education and Research Scientist at the Institute for Social Research. He received his doctorate in Social Psychology from the University of Michigan in 1956. He has published in many areas, including mental health, personality and social structure, adult socialization, and social influences, particularly in relation to educational settings and resocialization programs.

Shirley J. Hatchett, Ph.D., is Sociologist and Research Investigator at the Institute for Social Research at the University of Michigan. She has co-authored a recent book on black political attitudes and behaviors, as well as published books and articles about racial attitude change, racial and political socialization, social structural factors in black family structure and functioning, and selected issues in survey research methodology. She is currently analyzing data from a prospective study of first marriages, and is involved in the design of a major study of the national drug and alcohol treatment system and its clients.

James S. Jackson, Ph.D., is Professor of Social Psychology and Public Health and Research Scientist at the Institute for Social Research at the University of Michigan. He is the Director of the Program for Research on Black Americans and the African American Mental Health Research Center. He is a co-author of a recent book on black political attitudes and behavior and the editor of a book on the black elderly. He has directed five major national sample surveys of the black population and has conducted research and published in the areas of racial and ethnic influences on life-course development, attitude change, reciprocity, social support, and coping and health.

Wayne R. McCullough, Ph.D., received his doctoral degree from the University of Michigan in Social Psychology in 1982. After joining IBM he implemented the firm's first worldwide survey of company executives and developed its U.S. program for evaluating the effectiveness of communications programs. He currently manages a group of research professionals concerned with increasing the quality of communications activities. His research interests include the development of group identity, organizational commitment, and the utilization of scientific research to improve organizational effectiveness.

Norweeta G. Milburn, Ph.D., is Assistant Professor of Psychology at Hofstra University. After earning her doctoral degree in Community Psychology at the University of Michigan, she received postdoctoral training supported by the National Institute of Mental Health at the Institute for Social Research at the University of Michigan. She has worked as a Senior Research Associate at the Institute for Urban Affairs and Research at Howard University and was involved in epidemiologic research on the mental health of African American adults. Her current research focuses on substance abuse among homeless adults.

Harold W. Neighbors, Ph.D., is Assistant Professor in the School of Public Health and Faculty Associate at the Institute for Social Research at the University of Michigan. After receiving his doctoral degree in Social Psychology from the University of Michigan in 1982, he did postdoctoral work at the Institute for Social Research, receiving grants from the Rockefeller Foundation and the National Institute of Mental Health. His current research interests include psychiatric epidemiology, risk factor identification, methodological approaches to mental health need assessment, ethnic influences on the perception and classification of mental disorders, help seeking, and service utilization.

Robert Joseph Taylor, M.S.W., Ph.D., is Assistant Professor of Social Work and Faculty Associate at the Institute for Social Research at the University of Michigan. After earning his doctorate in Social Work and Sociology at the University of Michigan in 1983, he completed postdoctoral training sponsored by the National Institute on Aging and is currently a recipient of the National Institute on Aging's First Independent Research Support and Transition (FIRST) Award. His research focuses on family and friend social support networks across the life span, with a particular emphasis on the networks of older adults.